New Psalms for Common Worship

New Psalms for Common Worship

Compiled by Colin Mawby

kevin mayhew

We hope you enjoy *New Psalms for Common Worship*. Further copies are available from your local music shop or Christian bookshop.

In case of difficulty, please contact the publisher direct by writing to:

The Sales Department
KEVIN MAYHEW LTD
Buxhall
Stowmarket
Suffolk IP14 3BW

Phone 01449 737978
Fax 01449 737834
E-mail info@kevinmayhewltd.com

Please ask for our complete catalogue of outstanding Church Music.

The Publishers wish to express their gratitude to The Archbishops' Council of the Church of England, Church House, Great Smith Street, London SW1P 3NZ, for permission to use the *Revised Psalter*.

The *Revised Psalter* as used in *Common Worship* is copyright © The Archbishops' Council, 2000 and is reproduced by permission.

First published in Great Britain in 2004 by Kevin Mayhew Ltd.

© Copyright 2004 Kevin Mayhew Ltd.

ISBN 1 84417 299 6
ISMN M 57024 368 6
Catalogue No: 1450333

0 1 2 3 4 5 6 7 8 9

The texts and music in this book are protected by copyright and may not be reproduced in any way for sale or private use without the consent of the copyright owner. Please note, the music in this book is not covered by a C.C.L. Music Reproduction Licence.

Cover design by Angela Selfe
Music editor and setter: Donald Thomson
Proof reader: Linda Ottewell

Printed and bound in Great Britain

Foreword

This book builds on the great success of *Sunday Psalms, Musical Settings for Common Worship* which was compiled by Andrew Moore. It retains all the features of the original but gives an entirely new selection of easy and tuneful psalm tones and responses which are diatonically rather than modally based.

This collection of psalms and gospel acclamations is designed for use with *Common Worship* on Sundays and Principal Feasts. Its layout allows the psalms to be sung at any service (Principal, Second, Third or Evening Prayer, as appropriate) in a variety of ways.

Our subsequent Liturgical Calendar lists the psalms designated for each service on Sundays and Feasts. As some psalms are divided, the verses to be used on each day are listed at the top of each psalm.

For example:
The Liturgical Calendar shows that for the Principal Service on the First Sunday of Advent in Year B, Psalm 80 should be used, but it will be noted that for this particular Sunday, only verses 1-8 are laid down. However, the whole of the psalm is printed because on Proper 15 in Year C, verses 9-20 are used.

In *Common Worship* an alternative psalmody is often given for the Principal and Second Services. In this book, the alternative psalmody has usually been preferred as being more suitable for singing. Where verses of a psalm, designated for use on different feasts, have been found to be mutually exclusive for a sung setting, appropriate adjustments have been made.

Common Worship introduces acclamations to be sung before the Gospel. These, too, are all included in this volume.

Performance Notes

The Psalms

Each psalm has a response and a simple tone both of which are designed to lie well within the range of cantors and congregations. An optional instrumental descant is given to be played on C or B♭ instruments – a flute will be ideal.

The psalm may be sung responsorially, for example at the Principal Service, where the psalm provides a mediation for the following readings. The Cantor/Choir sing the response which is repeated by the people. The Cantor/Choir sing the verses and the people sing the response at the end of each verse.

Alternatively, and more appropriately at other services, the Response may be sung at the beginning and end of the psalm only. The psalm may then be sung in the following ways:

A Cantor/Choir alternating with the congregation
two sides of a choir alternating
two sides of a congregation alternating
sung straight through by all.

If the Gloria is to be sung after the final verse of a psalm or canticle (as is traditionally done at morning or evening prayer) it is pointed thus:

Glory to the Father and | to the Son
and to the | Holy Spirit;
as it was in | the beginning
is now and shall be for e | ver. Amen

The Gospel Acclamations

Except from Ash Wednesday to Maundy Thursday, they are sung as follows:

All	Alleluia
Cantor/Choir	sings the appropriate scriptural verse
All	Alleluia

From Ash Wednesday to Maundy Thursday the Alleluia is replaced by the response:

Praise to you, O Christ, King of eternal glory.

The texts and musical settings of the Acclamations will be found on pages 288-295. Any setting may be chosen for any text.

The composers of the psalm tones are:

KD	Keith Duke
SL	Simon Lesley
TB	Timothy Blinko
GN	Geoff Nobes
CM	Colin Mawby
AM	Andrew Moore

Liturgical Calendar

Square brackets indicate optional additional psalms, rather than a simple choice between two alternatives which is indicated by 'or' between the two psalm numbers or between psalm and canticle.

	YEAR A	YEAR B	YEAR C
ADVENT			
First Sunday of Advent			
Principal Service	Ps 122	Ps 80	Ps 25
Second Service	Ps 9	Ps 25	Ps 9
Third Service	Ps 44	Ps 44	Ps 44
Second Sunday of Advent			
Principal Service	Ps 72	Ps 85	Benedictus (p. 275)
Second Service	Ps 11 [28]	Ps 40	Ps 75 [76]
Third Service	Ps 80	Ps 80	Ps 80
Third Sunday of Advent			
Principal Service	Ps 146 or Magnificat (p. 276)	Ps 126 or Magnificat (p. 276)	Isaiah (p. 280)
Second Service	Ps 12 [14]	Ps 68	Ps 50 [62]
Third Service	Ps 68	Ps 50, 62	Ps 12, 14
Fourth Sunday of Advent			
Principal Service	Ps 80	Magnificat (p. 276) or Ps 89	Magnificat (p. 276) or Ps 80
Second Service	Ps 113 [126]	Ps 113 [131]	Ps 123 [131]
Third Service	Ps 144	Ps 144	Ps 144
CHRISTMAS			
Christmas Eve			
Morning Eucharist	Ps 89	Ps 89	Ps 89
Evening Prayer	Ps 85	Ps 85	Ps 85
Christmas Day			
Principal Service	Set I: Ps 96	Set II: Ps 97	Set III: Ps 98
Second Service	Ps 8	Ps 8	Ps 8
Third Service	Ps 110	Ps 110	Ps 110
First Sunday of Christmas			
Principal Service	Ps 148	Ps 148	Ps 148
Second Service	Ps 132	Ps 132	Ps 132
Third Service	Ps 105	Ps 105	Ps 105

Second Sunday of Christmas
Principal Service	Ps 147	Ps 147	Ps 147
Second Service	Ps 135	Ps 135	Ps 135
Third Service	Ps 87	Ps 87	Ps 87

EPIPHANY

The Epiphany
Evening Prayer on the Eve	Ps 96, 97	Ps 96, 97	Ps 96, 97
Principal Service	Ps 72	Ps 72	Ps 72
Second Service	Ps 98, 100	Ps 98, 100	Ps 98, 100
Third Service	Ps 113, 132	Ps 113, 132	Ps 113, 132

The Baptism of Christ (First Sunday of Epiphany)
Evening Prayer on the Eve	Ps 36	Ps 36	Ps 36
Principal Service	Ps 29	Ps 29	Ps 29
Second Service	Ps 46, 47	Ps 46, 47	Ps 46, 47
Third Service	Ps 89	Ps 89	Ps 89

Second Sunday of Epiphany
Principal Service	Ps 40	Ps 139	Ps 36
Second Service	Ps 96	Ps 96	Ps 96
Third Service	Ps 145	Ps 145	Ps 145

Third Sunday of Epiphany
Principal Service	Ps 27	Ps 128	Ps 19
Second Service	Ps 33	Ps 33	Ps 33
Third Service	Ps 113	Ps 113	Ps 113

Fourth Sunday of Epiphany
Principal Service	Ps 36	Ps 111	Ps 48
Second Service	Ps 34	Ps 34	Ps 34
Third Service	Ps 71	Ps 71	Ps 71

The Presentation of Christ in the Temple
Evening Prayer on the Eve	Ps 118	Ps 118	Ps 118
Principal Service	Ps 24	Ps 24	Ps 24
Second Service	Ps 122, 132	Ps 122, 132	Ps 122, 132
Third Service	Ps 42, 43, 48	Ps 42, 43, 48	Ps 42, 43, 48

ORDINARY TIME

Proper 1
Principal Service	Ps 112	Ps 147	Ps 138
Second Service	Ps [1, 3] 4	Ps 5	Ps 1 [2]
Third Service	Ps 5, 6	Ps 2, 3	Ps 3, 4

Proper 2
    Principal Service   Ps 119   Ps 30   Ps 1
    Second Service   Ps [7] 13   Ps 6   Ps [5] 6
    Third Service   Ps 10   Ps 7   Ps 7

Proper 3
    Principal Service   Ps 119   Ps 41   Ps 37
    Second Service   Ps 18   Ps 10   Ps [11] 13
    Third Service   Ps 21, 23   Ps 9   Ps 10

Second Sunday before Lent
    Principal Service   Ps 136   Ps 104   Ps 65
    Second Service   Ps 148   Ps 65   Ps 147
    Third Service   Ps 100, 150   Ps 29, 67   Ps 104

Sunday next before Lent
    Principal Service   Ps 2 or 99   Ps 50   Ps 99
    Second Service   Ps 84   Ps 2 [99]   Ps 89
    Third Service   Ps 72   Ps 27, 150   Ps 2

LENT

Ash Wednesday
    Principal Service   Ps 51   Ps 51   Ps 51
    Second Service   Ps 102   Ps 102   Ps 102
    Third Service   Ps 38   Ps 38   Ps 38

First Sunday of Lent
    Principal Service   Ps 32   Ps 25   Ps 91
    Second Service   Ps 50   Ps 119   Ps 119
    Third Service   Ps 119   Ps 77   Ps 50

Second Sunday of Lent
    Principal Service   Ps 121   Ps 22   Ps 27
    Second Service   Ps 135   Ps 135   Ps 135
    Third Service   Ps 74   Ps 105   Ps 119

Third Sunday of Lent
    Principal Service   Ps 95   Ps 19   Ps 63
    Second Service   Ps 40   Ps 11, 12   Ps 12, 13
    Third Service   Ps 46   Ps 18   Ps 26, 28

Fourth Sunday of Lent
    Principal Service   Ps 23   Ps 107   Ps 32
    Second Service   Ps 31   Ps 13, 14   Ps 30
    Third Service   Ps 19   Ps 27   Ps 84, 85

Mothering Sunday
    Principal Service   Ps 34 or 127   Ps 34 or 127   Ps 34 or 127

Fifth Sunday of Lent
Principal Service	Ps 130	Ps 51 or 119	Ps 126
Second Service	Ps 30	Ps 34	Ps 35
Third Service	Ps 86	Ps 107	Ps 111, 112

Palm Sunday
Liturgy of the Palms	Ps 118	Ps 118	Ps 118
Liturgy of the Passion	Ps 31	Ps 31	Ps 31
Second Service	Ps 80	Ps 69	Ps 69
Third Service	Ps 61, 62	Ps 61, 62	Ps 61, 62

Monday of Holy Week
Principal Service	Ps 36	Ps 36	Ps 36
Second Service	Ps 41	Ps 41	Ps 41
Third Service	Ps 25	Ps 25	Ps 25

Tuesday of Holy Week
Principal Service	Ps 71	Ps 71	Ps 71
Second Service	Ps 27	Ps 27	Ps 27
Third Service	Ps 55	Ps 55	Ps 55

Wednesday of Holy Week
Principal Service	Ps 70	Ps 70	Ps 70
Second Service	Ps 102	Ps 102	Ps 102
Third Service	Ps 88	Ps 88	Ps 88

Maundy Thursday
Principal Service	Ps 116	Ps 116	Ps 116
Second Service	Ps 39	Ps 39	Ps 39
Third Service	Ps 42, 43	Ps 42, 43	Ps 42, 43

Good Friday
Principal Service	Ps 22	Ps 22	Ps 22
Second Service	Ps 130, 143	Ps 130, 143	Ps 130, 143
Third Service	Ps 69	Ps 69	Ps 69

Easter Eve
(services other than Easter Vigil)
Principal Service	Ps 31	Ps 31	Ps 31
Second Service	Ps 142	Ps 142	Ps 142
Third Service	Ps 116	Ps 116	Ps 116

EASTER

Easter Vigil

Ps 136, 46, 16	Ps 136, 46, 16	Ps 136, 46, 16
Exodus (p. 278)	Exodus (p. 278)	Exodus (p. 278)
Isaiah (p. 280)	Isaiah (p. 280)	Isaiah (p. 280)
Ps 19, 42, 43, 143, 98	Ps 19, 42, 43, 143, 98	Ps 19, 42, 43, 143, 98
Ps 114	Ps 114	Ps 114

Easter Day
   Principal Service   Ps 118   Ps 118   Ps 118
   Second Service   Ps 114, 117   Ps 114, 117   Ps 114, 117, 66
   Third Service   Ps 105 or 66   Ps 105 or 66   Ps 114, 117

Second Sunday of Easter
   Principal Service   Ps 16   Ps 133   Ps 118 or 150
   Second Service   Ps 30   Ps 143   Ps 16
   Third Service   Ps 81   Ps 22   Ps 136

Third Sunday of Easter
   Principal Service   Ps 116   Ps 4   Ps 30
   Second Service   Ps 48   Ps 142   Ps 86
   Third Service   Ps 23   Ps 77   Ps 80

Fourth Sunday of Easter
   Principal Service   Ps 23   Ps 23   Ps 23
   Second Service   Ps 29   Ps 81   Ps 113, 114
   Third Service   Ps 106   Ps 119   Ps 146

Fifth Sunday of Easter
   Principal Service   Ps 31   Ps 22   Ps 148
   Second Service   Ps 147   Ps 96   Ps 98
   Third Service   Ps 30   Ps 44   Ps 16

Sixth Sunday of Easter
   Principal Service   Ps 66   Ps 98   Ps 67
   Second Service   Ps 87, 36   Ps 45   Ps 126, 127
   Third Service   Ps 73   Ps 104   Ps 40

Ascension Day
   Evening Prayer on the Eve   Ps 15, 24   Ps 15, 24   Ps 15, 24
   Principal Service   Ps 47 or 93   Ps 47 or 93   Ps 47 or 93
   Second Service   Ps 8   Ps 8   Ps 8
   Third Service   Ps 110   Ps 110   Ps 110

Seventh Sunday of Easter
   Principal Service   Ps 68   Ps 1   Ps 97
   Second Service   Ps 47   Ps 147   Ps 68
   Third Service   Ps 104   Ps 76   Ps 99

Day of Pentecost
   Evening Prayer on the Eve   Ps 48   Ps 48   Ps 48
   Principal Service   Ps 104   Ps 104   Ps 104
   Second Service   Ps 67, 133   Ps 139   Ps 36, 150
   Third Service   Ps 87   Ps 145   Ps 33

ORDINARY TIME

Trinity Sunday
    Evening Prayer on the Eve   Ps 97, 98   Ps 97, 98   Ps 97, 98
    Principal Service   Ps 8   Ps 29   Ps 8
    Second Service   Ps 93, 150   Ps 104   Ps 73
    Third Service   Ps 86   Ps 33   Ps 29

Corpus Christi
    Evening Prayer on the Eve   Ps 110, 111   Ps 110, 111   Ps 110, 111
    Eucharist   Ps 116   Ps 116   Ps 116
    Morning Prayer   Ps 147   Ps 147   Ps 147
    Evening Prayer   Ps 23, 42, 43   Ps 23, 42, 43   Ps 23, 42, 43

Proper 4
    Principal Service
      Continuous   Ps 46   Ps 139   Ps 96
      Related   Ps 31   Ps 81   Ps 96
    Second Service   Ps 33   Ps 35   Ps 39
    Third Service   Ps 37   Ps 28, 32   Ps 41

Proper 5
    Principal Service
      Continuous   Ps 33   Ps 138   Ps 146
      Related   Ps 50   Ps 130   Ps 30
    Second Service   Ps [39] 41   Ps 37   Ps 44
    Third Service   Ps 38   Ps 36   Ps 45

Proper 6
    Principal Service
      Continuous   Ps 116   Ps 20   Ps 5
      Related   Ps 100   Ps 92   Ps 32
    Second Service   Ps [42] 43   Ps 39   Ps 52 [53]
    Third Service   Ps 45   Ps 42, 43   Ps 49

Proper 7
    Principal Service
      Continuous   Ps 86   Ps 9 or 133   Ps 42, 43
      Related   Ps 69   Ps 107   Ps 22
    Second Service   Ps 46 [48]   Ps 49   Ps [50] 57
    Third Service   Ps 49   Ps 48   Ps 55

Proper 8
    Principal Service
      Continuous   Ps 13   Ps 130   Ps 77
      Related   Ps 89   Lamentations B (p. 282) or Ps 30   Ps 16
    Second Service   Ps 50   Ps [52] 53   Ps [59] 60
    Third Service   Ps 52, 53   Ps 56   Ps 64

Proper 9
  Principal Service
    Continuous   Ps 45 or Song of Solomon (p. 283)   Ps 48   Ps 30
    Related   Ps 145   Ps 123   Ps 66
  Second Service   Ps 56 [57]   Ps [63] 64   Ps 65 [70]
  Third Service   Ps 55   Ps 57   Ps 74

Proper 10
  Principal Service
    Continuous   Ps 119   Ps 24   Ps 82
    Related   Ps 65   Ps 85   Ps 25
  Second Service   Ps 60 [63]   Ps 66   Ps 77
  Third Service   Ps 64, 65   Ps 65   Ps 76

Proper 11
  Principal Service
    Continuous   Ps 139   Ps 89   Ps 52
    Related   Ps 86   Ps 23   Ps 15
  Second Service   Ps 67 [70]   Ps 73   Ps 81
  Third Service   Ps 71   Ps 67, 70   Ps 82, 100

Proper 12
  Principal Service
    Continuous   Ps 105 or 128   Ps 14   Ps 85
    Related   Ps 119   Ps 145   Ps 138
  Second Service   Ps 75 [76]   Ps 74   Ps 88
  Third Service   Ps 77   Ps 75   Ps 95

Proper 13
  Principal Service
    Continuous   Ps 17   Ps 51   Ps 107
    Related   Ps 145   Ps 78   Ps 49
  Second Service   Ps 80   Ps 88   Ps 107
  Third Service   Ps 85   Ps 86   Ps 106

Proper 14
  Principal Service
    Continuous   Ps 105   Ps 130   Ps 50
    Related   Ps 85   Ps 34   Ps 33
  Second Service   Ps 86   Ps 91   Ps 108 [116]
  Third Service   Ps 88   Ps 90   Ps 115

Proper 15
  Principal Service
    Continuous   Ps 133   Ps 111   Ps 80
    Related   Ps 67   Ps 34   Ps 82
  Second Service   Ps 90   Ps 92 [100]   Ps 119
  Third Service   Ps 92   Ps 106   Ps 119

Proper 16
  Principal Service
    Continuous   Ps 124   Ps 84   Ps 71
    Related   Ps 138   Ps 34   Ps 103
    Second Service   Ps 95   Ps 116   Ps 119
    Third Service   Ps 104   Ps 115   Ps 119

Proper 17
  Principal Service
    Continuous   Ps 105   Ps 45   Ps 81
    Related   Ps 26   Ps 15   Ps 112
    Second Service   Ps 105   Ps 119   Ps 119
    Third Service   Ps 107   Ps 119   Ps 119

Proper 18
  Principal Service
    Continuous   Ps 149   Ps 125   Ps 139
    Related   Ps 119   Ps 146   Ps 1
    Second Service   Ps 108 [115]   Ps 119   Ps [120] 121
    Third Service   Ps 119   Ps 119   Ps 122, 123

Proper 19
  Principal Service
    Continuous   Ps 114   Ps 19   Ps 14
                        or Exodus (p. 278)   or Wisdom B (p. 285)
    Related   Ps 103   Ps 116   Ps 51
    Second Service   Ps 119   Ps 119   Ps 124, 125
    Third Service   Ps 119   Ps 119   Ps 126, 127

Proper 20
  Principal Service
    Continuous   Ps 105   Ps 1   Ps 79
    Related   Ps 145   Ps 54   Ps 113
    Second Service   Ps 119   Ps 119   Ps [128] 129
    Third Service   Ps 119   Ps 119   Ps 130, 131

Proper 21
  Principal Service
    Continuous   Ps 78   Ps 124   Ps 91
    Related   Ps 25   Ps 19   Ps 146
    Second Service   Ps [120, 123] 124   Ps 120, 121   Ps 134, 135
    Third Service   Ps 125, 126, 127   Ps 122   Ps 132

Proper 22
  Principal Service
    Continuous   Ps 19   Ps 26   Lamentations A
                                                                            (p. 281) or Ps 137
    Related   Ps 80   Ps 8   Ps 37
    Second Service   Ps 136   Ps 125, 126   Ps 142
    Third Service   Ps 128, 129, 134   Ps 123, 124   Ps 141

Proper 23
Principal Service
Continuous	Ps 106	Ps 22	Ps 66
Related	Ps 23	Ps 90	Ps 111
Second Service	Ps 139	Ps 127 [128]	Ps 144
Third Service	Ps 138, 141	Ps 129, 130	Ps 143

Proper 24
Principal Service
Continuous	Ps 99	Ps 104	Ps 119
Related	Ps 96	Ps 91	Ps 121
Second Service	Ps 142 [143]	Ps 141	Ps [146] 149
Third Service	Ps 145, 149	Ps 133, 134, 137	Ps 147

Proper 25
Principal Service
Continuous	Ps 90	Ps 34	Ps 65
Related	Ps 1	Ps 126	Ps 84
Second Service	Ps 119	Ps 119	Ps 119
Third Service	Ps 119	Ps 119	Ps 119

Bible Sunday
Principal Service	Ps 119	Ps 19	Ps 119
Second Service	Ps 119	Ps 119	Ps 119
Third Service	Ps 119	Ps 119	Ps 119

Dedication Festival
Evening Prayer on the Eve	Ps 24	Ps 24	Ps 24
Principal Service	Ps 122	Ps 122	Ps 122
Second Service	Ps 132	Ps 132	Ps 132
Third Service	Ps 48	Ps 48	Ps 48

All Saints' Day
Evening Prayer on the Eve	Ps 1, 5	Ps 1, 5	Ps 1, 5
Principal Service	Ps 34	Ps 24	Ps 149
Morning Prayer	Ps 15, 84	Ps 15, 84	Ps 15, 84
Evening Prayer	Ps 148, 150	Ps 148, 150	Ps 148, 150

All Saints' Day
(on 1 November if the above is used on the Sunday)
Eucharist	Ps 33	Ps 33	Ps 33
Morning Prayer	Ps 111, 112, 117	Ps 111, 112, 117	Ps 111, 112, 117
Evening Prayer	Ps 145	Ps 145	Ps 145

Fourth Sunday before Advent
Principal Service	Ps 43	Ps 119	Ps 32
Second Service	Ps 111, 117	Ps 145	Ps 145
Third Service	Ps 33	Ps 112, 149	Ps 87

Third Sunday before Advent

Principal Service	Wisdom A (p. 284)	Ps 62 or Ps 70	Ps 17
Second Service	Ps [20] 82	Ps 46 [82]	Ps 40
Third Service	Ps 91	Ps 136	Ps 20, 90

Second Sunday before Advent

Principal Service	Ps 90	Ps 16	Ps 98
Second Service	Ps 89	Ps 95	Ps [93] 97
Third Service	Ps 98	Ps 96	Ps 132

Christ the King

Evening Prayer on the Eve	Ps 99, 100	Ps 99, 100	Ps 99, 100
Principal Service	Ps 95	Ps 93	Ps 46
Second Service	Ps 93 [97]	Ps 72	Ps 72
Third Service	Ps 29, 110	Ps 29, 110	Ps 29, 110

Psalm 1

PRINCIPAL SERVICE
Proper 2 C
7 Easter B
Proper 18 C (related)
Proper 20 B
Proper 25 A (related)
Also: Evening Prayer: All Saints' Eve

2ND SERVICE
Proper 1 A
Proper 1 C

3RD SERVICE

Response

Keith Duke

v. 6a For the Lord knows the way, the way of the right-eous.

Verse

* *Omit in verse 3*

C.M.

1 *1* Blessed are they who | have not walked
  in the counsel | of the wicked,
  nor lingered in the | way of sinners,
  nor sat in the assembly | of the scornful.
  2 Their delight is in the law | of the Lord
  and they meditate on his law | day and night.

2 *3* Like a tree planted by | streams of water
  bearing fruit | in due season,
  with leaves that | do not wither,
  whatever they do, | it shall prosper.
  4 As for the wicked, it is not | so with them;
  they are like chaff which the wind | blows away.

3 *5* Therefore the wicked shall | not be able
  to stand | in the judgement,
  nor the sinner in the congregation | of the righteous.
  6 For the Lord knows the way | of the righteous,
  but the way of the wick | ed shall perish.

C Instrument

B♭ Instrument

Psalm 2

PRINCIPAL SERVICE
1 before Lent A

2ND SERVICE
1 before Lent B
Proper 1 C

3RD SERVICE
Proper 1 B
1 before Lent C

Response Andrew Wright

cf. v. 12 Happy are all who take their refuge in him.

Verse

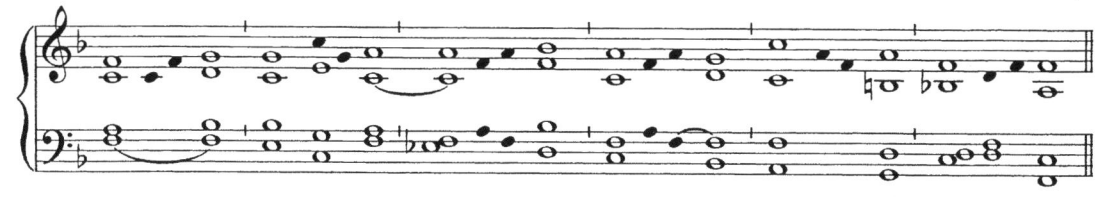

C.M.

1. *1* Why are the na | tions in tumult,
   and why do the peoples de | vise a vain plot?
   2 The kings of the earth rise up, and the rulers take coun | sel together,
   against the Lord and against | his anointed:
   3 'Let us break their | bonds asunder
   and cast a | way their cords from us.'

2. *4* He who dwells in heaven shall laugh | them to scorn;
   the Lord shall have them | in derision.
   5 Then shall he speak to them | in his wrath
   and terrify them | in his fury:
   6 'Yet have I | set my king
   upon my holy | hill of Zion.'

3. *7* I will proclaim the decree | of the Lord;
   he said to me: 'You are my Son; this day have | I begotten you.
   8 'Ask of me and I will give you the nations for | your inheritance
   and the ends of the earth for | your possession.
   9 'You shall break them with a | rod of iron
   and dash them in pieces like a | potter's vessel.'

4. *10* Now therefore be | wise, O kings;
   be prudent, you judges | of the earth.
   11 Serve the Lord with fear, and with trembling | kiss his feet,
   lest he be angry and you perish | from the way,
   for his wrath is | quickly kindled.
   12 Happy are all they who take ref | uge in him.

C Instrument

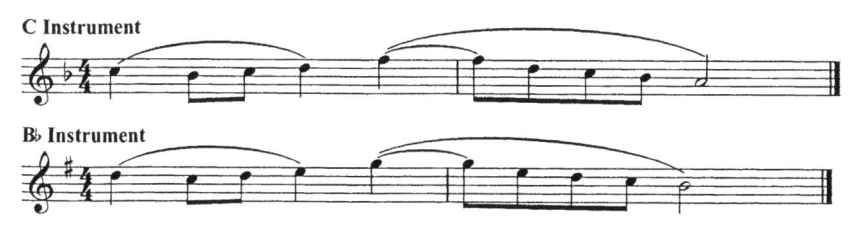

B♭ Instrument

Psalm 3

PRINCIPAL SERVICE

2ND SERVICE
Proper 1 A

3RD SERVICE
Proper 1 B
Proper 1 C

Keith Duke

Response

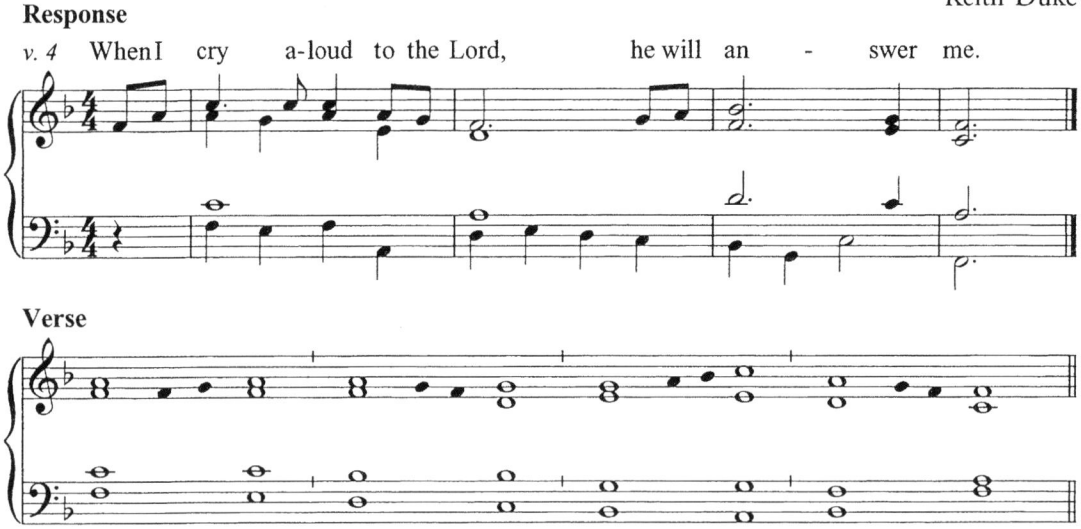

v. 4 When I cry aloud to the Lord, he will answer me.

Verse

T.B.

1. *1* Lord, how many | are my adversaries;
   many are they who rise | up against me.
   2 Many are they who say | to my soul,
   'There is no help for you | in your God.'

2. *3* But you, Lord, are a | shield about me;
   you are my glory, and the lifter up | of my head.
   4 When I cry aloud | to the Lord,
   he will answer me from his | holy hill;

3. *5* I lie down and sleep and | rise again,
   because the | Lord sustains me.
   6 I will not be afraid of hordes | of the peoples
   that have set themselves against me | all around.

4. *7* Rise up, O Lord, and deliver me, | O my God,
   for you strike all my enemies on the cheek and break the teeth | of the wicked.
   8 Salvation belongs | to the Lord:
   may your blessing be up | on your people.

C Instrument

B♭ Instrument

Psalm 4

PRINCIPAL SERVICE
3 Easter B

2ND SERVICE
Proper 1 A

3RD SERVICE
Proper 1 C

Andrew Wright

Response

cf. v. 8b It is you, O Lord, who make me dwell in safety.

Verse

* Omit in verse 4

S.L.

1 *1* Answer me | when I call,
   O God | of my righteousness;
   you set me at liberty when I | was in trouble;
   have mercy on me and | hear my prayer.

2 *2* How long will you nobles dishon | our my glory;
   how long will you love vain things and seek | after falsehood?
   3 But know that the Lord has shown me his mar | vellous kindness;
   when I call upon the Lord, | he will hear me.

3 *4* Stand in | awe, and sin not;
   commune with your own heart upon your bed, | and be still.
   5 Offer the sacrifi | ces of righteousness
   and put your trust | in the Lord.

4 *6* There are ma | ny that say,
   'Who will show us | any good?'
   Lord, lift up the light of your counte | nance upon us.

5 *7* You have put gladness | in my heart,
   more than when their corn and wine and | oil increase.
   8 In peace I will lie | down and sleep,
   for it is you Lord, only, who make me | dwell in safety.

C Instrument

B♭ Instrument

Psalm 5

PRINCIPAL SERVICE
Proper 6 C (vs. 1-8)
Also: Evening Prayer: All Saints' Eve

2ND SERVICE
Proper 1 B
Proper 2 C

3RD SERVICE
Proper 1 A

Keith Duke

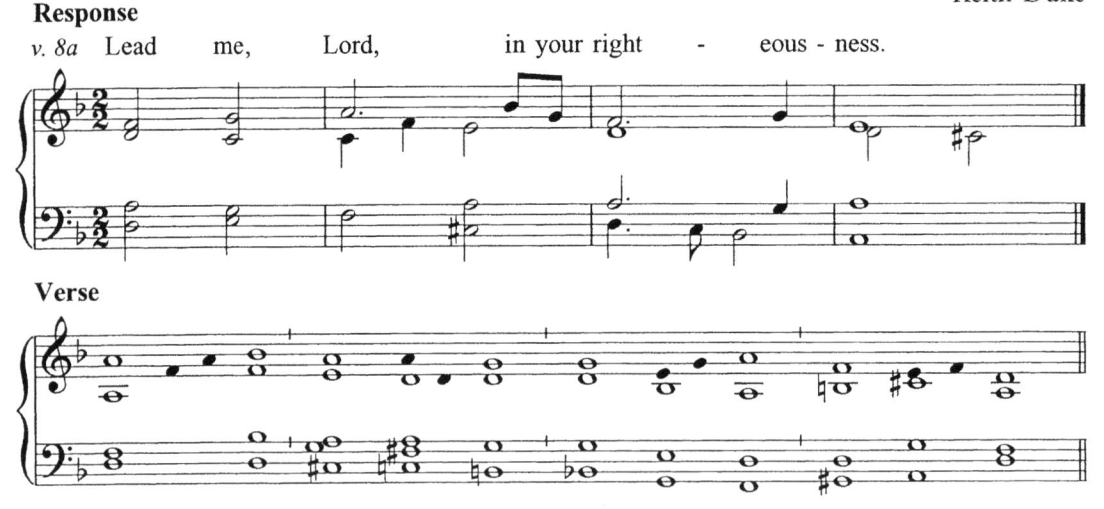

Response

v. 8a Lead me, Lord, in your right - eous - ness.

Verse

C.M.

1 *1* Give ear to my | words, O Lord;
   consider my | lamentation.
   2 Hearken to the voice of my crying, my King | and my God,
   for to you I | make my prayer.

2 *3* In the morning, Lord, you will | hear my voice;
   early in the morning I make my appeal to you, | and look up.
   4 For you are the God who takes no plea | sure in wickedness;
   no e | vil can dwell with you.

3 *5* The boastful cannot stand | in your sight;
   you hate all those | that work wickedness.
   6 You destroy those | who speak lies;
   the bloodthirsty and deceitful the Lord | will abhor.

4 *7* But as for me, through the greatness of your mercy, I will come in | to your house;
   I will bow down towards your holy tem | ple in awe of you.
   8 Lead me, Lord, in your righteousness, because | of my enemies;
   make your way straight be | fore my face.

5 *9* For there is no truth | in their mouth,
   in their heart | is destruction,
   their throat is an | open sepulchre,
   and they flatter | with their tongue.

6 *10* Punish | them, O God;
   let them fall through their | own devices.
   11 Because of their many transgressions | cast them out,
   for they have re | belled against you.

7 *12* But let all who take refuge in you be glad; let them sing out their | joy for ever.
   13 You will shelter them, so that those who love your name | may exult in you.
   14 For you, O Lord, will | bless the righteous;
   and with your favour you will defend them as | with a shield.

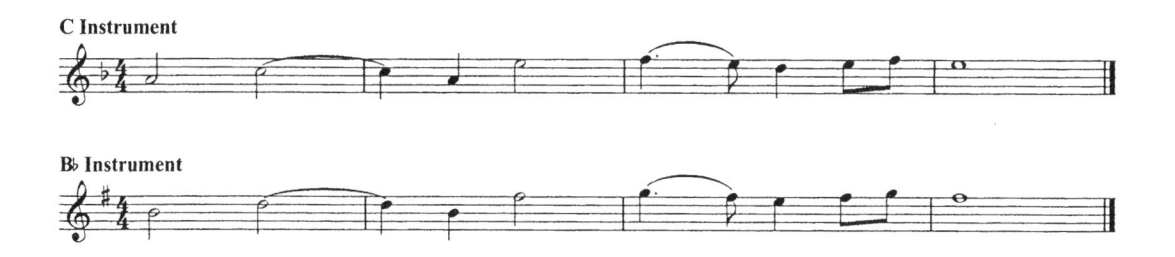

New Psalms for Common Worship

Psalm 6

PRINCIPAL SERVICE

2ND SERVICE
Proper 2 B
Proper 2 C

3RD SERVICE
Proper 1 A

Andrew Moore

Response
v. 9 The Lord has heard my sup-pli-ca-tion; the Lord will re-ceive my prayer.

Verse

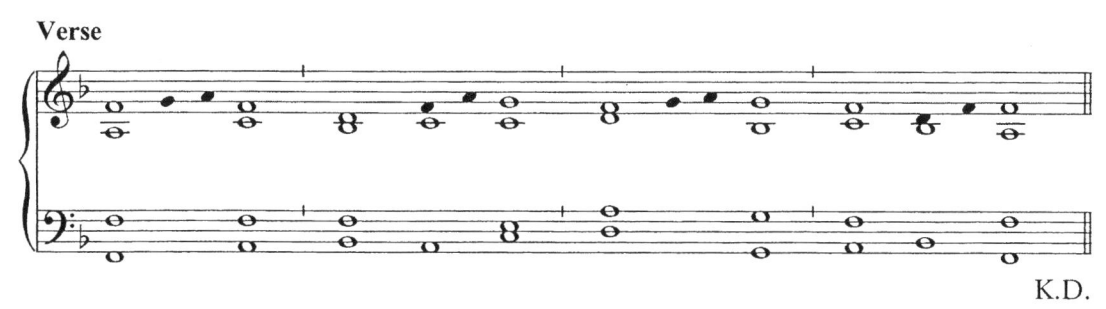

K.D.

1. *1* O Lord, rebuke me not | in your wrath;
   neither chasten me in | your fierce anger.
   2 Have mercy on me, Lord, for | I am weak;
   Lord, heal me, for my | bones are racked.

2. *3* My soul also shakes with terror; how long, O | Lord, how long?
   4 Turn again, O Lord, and deli | ver my soul;
   save me for your loving | mercy's sake.
   5 For in death no one remembers you; and who can give you thanks | in the grave?

3. *6* I am weary | with my groaning;
   every night I drench my pillow and flood my bed | with my tears.
   7 My eyes are was | ted with grief
   and worn away because of | all my enemies.

4. *8* Depart from me, all you | that do evil,
   for the Lord has heard the voice | of my weeping.
   9 The Lord has heard my supplication; the Lord will re | ceive my prayer.
   10 All my enemies shall be put to shame and confusion;
   they shall suddenly turn back | in their shame.

C Instrument

B♭ Instrument

Psalm 7

PRINCIPAL SERVICE

2ND SERVICE
Proper 2 A

3RD SERVICE
Proper 2 B
Proper 2 C

Gerry Fitzpatrick

Response

v. 1a O Lord my God, in you I take re-fuge.

Verse

K.D.

1 *1* O Lord my God, in you | I take refuge;
　　save me from all who pursue me, | and deliver me,
　2 Lest they rend me like a lion and tear | me in pieces
　　while there is no | one to help me.

2 *3* O Lord my God, if I have done these things:
　　if there is any wickedness | in my hands,
　4 If I have repaid my friend with evil,
　　or plundered my enemy with | out a cause,
　5 Then let my enemy pursue me and | overtake me,
　　trample my life to the ground, and lay my honour | in the dust.

3 *6* Rise up, O Lord, | in your wrath;
　　lift yourself up against the fury | of my enemies.
　　Awak | en, my God,
　　the judgement that you | have commanded.

4 *7* Let the assembly of the peoples | gather round you;
　　be seated high above them: O Lord, | judge the nations.
　8 Give judgement for me according to my righteous | ness, O Lord,
　　and according to the innocence | that is in me.

5 *9* Let the malice of the wicked come | to an end,
　　but esta | blish the righteous;
　　for you test the | mind and heart,
　　O | righteous God.

6 *10* God is my shield | that is over me;
   he saves the | true of heart.
  11 God is a | righteous judge;
   he is provoked | all day long.

7 *12* If they will not repent, God will | whet his sword;
   he has bent his bow and | made it ready.
  13 He has prepared the wea | pons of death;
   he makes his arrows | shafts of fire.

8 *14* Behold those who are in la | bour with wickedness,
   who conceive evil and give | birth to lies.
  15 They dig a pit and | make it deep
   and fall into the hole that they have | made for others.

9 *16* Their mischief rebounds on | their own head;
   their violence falls on | their own scalp.
  17 I will give thanks to the Lord | for his righteousness
   and I will make music to the name of the | Lord Most High.

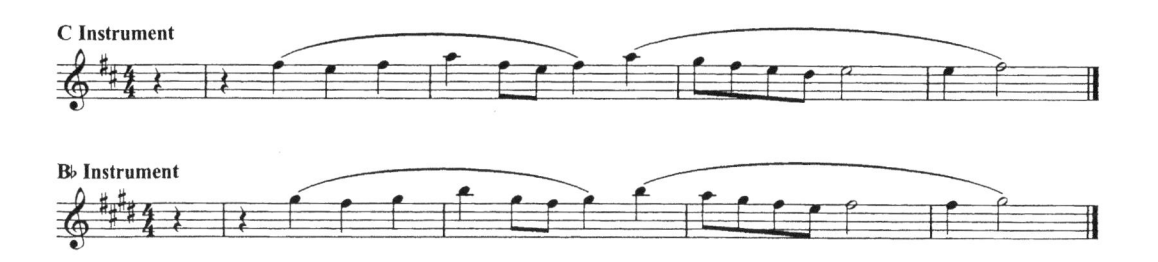

New Psalms for Common Worship

Psalm 8

PRINCIPAL SERVICE
Trinity A
Trinity C
Proper 22 B (related)

2ND SERVICE
Christmas Day ABC
Ascension ABC

3RD SERVICE

Keith Duke

Response
cf. v. 2 A-bove the hea-vens your ma-jes-ty be praised.

Verse

S.L.

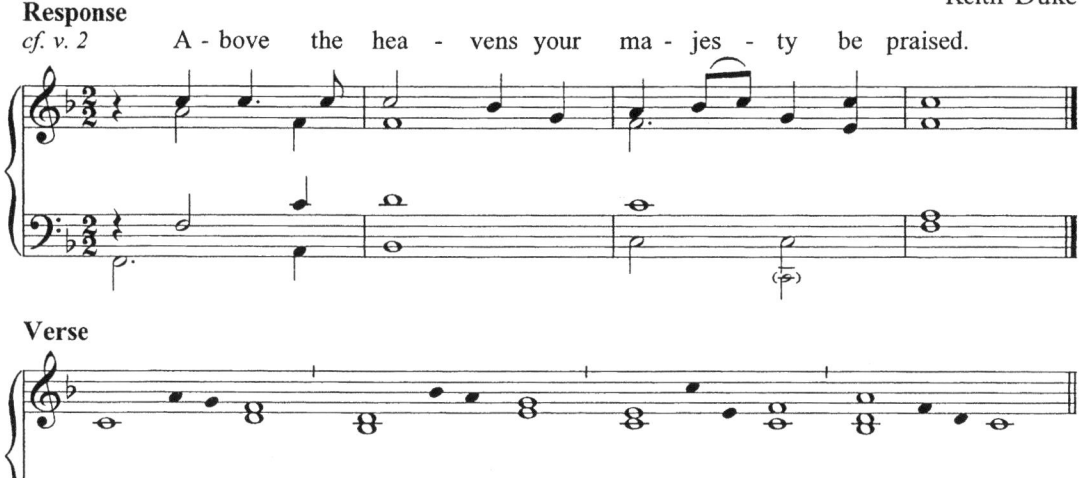

1 1 O Lord our governor, how glorious is your name in | all the world!
   2 Your majesty above the heavens is praised
       out of the mouths of babes | at the breast.
   3 You have founded a stronghold a | gainst your foes,
       that you might still the enemy and | the avenger.

2 4 When I consider your heavens, the work | of your fingers,
       the moon and the stars that you | have ordained,
   5 What are mortals, that you should be mind | ful of them;
       mere human beings, that you should | seek them out?

3 6 You have made them little lower | than the angels
       and crown them with glo | ry and honour.
   7 You have given them dominion over the works | of your hands
       and put all things un | der their feet,

4 8 All sheep and oxen, even the wild beasts | of the field,
   9 The birds of the air, the fish | of the sea
       and whatsoever moves in the paths | of the sea.
   10 O Lord our governor, how glorious is your name in | all the world!

C Instrument

B♭ Instrument

Psalm 9

PRINCIPAL SERVICE
Proper 7 B (vs. 9-20)

2ND SERVICE
1 Advent A (vs. 1-8)
1 Advent C (vs. 1-8)

3RD SERVICE
Proper 3 B

Keith Duke

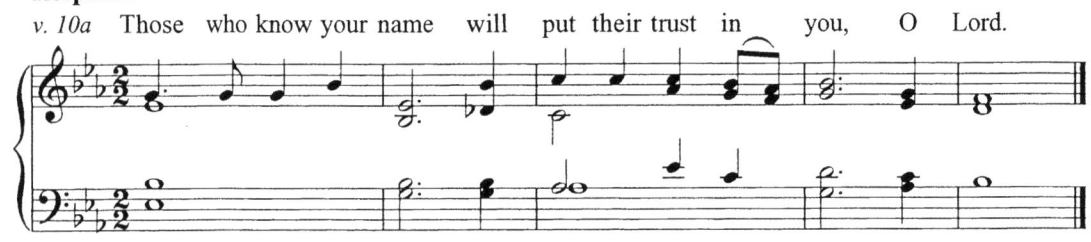

Response

v. 10a Those who know your name will put their trust in you, O Lord.

Verse

G.N.

1 *1* I will give thanks to you, Lord, with | my whole heart;
   I will tell of all your mar | vellous works.
   2 I will be glad | and rejoice in you;
   I will make music to your name, | O Most High.

2 *3* When my enemies are | driven back,
   they stumble and perish | at your presence.
   4 For you have maintained my right | and my cause;
   you sat on your throne giving | righteous judgement.

3 *5* You have rebuked the nations and des | troyed the wicked;
   you have blotted out their name for e | ver and ever.
   6 The enemy was utter | ly laid waste.
   You uprooted their cities; their very memo | ry has perished.

4 *7* But the Lord shall en | dure for ever;
   he has made fast his | throne for judgement.
   8 For he shall rule the | world with righteousness
   and govern the peo | ples with equity.

5 *9* Then will the Lord be a refuge for | the oppressed,
   a refuge in the | time of trouble.
   10 And those who know your name will | put their trust in you,
   for you, Lord, have never failed | those who seek you.

6 *11* Sing praises to the Lord who | dwells in Zion;
  declare among the peoples the things | he has done.
  12 The avenger of blood | has remembered them;
  he did not forget the cry of | the oppressed.

7 *13* Have mercy upon me, O Lord;
   consider the trouble I suffer from | those who hate me,
  you that lift me up from the | gates of death;
  14 That I may tell all your praises in the gates of the ci | ty of Zion
  and rejoice in | your salvation.

8 *15* The nations shall sink into the pit | of their making
  and in the snare which they set will their own | foot be taken.
  16 The Lord makes himself known by his | acts of justice;
  the wicked are snared in the works of | their own hands.

9 *17* They shall return to the | land of darkness,
  all the nations | that forget God.
  18 For the needy shall not always | be forgotten
  and the hope of the poor shall not pe | rish for ever.

10 *19* Arise, O Lord, and let not mortals have the | upper hand;
  let the nations be judged be | fore your face.
  20 Put them in | fear, O Lord,
  that the nations may know themselves to | be but mortal.

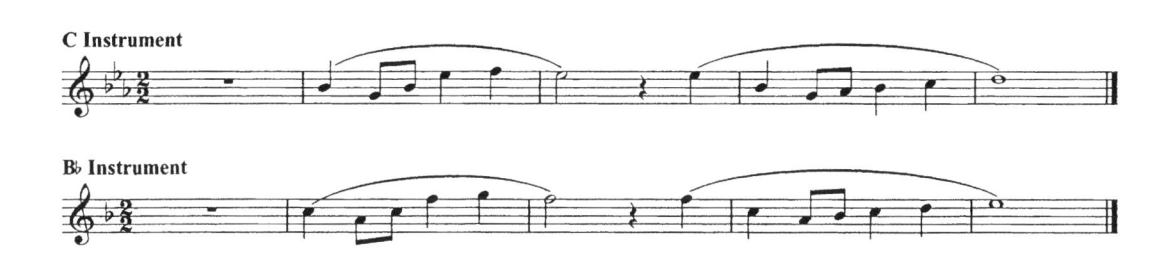

Psalm 10

PRINCIPAL SERVICE   2ND SERVICE   3RD SERVICE
                     Proper 3 B   Proper 2 A
                                    Proper 3 C

Gerry Fitzpatrick

Response
cf. v. 1 Do not hide your-self, O Lord, in time of trou-ble.

Verse

T.B.

1 *1* Why stand so far off, O Lord? Why hide yourself in | time of trouble?
  2 The wicked in their pride persecute the poor;
      let them be caught in the schemes they | have devised.
  3 The wicked boast of their | heart's desire;
      the covetous curse and re | vile the Lord.

2 *4* The wicked in their arrogance say, 'God will | not avenge it';
      in all their scheming God | counts for nothing.
  5 They are stubborn in all their ways,
      for your judgements are far above out | of their sight;
      they scoff at | all their adversaries.

3 *6* They say in their heart, 'I shall | not be shaken;
      no harm shall ever hap | pen to me.'
  7 Their mouth is full of cursing, de | ceit and fraud;
      under their tongue lie mis | chief and wrong.

4 *8* They lurk in the outskirts and in dark alleys they mur | der the innocent;
      their eyes are ever watching | for the helpless.
  9 They lie in wait, like a lion in his den;
      they lie in wait to | seize the poor;
      they seize the poor when they get them in | to their net.

5 *10* The innocent are broken and hum | bled before them;
   the helpless fall be | fore their power.
   11 They say in their heart, 'God | has forgotten;
   he hides his face away; he will | never see it.'

6 *12* Arise, O Lord God, and lift up your hand; forget | not the poor.
   13 Why should the wicked be scornful of God?
   Why should they say in their hearts, 'You will | not avenge it'?
   14 Surely, you behold trou | ble and misery;
   you see it and take it into | your own hand.

7 *15* The helpless commit them | selves to you,
   for you are the helper | of the orphan.
   16 Break the power of the wicked | and malicious;
   search out their wickedness un | til you find none.

8 *17* The Lord shall reign for ever and ever;
   the nations shall perish | from his land.
   18 Lord, you will hear the desire of the poor;
   you will incline your ear to the fullness | of their heart,
   19 To give justice to the orphan | and oppressed,
   so that people are no longer driven in terror | from the land.

Psalm 11

PRINCIPAL SERVICE

2ND SERVICE
2 Advent A
3 Lent B
Proper 3 C

3RD SERVICE

Simon Lesley

Response
cf. v. 8 For the Lord is right-eous, and those who are up-right shall be-hold his face.

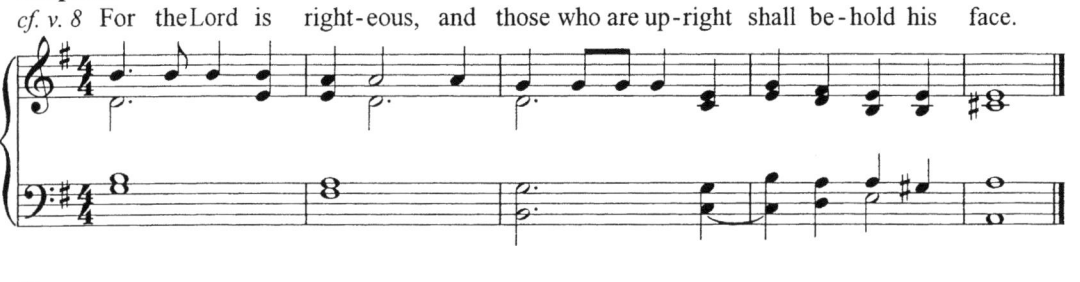

Verse

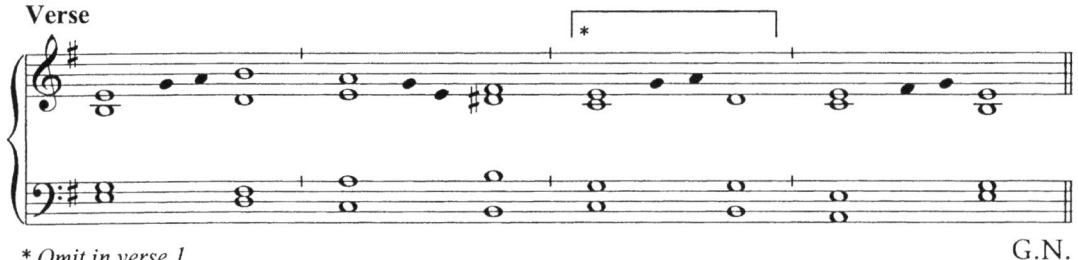

* Omit in verse 1

G.N.

1 *1* In the Lord have I | taken refuge;
how then | can you say to me,
'Flee like a bird | to the hills,

2 *2* 'For see how the wicked | bend the bow
and fit their arrows | to the string,
to shoot from the shadows at the | true of heart.
3 'When the foundations are destroyed, what | can the righteous do?'

3 *4* The Lord is in his holy temple; the Lord's throne | is in heaven.
5 His eyes behold, his eyelids try every | mortal being.
6 The Lord tries the righteous as well | as the wicked,
but those who delight in violence his | soul abhors.

4 *7* Upon the wicked he shall rain coals of fire and | burning sulphur;
scorching wind shall be their por | tion to drink.
8 For the Lord is righteous; he loves | righteous deeds,
and those who are upright shall be | hold his face.

C Instrument

B♭ Instrument

Psalm 12

PRINCIPAL SERVICE

2ND SERVICE
3 Advent A
3 Lent B
3 Lent C

3RD SERVICE
3 Advent C

Andrew Moore

Response

v. 7a You, O Lord, you, O Lord, will watch o-ver us.

Verse

T.B.

1 *1* Help me, Lord, for no one god | ly is left;
   the faithful have vanished from the whole | human race.
   2 They all speak falsely | with their neighbour;
   they flatter with their lips, but speak from a | double heart.

2 *3* O that the Lord would cut off all flat | tering lips
   and the tongue that | speaks proud boasts!
   4 Those who say, 'With our tongue will | we prevail;
   our lips we will use; who is lord | over us?'

3 *5* 'Because of the oppression of the needy, and the groaning | of the poor,
   I will rise up now,' says the Lord, 'and set them in the safety | that they long for.'
   6 The words of the Lord | are pure words,
   like silver refined in the furnace and purified seven times | in the fire.

4 *7* You, O Lord, | will watch over us
   and guard us from this genera | tion for ever.
   8 The wicked strut on | every side,
   when what is vile is exalted by the whole | human race.

C Instrument

B♭ Instrument

Psalm 13

PRINCIPAL SERVICE
Proper 8 A

2ND SERVICE
Proper 2 A
Proper 3 C
3 Lent C
4 Lent B

3RD SERVICE

Andrew Moore

Response

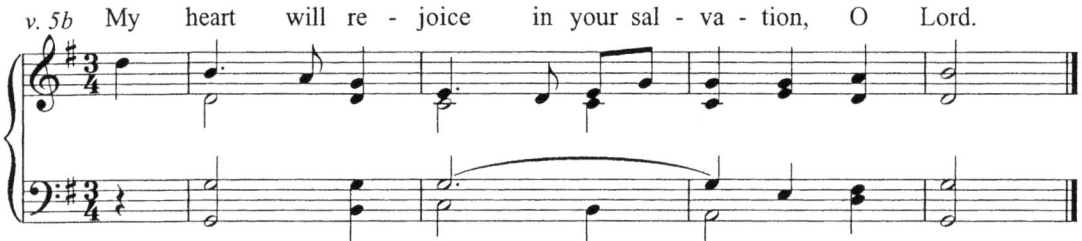

v. 5b My heart will re-joice in your sal-va-tion, O Lord.

Verse

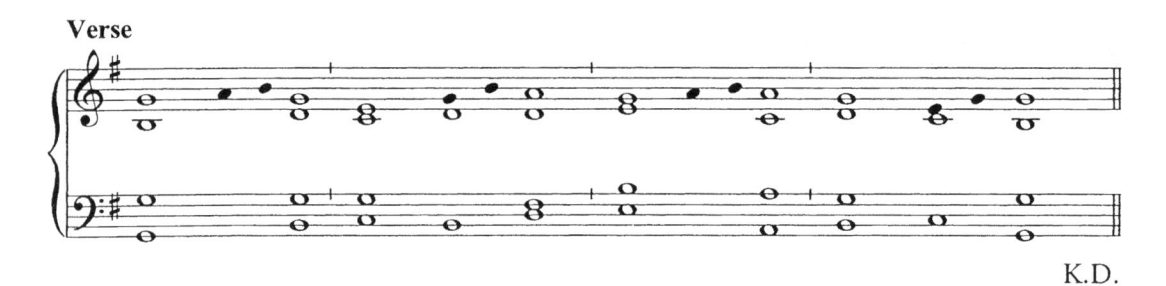

K.D.

1 *1* How long will you forget me, O | Lord; for ever?
   How long will you | hide your face from me?
  2 How long shall I have anguish in my soul
   and grief in my heart, day | after day?
   How long shall my enemy triumph | over me?

2 *3* Look upon me and answer, O | Lord my God;
   lighten my eyes, lest I | sleep in death;
  4 Lest my enemy say, 'I have pre | vailed against him,'
   and my foes rejoice that | I have fallen.

3 *5* But I put my trust in your | steadfast love;
   my heart will rejoice in | your salvation.
  6 I will sing | to the Lord,
   for he has dealt so bounti | fully with me.

C Instrument

B♭ Instrument

Psalm 14

PRINCIPAL SERVICE	2ND SERVICE	3RD SERVICE
Proper 12 B	3 Advent A	3 Advent C
Proper 19 C	4 Lent B	

Andrew Wright

Response

cf. v. 6 The Lord is the re-fuge of the poor.

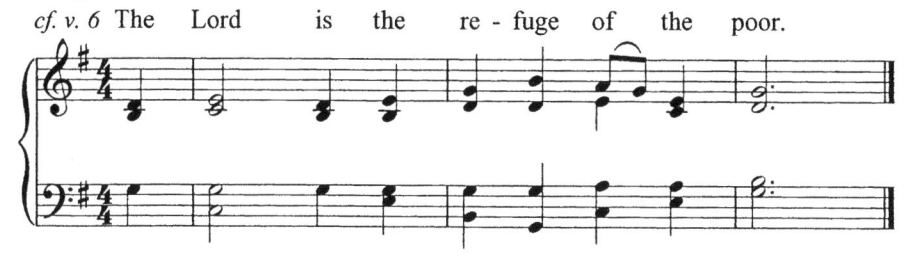

Verse

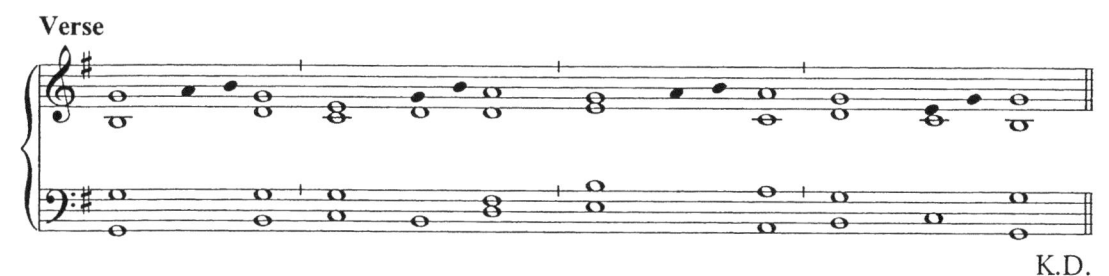

K.D.

1 *1* The fool has said in his heart, 'There | is no God.'
   Corrupt are they, and abominable in their wickedness;
      there is no one | that does good.
   2 The Lord has looked down from heaven upon the child | ren of earth,
      to see if there is anyone who is wise and seeks | after God.

2 *3* But every one has turned back; all alike have be | come corrupt:
      there is none that does good; | no, not one.
   4 Have they no knowledge, those | evildoers,
      who eat up my people as if they ate bread and do not call up | on the Lord?

3 *5* There shall they be | in great fear;
      for God is in the company | of the righteous.
   6 Though they would confound the counsel | of the poor,
      yet the Lord shall | be their refuge.

4 *7* O that Israel's salvation would come | out of Zion!
      When the Lord restores the fortunes | of his people,
      then will Ja | cob rejoice
      and Isra | el be glad.

C Instrument

B♭ Instrument

New Psalms for Common Worship

Psalm 15

PRINCIPAL SERVICE
Proper 11 C (related)
Proper 17 B (related)
Also: Evening Prayer: Ascension Day Eve ABC

2ND SERVICE
All Saints ABC

3RD SERVICE

Colin Mawby

Response

v. 1a O Lord, who may dwell in your ta-ber-na-cle?

Verse

S.L.

1 *1* Lord, who may dwell | in your tabernacle?
   Who may rest upon your | holy hill?
  2 Whoever leads an un | corrupt life
   and does the thing | that is right;

2 *3* Who speaks the truth | from the heart
   and bears no deceit | on the tongue;
  4 Who does no evil | to a friend
   and pours no scorn | on a neighbour;

3 *5* In whose sight the wicked are | not esteemed,
   but who honours those who | fear the Lord.
  6 Whoever has sworn | to a neighbour
   and never goes back | on that word;

4 *7* Who does not lend money in | hope of gain,
   nor takes a bribe a | gainst the innocent;
  8 Whoever | does these things
   shall | never fall.

C Instrument

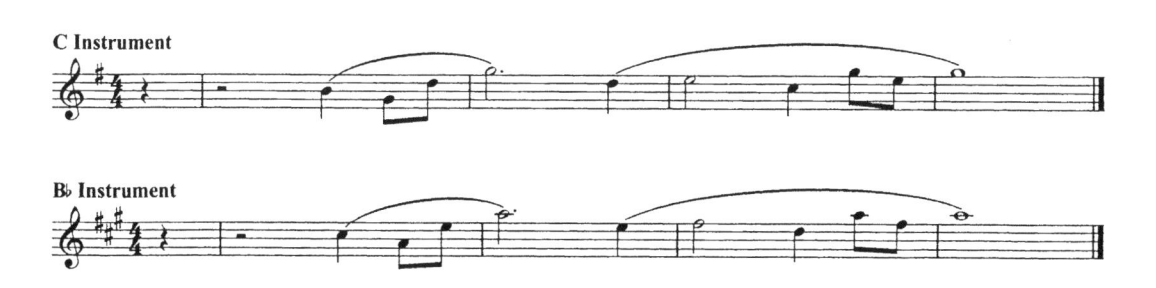

B♭ Instrument

Psalm 16

PRINCIPAL SERVICE
2 Easter A
Proper 8 C (related)
2 before Advent B
Also: Easter Vigil ABC

2ND SERVICE
2 Easter C

3RD SERVICE
5 Easter C

Simon Lesley

Response

cf. v. 10 In your presence, O Lord, is the full-ness of joy.

Verse

C.M.

1 *1* Preserve me, O God, for in you have I | taken refuge;
   I have said to the Lord, 'You are my lord,
      all my good de | pends on you.'
  2 All my delight is upon the godly that are in the land,
      upon those who are no | ble in heart.

2 *3* Though the idols are legion that ma | ny run after,
   their drink offerings of blood I | will not offer,
   neither make mention of their names up | on my lips.

3 *4* The Lord himself is my portion | and my cup;
   in your hands alone | is my fortune.
  5 My share has fallen in a fair land;
      indeed, I have a | goodly heritage.

4 *6* I will bless the Lord who has gi | ven me counsel,
   and in the night watches he in | structs my heart.
  7 I have set the Lord always before me;
      he is at my right hand; I | shall not fall.

5 *8* Wherefore my heart is glad and my spi | rit rejoices;
   my flesh also shall | rest secure.
 9 For you will not abandon my soul to Death,
   nor suffer your faithful one to | see the Pit.

6 *10* You will show me the | path of life;
   in your presence is the full | ness of joy
   and in your right hand are pleasures for | evermore.

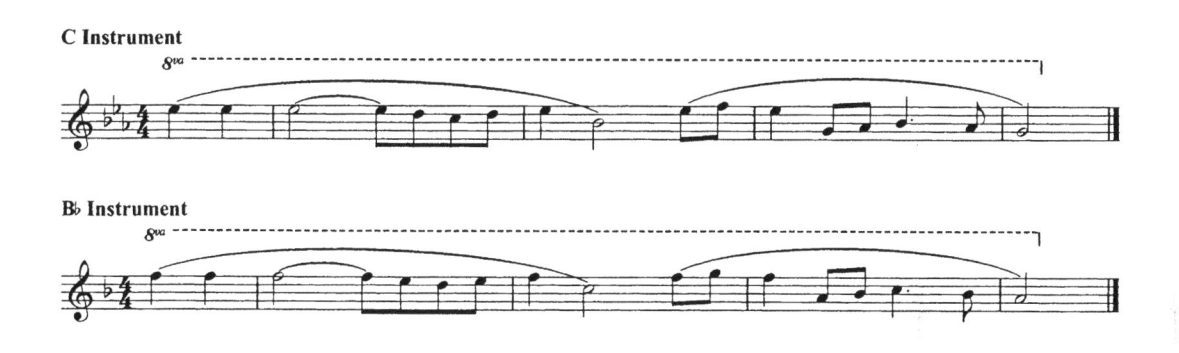

New Psalms for Common Worship

Psalm 17

vs. 9-15 are omitted
PRINCIPAL SERVICE
Proper 13 A (vs. 1-7, 16)
3 before Advent C (vs. 1-8)

2ND SERVICE

3RD SERVICE

Colin Mawby

Response

cf. v. 6 In-cline your ear to me, O Lord, and lis-ten to my words.

Verse

* Omit in verse 4

G.N.

1 ₁ Hear my just cause, O Lord; consider | my complaint;
   listen to my prayer, which comes not from | lying lips.
   ₂ Let my vindication come forth | from your presence;
   let your eyes behold | what is right.

2 ₃ Weigh my heart, examine | me by night,
   refine me, and you will find no impuri | ty in me.
   ₄ My mouth does not trespass for earth | ly rewards;
   I have heeded the words of your lips.

3 ₅ My footsteps hold fast in the ways of | your commandments;
   my feet have not stumbled | in your paths.
   ₆ I call upon you, O God, for | you will answer me;
   incline your ear to me, and listen | to my words.

4 ₇ Show me your marvellous | loving-kindness,
   O Saviour of those who take refuge at | your right hand
       from those who rise | up against them.

5 ₈ Keep me as the apple | of your eye;
   hide me under the shadow | of your wings.
   ₁₆ As for me, I shall see your | face in righteousness;
   when I awake and behold your likeness, I | shall be satisfied.

C Instrument

B♭ Instrument

Psalm 18

vs. 31-51 are omitted

PRINCIPAL SERVICE

2ND SERVICE
Proper 3 A (vs. 1-20)
(or vs. 21-30)

3RD SERVICE
3 Lent B (vs. 1-25)

John McCann

Response

cf. v. 3 I cried to the Lord, and was saved from my e-ne-mies.

Verse

T.B.

1 *1* I love you, O | Lord my strength.
   The Lord is my crag, my fortress and | my deliverer,
   2 My God, my rock in whom | I take refuge,
   my shield, the horn of my salvation | and my stronghold.

2 *3* I cried to the Lord | in my anguish
   and I was saved | from my enemies.
   4 The cords of death entwined me and the
   torrents of destruction | overwhelmed me.
   5 The cords of the Pit fastened about me
   and the snares of | death entangled me.

3 *6* In my distress I called up | on the Lord
   and cried out to my | God for help.
   7 He heard my voice | in his temple
   and my cry came | to his ears.

4 *8* The earth trem | bled and quaked;
   the foundations of the mountains shook;
   they reeled because | he was angry.
   9 Smoke rose from his nostrils
   and a consuming fire went out | of his mouth;
   burning coals blazed | forth from him.

5 *10* He parted the heavens | and came down
   and thick darkness was un | der his feet.
   11 He rode upon the cheru | bim and flew;
   he came flying on the wings | of the wind.

6 *12* He made darkness his covering | round about him,
   dark waters and thick clouds | his pavilion.
   13 From the brightness of his presence, | through the clouds
   burst hailstones and | coals of fire.

7 ₁₄ The Lord also thundered | out of heaven;
  the Most High uttered his voice with hailstones and | coals of fire.
 ₁₅ He sent out his ar | rows and scattered them;
  he hurled down lightnings and put | them to flight.

8 ₁₆ The springs of the o | cean were seen,
  and the foundations of the | world uncovered
  at your re | buke, O Lord,
  at the blast of the breath of | your displeasure.

9 ₁₇ He reached down from on | high and took me;
  he drew me out of the | mighty waters.
 ₁₈ He delivered me from | my strong enemy,
  from foes that were too migh | ty for me.

10 ₁₉ They came upon me in the day | of my trouble;
  but the Lord was | my upholder.
 ₂₀ He brought me out into a | place of liberty;
  he rescued me because he deligh | ted in me.

11 ₂₁ The Lord rewarded me after my | righteous dealing;
  according to the cleanness of my hands he | recompensed me,
 ₂₂ Because I had kept the ways | of the Lord
  and had not gone wickedly away | from my God,

12 ₂₃ For I had an eye to all his laws, and did not
  cast out his com | mandments from me.
 ₂₄ I was also wholehearted before him and kept myself | from iniquity;
 ₂₅ Therefore the Lord rewarded me after my | righteous dealing,
  and according to the cleanness of my hands | in his sight.

13 ₂₆ With the faithful you show | yourself faithful;
  with the true you show | yourself true;
 ₂₇ With the pure you show | yourself pure,
  but with the crooked you show your | self perverse.

14 ₂₈ For you will save a lowly people and bring down
  the high looks | of the proud.
 ₂₉ You also shall light my candle; the Lord my God
  shall make my darkness | to be bright.
 ₃₀ By your help I shall run at an e | nemy host;
  with the help of my God I can leap o | ver a wall.

Psalm 19

PRINCIPAL SERVICE
3 Epiphany C (vs. 1-6)
3 Lent B (vs. 7-14)
Proper 19 B (vs. 1-6)
Proper 21 B (related) (vs. 7-14)
Proper 22 A (vs. 7-14)
Bible Sunday B (vs. 7-14)
Also: Easter Vigil ABC

2ND SERVICE

3RD SERVICE
4 Lent A

Gerry Fitzpatrick

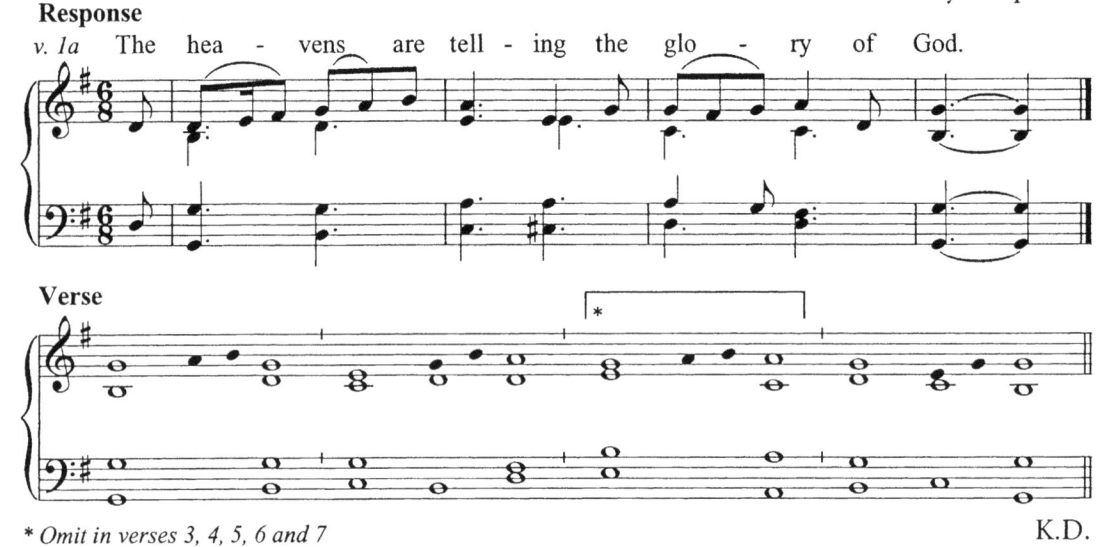

Response

v. 1a The heavens are telling the glory of God.

Verse

Omit in verses 3, 4, 5, 6 and 7

K.D.

1 *1* The heavens are telling the glo | ry of God
and the firmament pro | claims his handiwork.
2 One day pours out its song | to another
and one night unfolds knowledge | to another.

2 *3* They have neither | speech nor language
and their voices | are not heard,
4 Yet their sound has gone out in | to all lands
and their words to the ends | of the world.

3 *5* In them has he set a tabernacle | for the sun,
that comes forth as a bridegroom out | of his chamber
and rejoices as a champion to | run his course.

4 *6* It goes forth from the end | of the heavens
and runs to the very | end again,
and there is nothing hidden | from its heat.

5 *7* The law of the Lord is perfect, reviv | ing the soul;
the testimony of the | Lord is sure
and gives wisdom | to the simple.

46

6 *8* The statutes of the Lord are right and re | joice the heart;
　　the commandment of the | Lord is pure
　　and gives light | to the eyes.

7 *9* The fear of the Lord is clean and en | dures for ever;
　　the judgements of the | Lord are true
　　and righteous | altogether.

8 *10* More to be desired are | they than gold,
　　more than | much fine gold,
　　sweeter al | so than honey,
　　dripping | from the honeycomb.

9 *11* By them also is your | servant taught
　　and in keeping them there is | great reward.
　12 Who can tell how often | they offend?
　　O cleanse me from my | secret faults!

10 *13* Keep your servant also from pre | sumptuous sins
　　lest they get do | minion over me;
　　so shall I be | undefiled,
　　and innocent of | great offence.

11 *14* Let the words | of my mouth
　　and the meditation | of my heart
　　be acceptable | in your sight,
　　O Lord, my strength and | my redeemer.

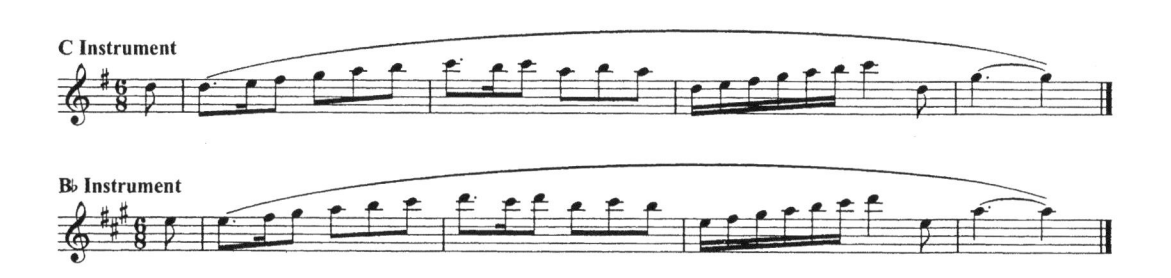

New Psalms for Common Worship

Psalm 20

PRINCIPAL SERVICE
Proper 6 B

2ND SERVICE
3 before Advent A

3RD SERVICE
3 before Advent C

Andrew Wright

Response

cf. v. 9 Answer us, O Lord, when we call.

Verse

C.M.

1 ₁ May the Lord hear you in the | day of trouble,
   the name of the God of Ja | cob defend you;
  ₂ Send you help | from his sanctuary
   and strengthen you | out of Zion;

2 ₃ Remember all your offerings and accept | your burnt sacrifice;
  ₄ Grant you your heart's desire and fulfil | all your mind.
  ₅ May we rejoice in your salvation and triumph in the name | of our God;
   may the Lord perform all | your petitions.

3 ₆ Now I know that the Lord will save | his anointed;
   he will answer him from his holy heaven,
    with the mighty strength | of his right hand.
  ₇ Some put their trust in chariots and | some in horses,
   but we will call only on the name of the | Lord our God.

4 ₈ They are brought | down and fallen,
   but we are risen | and stand upright.
  ₉ O Lord, | save the king
   and answer us when we | call upon you.

C Instrument

B♭ Instrument

Psalm 21

PRINCIPAL SERVICE   2ND SERVICE   3RD SERVICE
Proper 3 A

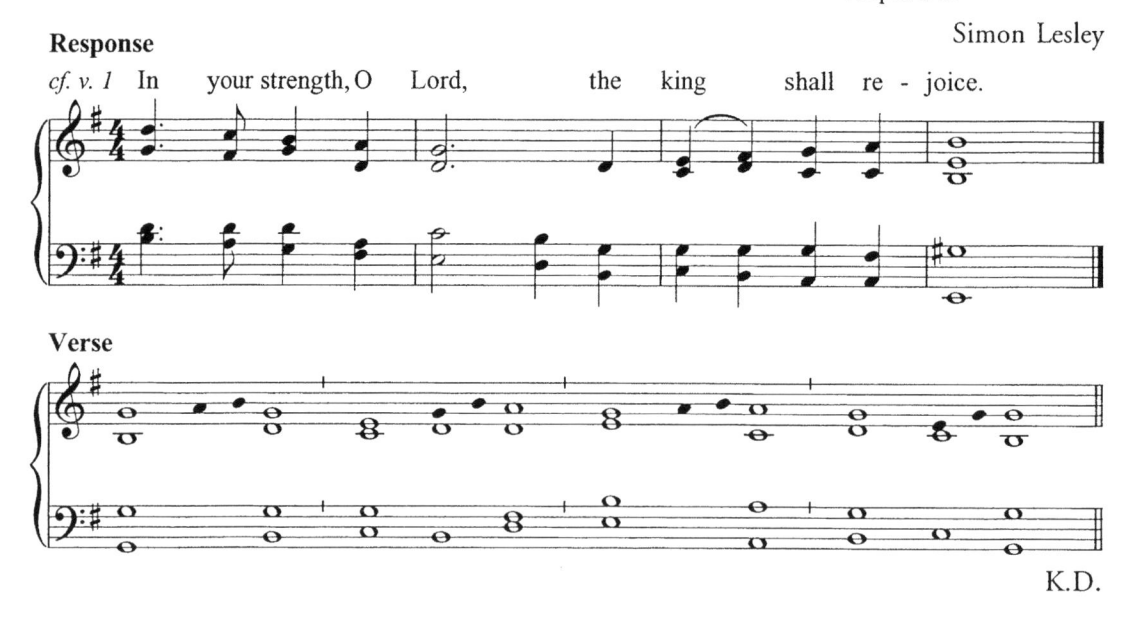

Simon Lesley

Response

cf. v. 1 In your strength, O Lord, the king shall re-joice.

Verse

K.D.

1 *1* The king shall rejoice in your | strength, O Lord;
how greatly shall he rejoice in | your salvation!
2 You have given him his | heart's desire
and have not denied the request | of his lips.

2 *3* For you come to meet him with bles | sings of goodness
and set a crown of pure gold u | pon his head.
4 He asked of you life | and you gave it him,
length of days, for e | ver and ever.

3 *5* His honour is great because of | your salvation;
glory and majesty have you | laid upon him.
6 You have granted him everlas | ting felicity
and will make him glad with joy | in your presence.

4 *7* For the king puts his trust | in the Lord;
because of the loving-kindness of the Most High,
he shall not be | overthrown.
8 Your hand shall mark down | all your enemies;
your right hand will find out | those who hate you.

5 *9* You will make them like a | fiery oven
in the time | of your wrath;
the Lord will swallow them up | in his anger
and the fire | will consume them.

6 *10* Their fruit you will root out | of the land
  and their seed from among | its inhabitants.
  11 Because they intend evil against you and devise | wicked schemes
  which they can | not perform,

7 *12* You will put | them to flight
  when you aim your bow | at their faces.
  13 Be exalted, O Lord, in | your own might;
  we will make music and sing | of your power.

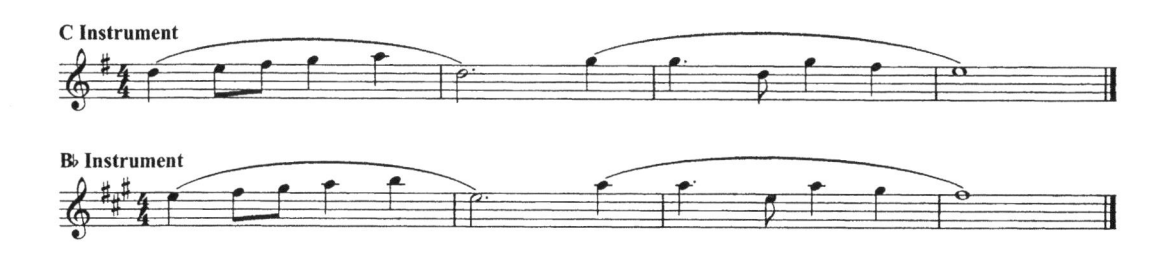

Psalm 22

PRINCIPAL SERVICE
2 Lent B (vs. 23-31)
Good Friday ABC
  (all, or vs. 1-11, or vs. 1-21)
5 Easter B (vs. 25-31)
Proper 7 C (related) (vs. 19-28)
Proper 23 B (vs. 1-15)

2ND SERVICE

3RD SERVICE
2 Easter B (vs. 19-32)

Andrew Moore

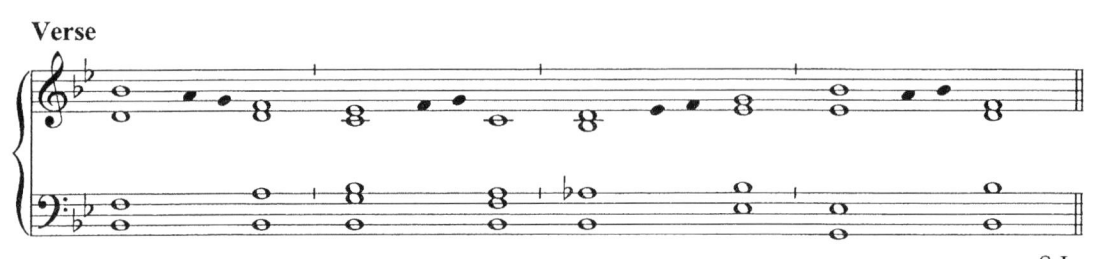

Response (v. 1): My God, my God, why have you forsaken me?

Verse

S.L.

1 *1* My God, my God, why have | you forsaken me,
   and are so far from my salvation, from the words of | my distress?
 2 O my God, I cry in the daytime, but you | do not answer;
   and by night also, but I | find no rest.

2 *3* Yet you are the Holy One, enthroned upon the prai | ses of Israel.
 4 Our forebears trusted in you; they trusted, and | you delivered them.
 5 They cried out to you and | were delivered;
   they put their trust in you and were | not confounded.

3 *6* But as for me, I am a worm | and no man,
   scorned by all and despised | by the people.
 7 All who see me laugh | me to scorn;
   they curl their lips and wag | their heads, saying,

4 *8* 'He trusted in the Lord; let | him deliver him;
   let him deliver him, if | he delights in him.'
 9 But it is you that took me out | of the womb
   and laid me safe upon my | mother's breast.

5 *10* On you was I cast ever since | I was born;
   you are my God even from my | mother's womb.
 11 Be not far from me, for trouble is | near at hand
   and there is | none to help.

6 *12* Mighty oxen | come around me;
   fat bulls of Bashan close me in on | ev'ry side.
 13 They gape upon me | with their mouths,
   as it were a ramping and a | roaring lion.

7 *14* I am poured out like water; all my bones are | out of joint;
  my heart has become like wax melting in the depths | of my body.
 15 My mouth is dried up like a potsherd; my tongue cleaves | to my gums;
  you have laid me in the | dust of death.

8 *16* For the hounds are all about me, the pack of evildo | ers close in on me;
  they pierce my hands | and my feet.
 17 I can count all my bones; they stand staring and look | ing upon me.
 18 They divide my garments among them; they cast lots | for my clothing.

9 *19* Be not far from me, O Lord; you are my strength; has | ten to help me.
 20 Deliver my soul | from the sword,
  my poor life from the power | of the dog.
 21 Save me from the lion's mouth,
   from the horns of wild oxen. | You have answered me!

10 *22* I will tell of your name | to my people;
  in the midst of the congregation | will I praise you.
 23 Praise the Lord, | you that fear him;
  O seed of Jacob, glorify him; stand in awe of him, O | seed of Israel.

11 *24* For he has | not despised
  nor abhorred the suffering | of the poor;
  neither has he hid | den his face from them;
  but when they cried to | him he heard them.

12 *25* From you comes my praise in the great | congregation;
  I will perform my vows in the presence of | those that fear you.
 26 The poor shall eat | and be satisfied;
  those who seek the Lord shall praise him; their hearts shall | live for ever.

13 *27* All the ends of the earth shall remember and turn | to the Lord,
  and all the families of the nations shall | bow before him.
 28 For the kingdom | is the Lord's
  and he rules o | ver the nations.

14 *29* How can those who sleep in the earth bow down in worship,
  or those who go down to the dust | kneel before him?
 30 He has saved my life for himself; my descen | dants shall serve him;
  this shall be told of the Lord for genera | tions to come.
 31 They shall come and make known his salvation, to a people yet unborn,
   declaring that he, the | Lord, has done it.

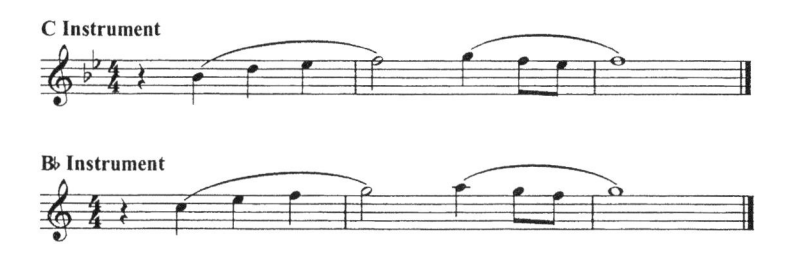

New Psalms for Common Worship

Psalm 23

PRINCIPAL SERVICE
4 Lent A
4 Easter ABC
Proper 11 B (related)
Proper 23 A (related)

2ND SERVICE

3RD SERVICE
Proper 3 A
3 Easter A
Corpus Christi ABC

Geoff Nobes

Response

cf. v. 1 The Lord is my shep-herd, there is no-thing I shall want.

Verse

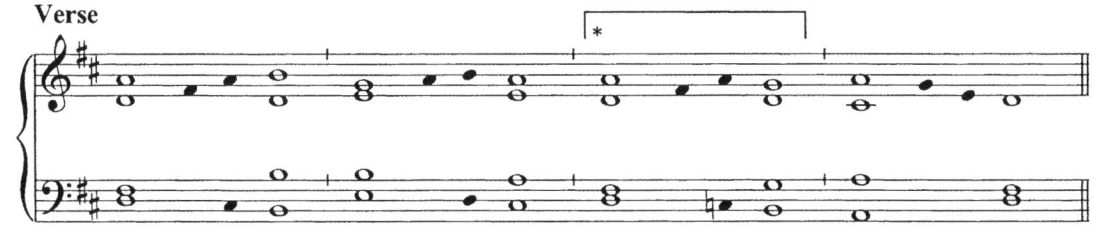

* Omit in verse 4

K.D.

1 *1* The Lord is my shepherd; therefore can | I lack nothing.
  2 He makes me lie down in green pastures and leads me be | side still waters.
  3 He shall re | fresh my soul
     and guide me in the paths of righteousness | for his name's sake.

2 *4* Though I walk through the valley of the sha | dow of death,
     I will | fear no evil;
     for | you are with me;
     your rod and your | staff, they comfort me.

3 *5* You spread a ta | ble before me
     in the presence of | those who trouble me;
     you have anointed my | head with oil
     and my cup | shall be full.

4 *6* Surely goodness and loving mer | cy shall follow me
     all the days | of my life,
     and I will dwell in the house of the | Lord for ever.

C Instrument

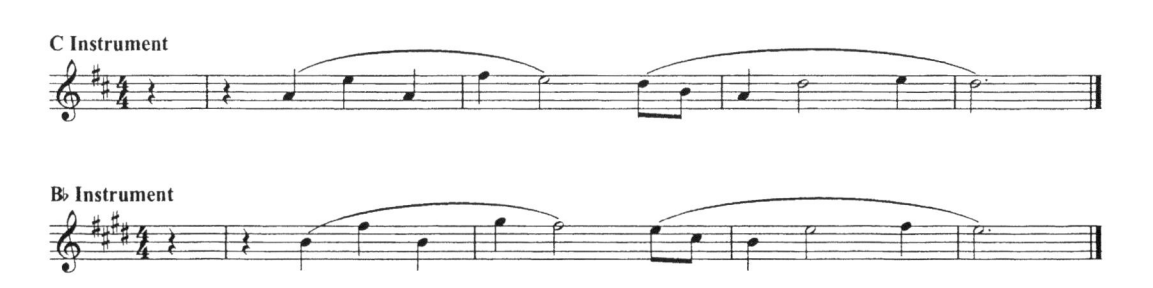

B♭ Instrument

Psalm 24

PRINCIPAL SERVICE
Presentation ABC (vs. 7-10)
Proper 10 B
All Saints B (vs. 1-6)
Also: Evening Prayer: Ascension ABC; Dedication ABC

2ND SERVICE

3RD SERVICE

John McCann

Response
v. 10b The Lord of hosts, he is the King of glory.

Verse

* Omit in verses 4-7

G.N.

1 ₁ The earth is the Lord's and | all that fills it,
   the compass of the world and all who | dwell therein.
  ₂ For he has founded it up | on the seas
   and set it firm upon the rivers | of the deep.

2 ₃ 'Who shall ascend the hill | of the Lord,
   or who can rise up in his | holy place?'
  ₄ 'Those who have clean hands | and a pure heart,
   who have not lifted up their soul to an idol, nor sworn an oath | to a lie;

3 ₅ 'They shall receive a blessing | from the Lord,
   a just reward from the God of | their salvation.'
  ₆ Such is the company of | those who seek him,
   of those who seek your face, O | God of Jacob.

4 ₇ Lift up your | heads, O gates;
   be lifted up, you ever | lasting doors;
   and the King of glory | shall come in.

5 *8* 'Who is the | King of glory?'
   'The Lord, | strong and mighty,
   the Lord who is migh | ty in battle.'

6 *9* Lift up your | heads, O gates;
   be lifted up, you ever | lasting doors;
   and the King of glory | shall come in.

7 *10* 'Who is this | King of glory?'
   'The | Lord of hosts,
   he is the | King of glory.'

Psalm 25

PRINCIPAL SERVICE
1 Advent C (vs. 1-9)
1 Lent B (vs. 1-9)
Proper 10 C (related) (vs. 1-9)
Proper 21 A (related) (vs. 1-9)

2ND SERVICE
1 Advent B (vs. 1-9)

3RD SERVICE
Monday of Holy Week ABC

Alan Rees

Response
v. 1 To you, O Lord, I lift up my soul.

Verse

* Omit in verse 10

G.N.

1 *1* To you, O Lord, I lift up my soul; O my God, in | you I trust;
   let me not be put to shame; let not my enemies | triumph over me.
  2 Let none who look to you be | put to shame,
   but let the treacherous be shamed | and frustrated.

2 *3* Make me to know your ways, O Lord, and teach | me your paths.
  4 Lead me in your | truth and teach me,
   for you are the God of | my salvation;
   for you have I hoped all | the day long.

3 *5* Remember, Lord, your compas | sion and love,
   for they are from | everlasting.
  6 Remember not the sins of my youth or | my transgressions,
   but think on me in your goodness, O Lord, according to your | steadfast love.

4 *7* Gracious and upright | is the Lord;
   therefore shall he teach sinners | in the way.
  8 He will guide the humble in doing right and teach his way | to the lowly.
  9 All the paths of the Lord are mercy and truth
   to those who keep his covenant | and his testimonies.

5 *10* For your name's | sake, O Lord,
   be merciful to my sin, for | it is great.
  11 Who are those who | fear the Lord?
   Them will he teach in the way that | they should choose.

6 *12* Their soul shall | dwell at ease
and their offspring shall inher | it the land.
 13 The hidden purpose of the Lord is for | those who fear him
and he will show | them his covenant.

7 *14* My eyes are ever looking | to the Lord,
for he shall pluck my feet out | of the net.
 15 Turn to me and be gra | cious to me,
for I am alone and brought | very low.

8 *16* The sorrows of my heart | have increased;
O bring me out of | my distress.
 17 Look upon my adversi | ty and misery
and forgive me | all my sin.

9 *18* Look upon my enemies, for | they are many
and they bear a violent ha | tred against me.
 19 O keep my soul | and deliver me;
let me not be put to shame, for I have put my | trust in you.

10 *20* Let integrity and upright | ness preserve me,
for my hope has | been in you.
 21 Deliver Israel, O God,
out of | all his troubles.

Psalm 26

PRINCIPAL SERVICE
Proper 17A (related) (vs. 1-8)
Proper 22 B

2ND SERVICE

3RD SERVICE
3 Lent C

Simon Lesley

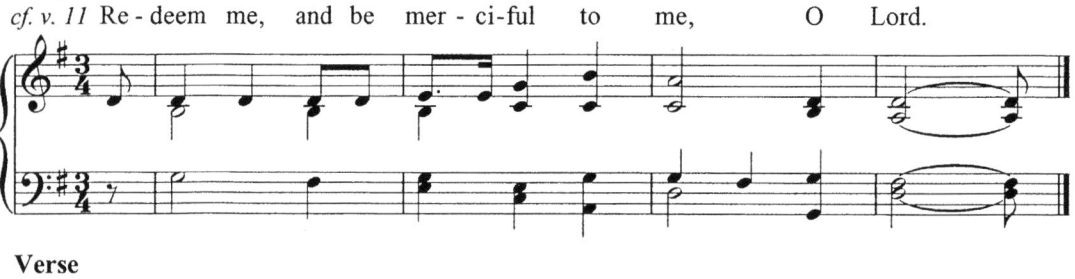

Response

cf. v. 11 Redeem me, and be merciful to me, O Lord.

Verse

S.L.

1 *1* Give judgement for me, O Lord, for I have walked | with integrity;
   I have trusted in the Lord and | have not faltered.
   2 Test me, O | Lord, and try me;
   examine my heart | and my mind.

2 *3* For your love is be | fore my eyes;
   I have walked | in your truth.
   4 I have not joined the company | of the false,
   nor consorted with | the deceitful.

3 *5* I hate the gathe | ring of evildoers
   and I will not sit down | with the wicked.
   6 I will wash my hands in inno | cence, O Lord,
   that I may go a | bout your altar,

4 *7* To make heard the voice | of thanksgiving
   and tell of all your won | derful deeds.
   8 Lord, I love the house of your | habitation
   and the place where your glo | ry abides.

5 ⁹Sweep me not a | way with sinners,
　　nor my life | with the bloodthirsty,
　¹⁰Whose hands are full of | wicked schemes
　　and their right hand | full of bribes.

6 ¹¹As for me, I will walk | with integrity;
　　redeem me, Lord, and be merci | ful to me.
　¹²My | foot stands firm;
　　in the great congregation I will | bless the Lord.

C Instrument

B♭ Instrument

Psalm 27

PRINCIPAL SERVICE
3 Epiphany A (vs. 1-10)
2 Lent C

2ND SERVICE
Tuesday of Holy Week ABC

3RD SERVICE
1 before Lent B
4 Lent B

Keith Duke

Response

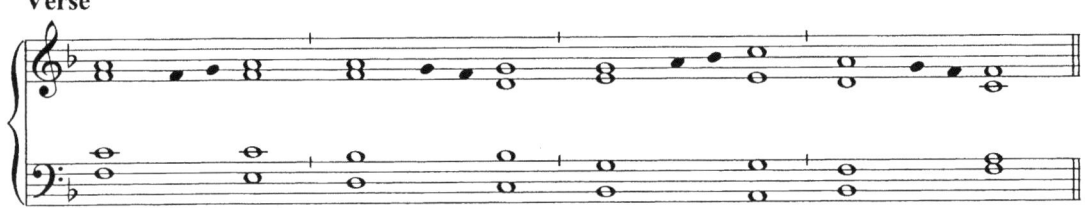

v. 1b The Lord is the strength of my life, of whom then shall I be afraid?

Verse

T.B.

1 *1* The Lord is my light and | my salvation;
   whom then | shall I fear?
   The Lord is the strength | of my life;
   of whom then shall I | be afraid?

2 *2* When the wicked, even my enemies | and my foes,
   came upon me to eat up my flesh, they stum | bled and fell.
   3 Though a host encamp against me, my heart shall not | be afraid,
   and though there rise up war against me, yet will I | put my trust in him.

3 *4* One thing have I asked of the Lord and that a | lone I seek:
   that I may dwell in the house of the Lord all the days | of my life,
   5 To behold the fair beauty | of the Lord
   and to seek his will | in his temple.

4 *6* For in the | day of trouble
   he shall hide me | in his shelter;
   in the secret place of his dwelling | shall he hide me
   and set me high u | pon a rock.

5 *7* And now shall he lift | up my head
   above my enemies | round about me;
   8 Therefore will I offer in his dwelling an oblation | with great gladness;
   I will sing and make music | to the Lord.

6 *9* Hear my voice, O Lord, | when I call;
   have mercy upon | me and answer me.
   10 My heart tells of your word, | 'Seek my face.'
   Your face, Lord, | will I seek.

7 *11* Hide not your face from me, nor cast your servant away | in displeasure.
   12 You have been my helper; leave me not, neither forsake me,
      O God of | my salvation.
   13 Though my father and my mo | ther forsake me,
      the Lord will | take me up.

8 *14* Teach me your | way, O Lord;
      lead me on a level path, because of those who | lie in wait for me.
   15 Deliver me not into the will | of my adversaries,
      for false witnesses have risen up against me,
         and those who | breathe out violence.

9 *16* I believe that I shall see the goodness | of the Lord
      in the land | of the living.
   17 Wait for the Lord; be strong and he shall com | fort your heart;
      wait patiently | for the Lord.

Psalm 28

PRINCIPAL SERVICE | 2ND SERVICE | 3RD SERVICE
 | 2 Advent A | 3 Lent C
 | | Proper 4 B

Richard Lloyd

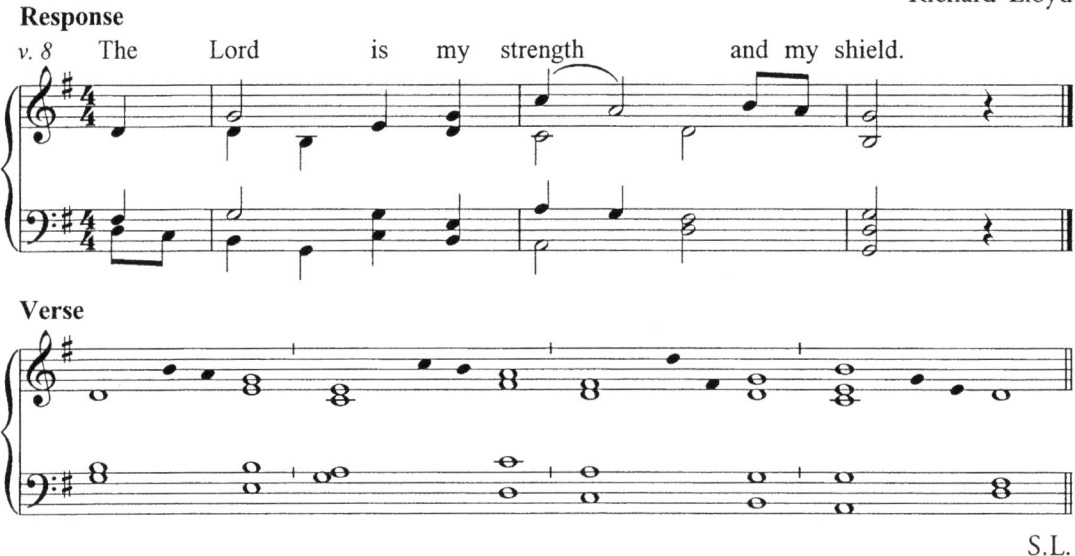

Response

v. 8 The Lord is my strength and my shield.

Verse

S.L.

1 *1* To you I call, O Lord my rock; be not deaf | to my cry,
   lest, if you do not hear me, I become like those who go down | to the Pit.
  2 Hear the voice of my prayer when | I cry out to you,
   when I lift up my hands to your ho | ly of holies.

2 *3* Do not snatch me away | with the wicked,
   with the | evildoers,
   who speak peaceably | with their neighbours,
   while malice is | in their hearts.

3 *4* Repay them according | to their deeds
   and according to the wickedness of | their devices.
  5 Reward them according to the work | of their hands
   and pay them their | just deserts.

4 *6* They take no heed of | the Lord's doings,
   nor of the works | of his hands;
   therefore shall he | break them down
   and not | build them up.

5 ⁷ Blessed be the Lord, for he has heard the voice | of my prayer.
  ⁸ The Lord is my strength and my shield;
     my heart has trusted in him and | I am helped;
  ⁹ Therefore my heart dan | ces for joy
    and in my song | will I praise him.

6 ¹⁰ The Lord is the strength | of his people,
    a safe refuge for | his anointed.
   ¹¹ Save your people and bless | your inheritance;
    shepherd them and carry | them for ever.

Psalm 29

PRINCIPAL SERVICE
Baptism ABC
Trinity B

2ND SERVICE
4 Easter A (vs. 1-10)

3RD SERVICE
2 before Lent B
Trinity C
Christ the King ABC

Colin Mawby

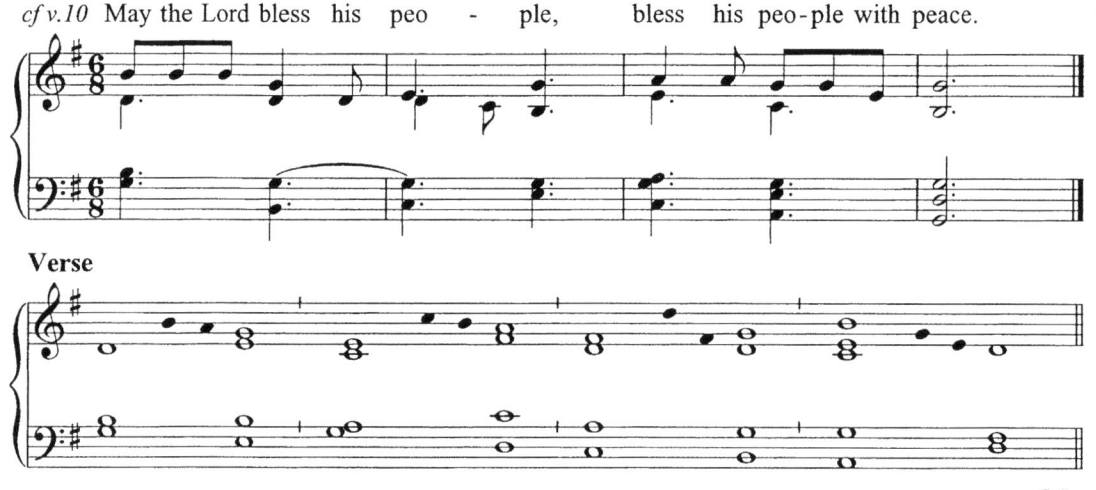

Response

cf v.10 May the Lord bless his peo - ple, bless his peo-ple with peace.

Verse

* Omit in verses 4 and 5

S.L.

1. 1 Ascribe to the Lord, you po | wers of heaven,
   ascribe to the Lord glo | ry and strength.
   2 Ascribe to the Lord the honour due | to his name;
   worship the Lord in the beau | ty of holiness.

2. 3 The voice of the Lord is u | pon the waters;
   the God of glory thunders; the Lord is upon the | mighty waters.
   4 The voice of the Lord is mighty in | operation;
   the voice of the Lord is a glo | rious voice.

3. 5 The voice of the Lord | breaks the cedar trees;
   the Lord breaks the ce | dars of Lebanon;
   6 He makes Lebanon skip | like a calf
   and Sirion like a | young wild ox.

4. 7 The voice of the Lord splits the | flash of lightning;
   the voice of the Lord | shakes the wilderness;
   the Lord shakes the wilder | ness of Kadesh.

5 *8* The voice of the Lord makes the | oak trees writhe
    and strips the | forests bare;
    in his temple | all cry, 'Glory!'

6 *9* The Lord sits enthroned a | bove the water flood;
    the Lord sits enthroned as king for | evermore.
 10 The Lord shall give strength | to his people;
    the Lord shall give his people the bles | sing of peace.

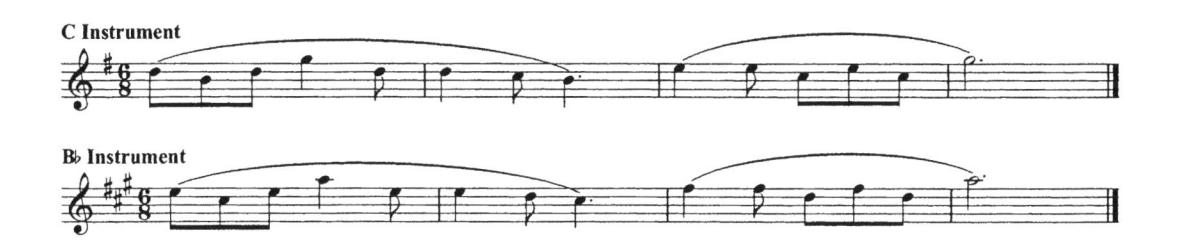

Psalm 30

PRINCIPAL SERVICE
Proper 2 B
3 Easter C
Proper 5 C (related)
Proper 8 B (related)
Proper 9 C

2ND SERVICE
4 Lent C
5 Lent A
2 Easter A (vs. 1-5)

3RD SERVICE
5 Easter A

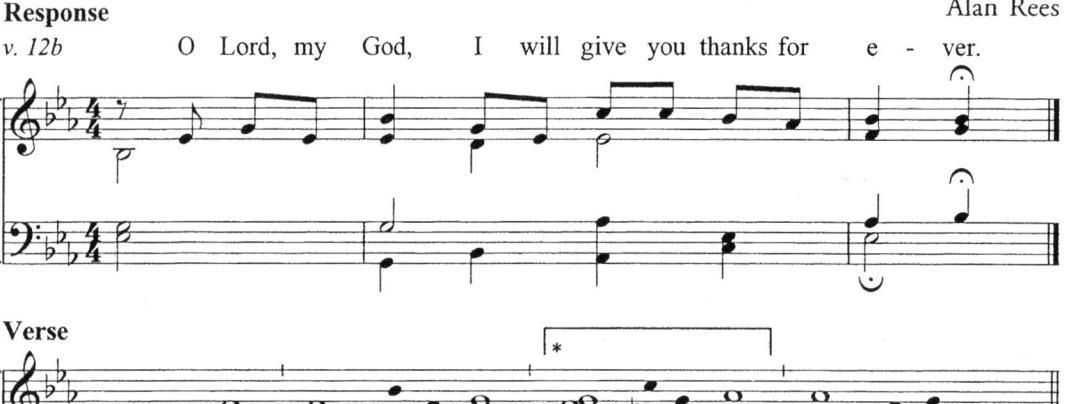

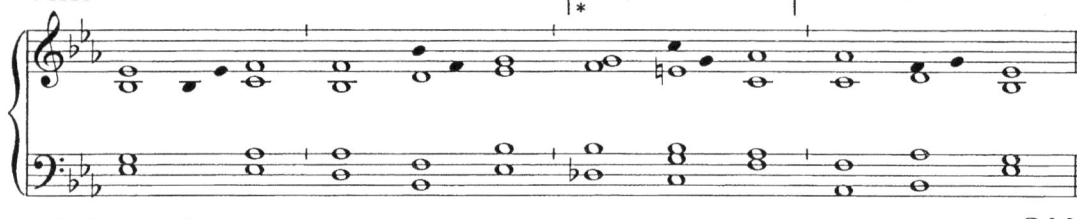

Response Alan Rees

v. 12b O Lord, my God, I will give you thanks for e - ver.

Verse

* *Omit in verse 1* C.M.

1 *1* I will exalt | you, O Lord,
   because you have | raised me up
   and have not let my foes | triumph over me.

2 *2* O Lord my God, | I cried out to you
   and | you have healed me.
   3 You brought me up, O Lord, | from the dead;
   you restored me to life from among those that go down | to the Pit.

3 *4* Sing to the Lord, you servants of his; give thanks to his | holy name.
   5 For his wrath endures but the twinkling of an eye, his favour | for a lifetime.
   Heaviness may endure | for a night,
   but joy comes | in the morning.

4 *6* In my prosperity I said, 'I shall ne | ver be moved.
   You, Lord, of your goodness, have made my | hill so strong.'
   7 Then you | hid your face from me
   and I was utter | ly dismayed.

5 *8* To you, O Lord, I cried; to the Lord I made my | supplication:
   9 'What profit is there in my blood, if I go down | to the Pit?
   Will the dust praise you or de | clare your faithfulness?
   10 'Hear, O Lord, and have mercy upon me; O Lord, | be my helper.'

6 *11* You have turned my mourning | into dancing;
   you have put off my sackcloth and girded | me with gladness;
   12 Therefore my heart sings to you | without ceasing;
   O Lord my God, I will give you | thanks for ever.

Psalm 31

PRINCIPAL SERVICE
Palm Sunday:
   Liturgy of the Passion ABC (vs. 9-16)
Easter Eve ABC (vs. 1-5)
5 Easter A (vs. 1-5)
Proper 4 A (related) (vs. 19-24)

2ND SERVICE
4 Lent A (vs. 1-16)
   (or vs. 1-8)

3RD SERVICE

Andrew Moore

Response
cf. v. 14   I trust in you, O Lord, for you are my God.

Verse

G.N.

1 *1* In you, O Lord, have I taken refuge;
    let me never be | put to shame;
    deliver me | in your righteousness.
  2 Incline your ear to me; make haste | to deliver me.
  3 Be my strong rock, a fortress to save me,
    for you are my rock | and my stronghold.

2   Guide me, and lead me for | your name's sake.
  4 Take me out of the net that they have laid secretly for me,
    for you | are my strength.
  5 Into your hands I com | mend my spirit,
    for you have redeemed me, O Lord | God of truth.

3 *6* I hate those who cling to worthless idols;
    I put my trust | in the Lord.
  7 I will be glad and rejoice in your mercy,
    for you have seen my affliction and known my soul | in adversity.
  8 You have not shut me up in the hand | of the enemy;
    you have set my feet in an | open place.

4 *9* Have mercy on me, Lord, for I | am in trouble;
    my eye is consumed with sorrow, my soul and my | body also.
  10 For my life is wasted with grief, and my | years with sighing;
    my strength fails me because of my affliction,
      and my bones | are consumed.

5 *11* I have become a reproach to all my enemies
    and even | to my neighbours,
  an object of dread to my acquaintances;
    when they see me in the | street they flee from me.
  12 I am forgotten like one that is dead, | out of mind;
  I have become like a | broken vessel.

6 *13* For I have heard the whispering | of the crowd;
  fear is on | ev'ry side;
  they scheme together against me, and plot to | take my life.
  14 But my trust is in you, O Lord. I have said, 'You | are my God.

7 *15* 'My times are in your hand; deliver me from the hand | of my enemies,
  and from | those who persecute me.
  16 'Make your face to shine u | pon your servant,
  and save me for your | mercy's sake.'

8 *17* Lord, let me not be confounded for I have | called upon you;
  but let the wicked be put to shame; let them be silent | in the grave.
  18 Let the lying lips be | put to silence
  that speak against the righteous with arrogance, disdain | and contempt.

9 *19* How abundant is your goodness, O Lord,
    which you have laid up for | those who fear you;
  which you have prepared in the sight of all for those
    who | put their trust in you.
  20 You hide them in the shelter of your presence from | those who slander them;
  you keep them safe in your refuge from the | strife of tongues.

10 *21* Blessed be the Lord! For he has shown me his | steadfast love
  when I was as a ci | ty besieged.
  22 I had said in my alarm, 'I have been cut off from the sight | of your eyes.'
  Nevertheless, you heard the voice of my prayer when | I cried out to you.

11 *23* Love the Lord, all | you his servants;
  for the Lord protects the faithful, but repays to the | full the proud.
  24 Be strong and let your | heart take courage,
  all you who wait in hope | for the Lord.

Psalm 32

PRINCIPAL SERVICE
1 Lent A
4 Lent C
Proper 6 C (related)
4 before Advent C (vs. 1-8)

2ND SERVICE

3RD SERVICE
Proper 4 B

Gerry Fitzpatrick

Response

cf. v. 5 For-give me, O Lord, the guilt of my sin.

Verse

T.B.

1 *1* Happy the one whose transgression | is forgiven,
  and whose | sin is covered.
 2 Happy the one to whom the Lord im | putes no guilt,
  and in whose spirit there | is no guile.

2 *3* For I | held my tongue;
  my bones wasted away through my groaning all | the day long.
 4 Your hand was heavy upon me | day and night;
  my moisture was dried up like the | drought in summer.

3 *5* Then I acknowledged my | sin to you
  and my iniquity I | did not hide.
 6 I said, 'I will confess my transgressions | to the Lord,'
  and you forgave the guilt | of my sin.

4 *7* Therefore let all the faithful make their prayers to you in | time of trouble;
  in the great water flood, it | shall not reach them.
 8 You are a place for me to hide in; you preserve | me from trouble;
  you surround me with songs | of deliverance.

5 *9* 'I will instruct you and teach you
    in the way that | you should go;
  I will guide you | with my eye.
 10 'Be not like horse and mule which have no | understanding;
  whose mouths must be held with bit and bridle,
    or else they will | not stay near you.'

6 *11* Great tribulations remain | for the wicked,
   but mercy embraces those who trust | in the Lord.
 12 Be glad, you righteous, and rejoice | in the Lord;
   shout for joy, all who are | true of heart.

Psalm 33

PRINCIPAL SERVICE
Proper 5 A (vs. 1-12)
Proper 14 C (related) (vs. 13-22)

2ND SERVICE
3 Epiphany ABC (vs. 1-12)
Proper 4 A (vs. 13-22)

3RD SERVICE
Pentecost C (vs. 1-12)
Trinity B (vs. 1-12)
4 before Advent A

Also: All Saints ABC (Alternative set of readings)

Geoff Nobes

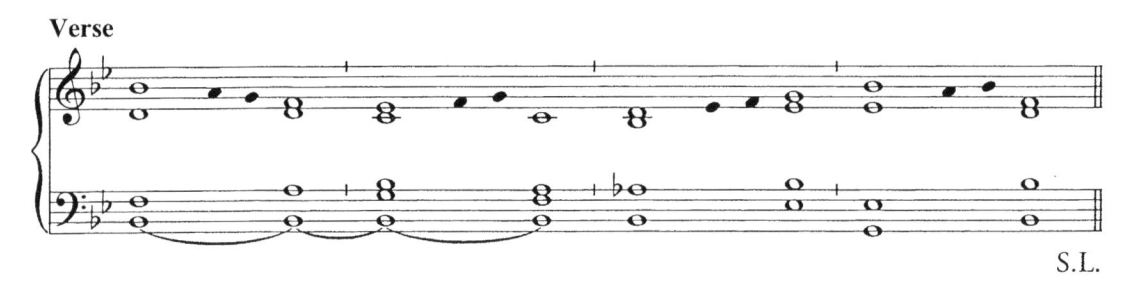

Response

v. 22 Let your lov-ing-kind-ness be up-on us, O Lord.

Verse

S.L.

1 ₁ Rejoice in the Lord, | O you righteous,
   for it is good for the just | to sing praises.
  ₂ Praise the Lord with the lyre;
   on the ten-stringed harp | sing his praise.
  ₃ Sing for him a new song; play skilfully, with | shouts of praise.

2 ₄ For the word of the Lord is true and all his | works are sure.
  ₅ He loves righteousness and justice;
   the earth is full of the loving-kindness | of the Lord.
  ₆ By the word of the Lord were the | heavens made
   and all their host by the breath | of his mouth.

3 ₇ He gathers up the waters of the sea as | in a waterskin
   and lays up the deep | in his treasury.
  ₈ Let all the earth fear the Lord;
   stand in awe of him, all who dwell | in the world.
  ₉ For he spoke, and it was done; he commanded, and | it stood fast.

4 ₁₀ The Lord brings the counsel of the nations to naught;
   he frustrates the designs | of the peoples.
  ₁₁ But the counsel of the Lord shall endure for ever
   and the designs of his heart from generation to | generation.
  ₁₂ Happy the nation whose God | is the Lord
   and the people he has chosen | for his own.

5 *13* The Lord looks down from heaven
    and beholds all the chil | dren of earth.
  14 From where he sits enthroned he turns his gaze
    on all who dwell | on the earth.
  15 He fashions | all the hearts of them
    and understands | all their works.

6 *16* No king is saved by the might | of his host;
    no warrior delivered by | his great strength.
  17 A horse is a vain hope | for deliverance;
    for all its strength it | cannot save.

7 *18* Behold, the eye of the Lord is upon | those who fear him,
    on those who wait in hope for his | steadfast love,
  19 To deliver their | soul from death
    and to feed them in | time of famine.

8 *20* Our soul waits longingly for the Lord;
    he is our help | and our shield.
  21 Indeed, our heart rejoices in him;
    in his holy name have we | put our trust.
  22 Let your loving-kindness, O Lord, | be upon us,
    as we have set our | hope on you.

C Instrument

B♭ Instrument

Psalm 34

PRINCIPAL SERVICE
Mothering Sunday (vs. 11-20) ABC
Proper 14 B (related) (vs. 1-8)
Proper 15 B (related) (vs. 9-14)
Proper 16 B (related) (vs. 15-22)
Proper 25 B (vs. 1-8)
All Saints A (vs. 1-10)

2ND SERVICE
4 Epiphany ABC (vs. 1-10)
5 Lent B (vs. 1-10)

3RD SERVICE

Andrew Moore

Response
v. 8 O taste and see, O taste and see that the Lord is gracious.

Verse

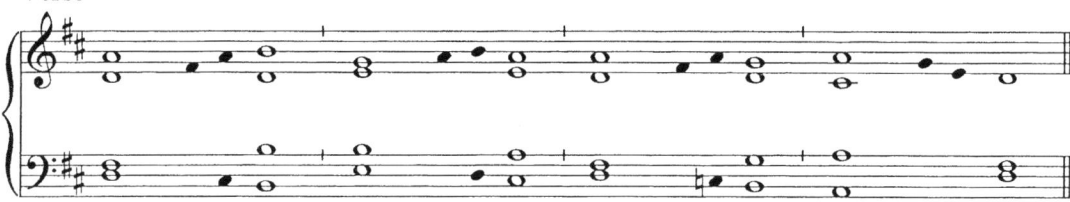

K.D.

1 *1* I will bless the Lord | at all times;
   his praise shall ever be | in my mouth.
   2 My soul shall glory | in the Lord;
   let the humble hear | and be glad.

2 *3* O magnify the | Lord with me;
   let us exalt his | name together.
   4 I sought the Lord | and he answered me
   and delivered me from | all my fears.

3 *5* Look upon him | and be radiant
   and your faces shall not | be ashamed.
   6 This poor soul cried, and | the Lord heard me
   and saved me from | all my troubles.

4 *7* The angel | of the Lord
   encamps around those who fear him | and delivers them.
   8 O taste and see that the | Lord is gracious;
   blessed is the | one who trusts in him.

5 *9* Fear the Lord, all | you his holy ones,
   for those who fear | him lack nothing.
   10 Lions may lack and | suffer hunger,
   but those who seek the Lord lack nothing | that is good.

6 *11* Come, my child | ren, and listen to me;
   I will teach you the fear | of the Lord.
  12 Who is there who de | lights in life
   and longs for days to en | joy good things?

7 *13* Keep your | tongue from evil
   and your lips from | lying words.
  14 Turn from evil | and do good;
   seek peace | and pursue it.

8 *15* The eyes of the Lord are u | pon the righteous
   and his ears are open | to their cry.
  16 The face of the Lord is against those | who do evil,
   to root out the remembrance of them | from the earth.

9 *17* The righteous cry and the | Lord hears them
   and delivers them out of | all their troubles.
  18 The Lord is near to the | brokenhearted
   and will save those who are | crushed in spirit.

10 *19* Many are the troubles | of the righteous;
   from them all will the | Lord deliver them.
  20 He keeps | all their bones,
   so that not one of | them is broken.

11 *21* But evil shall | slay the wicked
   and those who hate the righteous will | be condemned.
  22 The Lord ransoms the life | of his servants
   and will condemn none who seek re | fuge in him.

New Psalms for Common Worship

Psalm 35

vs. 11-29 are omitted

PRINCIPAL SERVICE

2ND SERVICE
5 Lent C
Proper 4 B

3RD SERVICE

Alan Rees

Response

v. 10b You deliver the poor from those that are too strong for them.

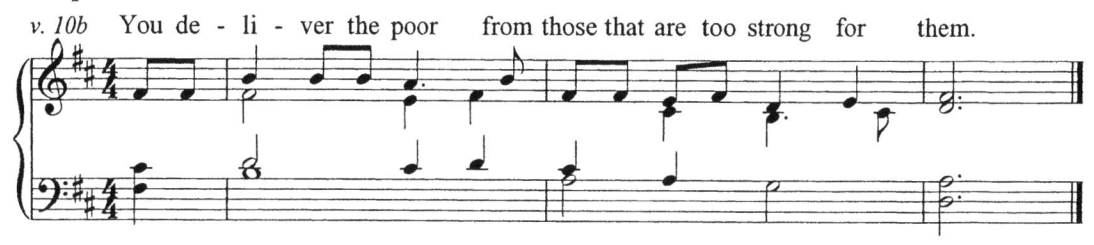

Verse

K.D.

1. *1* Contend, O Lord, with those that con | tend with me;
   fight against those that | fight against me.
   2 Take up | shield and buckler
   and rise | up to help me.

2. *3* Draw the spear and bar the way against those | who pursue me;
   say to my soul, 'I am | your salvation.'
   4 Let those who seek after my life be shamed | and disgraced;
   let those who plot my ruin fall back and be put | to confusion.

3. *5* Let them be as chaff be | fore the wind,
   with the angel of the Lord thrust | ing them down.
   6 Let their way be | dark and slippery,
   with the angel of the | Lord pursuing them.

4. *7* For they have secretly spread a net for me with | out a cause;
   without any cause they have dug a pit | for my soul.
   8 Let ruin come upon them | unawares;
   let them be caught in the net they laid;
   let them fall in it to | their destruction.

5. *9* Then will my soul be joyful in the Lord and glory in | his salvation.
   10 My very bones will say, 'Lord, | who is like you?
   You deliver the poor from those that | are too strong for them,
   the poor and needy from those who | would despoil them.'

C Instrument

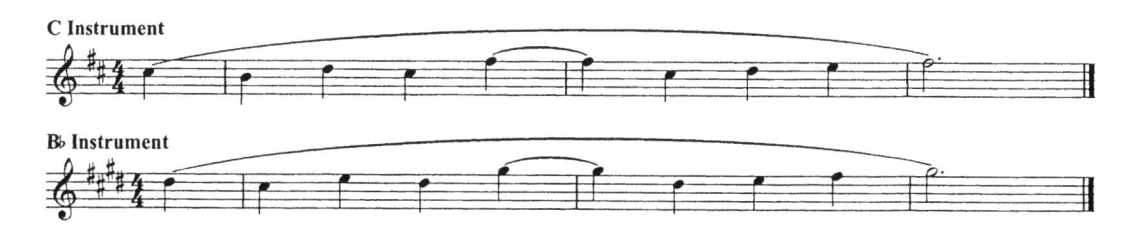

B♭ Instrument

Psalm 36

PRINCIPAL SERVICE
2 Epiphany C (vs. 5-10)
4 Epiphany A (vs. 5-10)
Monday of Holy Week ABC (vs. 5-10)
Also: Evening Prayer: Baptism ABC

2ND SERVICE
6 Easter A (vs. 5-10)
Pentecost C (vs. 5-10)

3RD SERVICE
Proper 5 B

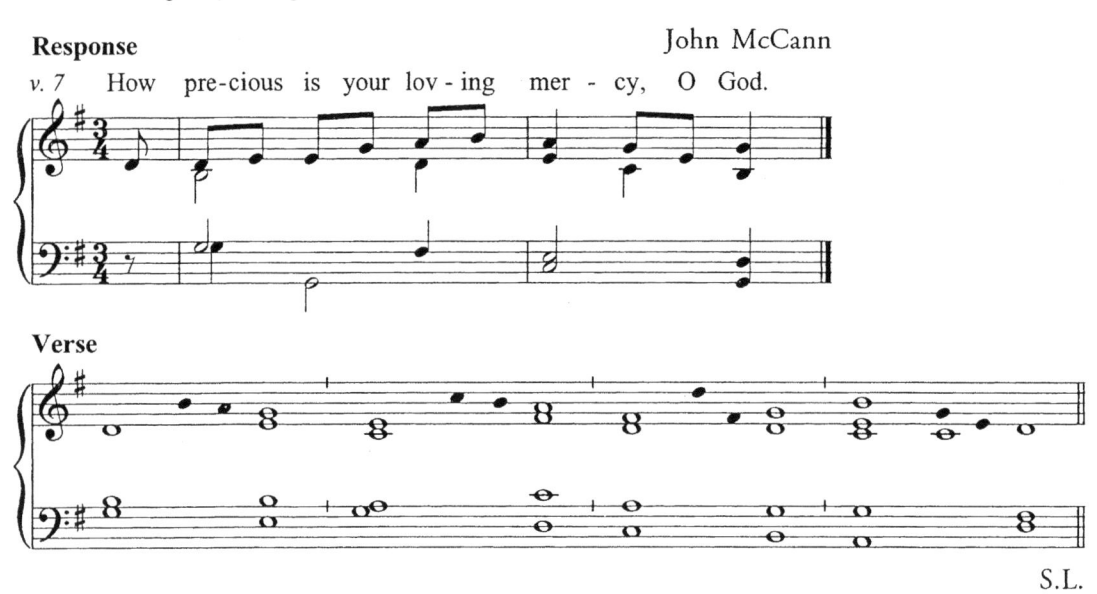

Response John McCann

v. 7 How precious is your loving mercy, O God.

Verse

S.L.

1 *1* Sin whispers to the wicked, in the depths | of their heart;
    there is no fear of God be | fore their eyes.
  2 They flatter themselves in | their own eyes
    that their abominable sin will | not be found out.

2 *3* The words of their mouth are unrighteous and full | of deceit;
    they have ceased to act wisely and | to do good.
  4 They think out mischief upon their beds
    and have set themselves in | no good way;
    nor do they abhor that | which is evil.

3 *5* Your love, O Lord, reaches | to the heavens
    and your faithfulness | to the clouds.
  6 Your righteousness stands like the strong mountains,
    your justice | like the great deep;
    you, Lord, shall save both | man and beast.

4 *7* How precious is your loving mer | cy, O God!
    All mortal flesh shall take refuge under the shadow | of your wings.
  8 They shall be satisfied with the abundance | of your house;
    they shall drink from the river of | your delights.

5 *9* For with you is the | well of life
   and in your light shall | we see light.
  10 O continue your loving-kindness to | those who know you
   and your righteousness to those who are | true of heart.

6 *11* Let not the foot of pride | come against me,
   nor the hand of the ungodly thrust | me away.
  12 There are they fallen, all | who work wickedness.
   They are cast down and shall not be a | ble to stand.

C Instrument

B♭ Instrument

Psalm 37

vs. 19-41 are omitted

PRINCIPAL SERVICE
Proper 3 C (vs. 1-7)
Proper 22 C (related) (vs. 1-9)

2ND SERVICE
Proper 5 B (vs. 1-11)

3RD SERVICE
Proper 4 A (vs. 1-18)

Gerry Fitzpatrick

Response

v. 7 Be still be-fore the Lord and wait for him.

Verse

C.M.

1 *1* Fret not because of evildoers;
    be not jealous of those | who do wrong.
  2 For they shall soon wither like grass
    and like the green herb | fade away.
  3 Trust in the Lord and be | doing good;
    dwell in the land and be nour | ished with truth.

2 *4* Let your delight be | in the Lord
    and he will give you your | heart's desire.
  5 Commit your way to the Lord and | put your trust in him,
    and he will bring | it to pass.

3 *6* He will make your righteousness as clear | as the light
    and your just dealing | as the noonday.
  7 Be still before the | Lord and wait for him;
    do not fret over those that prosper
      as they follow their | evil schemes.

4 *8* Refrain from anger and a | bandon wrath;
    do not fret, lest you be moved | to do evil.
  9 For evildoers shall | be cut off,
    but those who wait upon the Lord shall pos | sess the land.

5 *10* Yet a little while and the wicked shall | be no more;
    you will search for their place and | find them gone.
  11 But the lowly shall pos | sess the land
    and shall delight in abun | dance of peace.

6 *12* The wicked plot a | gainst the righteous
    and gnash at them | with their teeth.
  13 The Lord shall laugh | at the wicked,
    for he sees that their | day is coming.

7 *14* The wicked draw their sword
      and bend their bow to strike down the | poor and needy,
    to slaughter those who | walk in truth.
  15 Their sword shall go through | their own heart
    and their bows | shall be broken.

8 *16* The little that the righteous have
    is better than great riches | of the wicked.
  17 For the arms of the wicked shall be broken,
    but the Lord up | holds the righteous.
  18 The Lord knows the days | of the godly,
    and their inheritance shall | stand for ever.

Psalm 38

PRINCIPAL SERVICE   2ND SERVICE   3RD SERVICE
                                                                                         Ash Wednesday ABC
                                                                                         Proper 5 A

Response   Simon Lesley
cf. vs. 21, 22

Do not forsake me, O Lord, make haste to help me.

Verse

T.B.

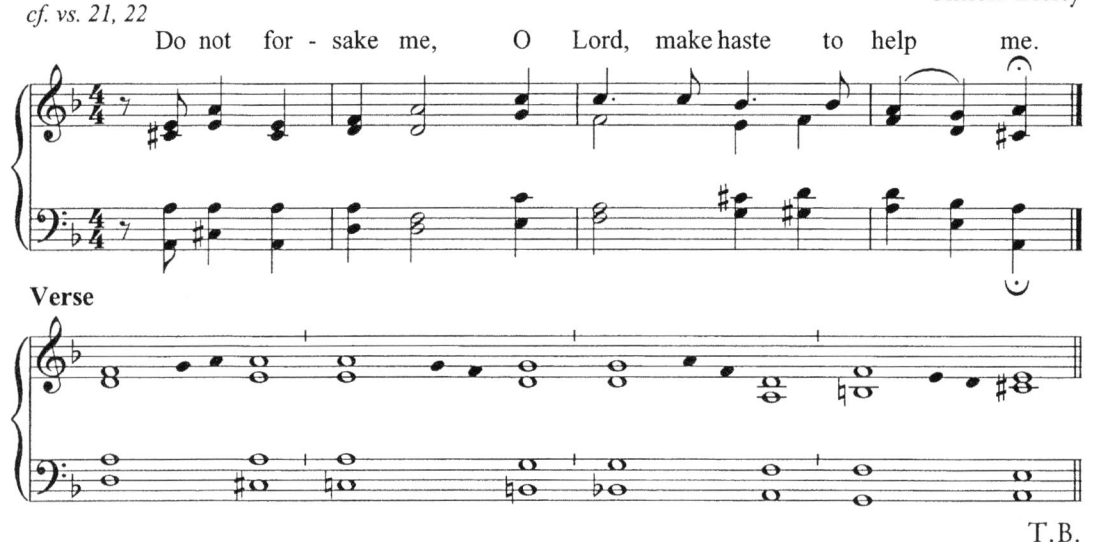

1 *1* Rebuke me not, O Lord, | in your anger,
     neither chasten me in your hea | vy displeasure.
  2 For your arrows | have stuck fast in me
     and your hand presses | hard upon me.

2 *3* There is no health in my flesh because of your | indignation;
     there is no peace in my bones because | of my sin.
  4 For my iniquities have gone o | ver my head;
     their weight is a burden too hea | vy to bear.

3 *5* My wounds stink and fester because | of my foolishness.
  6 I am utterly bowed down and brought very low;
     I go about mourning all | the day long.
  7 My loins are filled with searing pain;
     there is no health | in my flesh.
  8 I am feeble and utterly crushed;
     I roar aloud because of the disquiet | of my heart.

4 *9* O Lord, you know | all my desires
     and my sighing is not hid | den from you.
  10 My heart is pounding, my | strength has failed me;
     the light of my | eyes is gone from me.

5 *11* My friends and companions stand apart from | my affliction;
     my neighbours stand | afar off.
  12 Those who seek after my | life lay snares for me;
     and those who would harm me whisper evil
        and mutter slander all | the day long.

6 *13* But I am like one who is | deaf and hears not,
   like one that is dumb, who does not o | pen his mouth.
   14 I have become like one who | does not hear
   and from whose mouth comes | no retort.

7 *15* For in you, Lord, have I | put my trust;
   you will answer me, O | Lord my God.
   16 For I said, 'Let them not | triumph over me,
   those who exult over me | when my foot slips.'

8 *17* Truly, I am on the | verge of falling
   and my pain is | ever with me.
   18 I will confess | my iniquity
   and be sorry | for my sin.

9 *19* Those that are my enemies without any | cause are mighty,
   and those who hate me wrongfully are ma | ny in number.
   20 Those who repay evil for good | are against me,
   because the good is | what I seek.

10 *21* Forsake me | not, O Lord;
   be not far from me, | O my God.
   22 Make | haste to help me,
   O Lord of | my salvation.

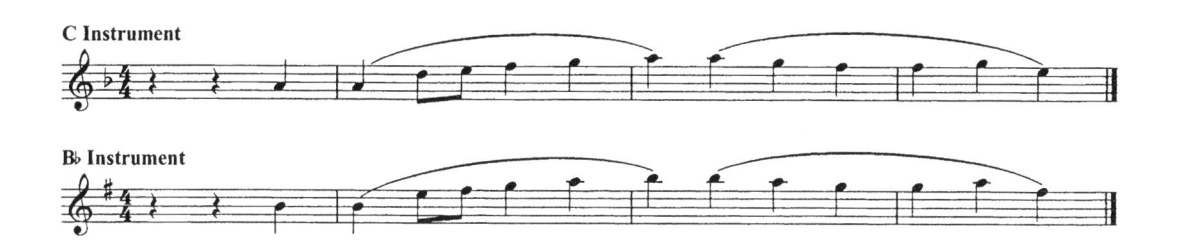

Psalm 39

PRINCIPAL SERVICE | 2ND SERVICE | 3RD SERVICE
Maundy Thursday ABC
Proper 4 C
Proper 5 A
Proper 6 B

Colin Mawby

Response
v. 13 Hear my prayer, O Lord, and give ear to my cry.

Verse

* *Omit in verses 2 and 5*

C.M.

1 *1* I said, 'I will keep watch o | ver my ways,
   so that I offend not | with my tongue.
  2 'I will guard my mouth | with a muzzle,
   while the wicked are | in my sight.'
  3 So I held my tongue | and said nothing;
   I kept silent but to | no avail.

2 *4* My distress increased, my heart grew | hot within me;
   while I mused, the | fire was kindled
   and I spoke out | with my tongue:
  5 'Lord, let me know my end and the number | of my days,
   that I may know how | short my time is.

3 *6* 'You have made my days | but a handsbreadth,
   and my lifetime is as nothing | in your sight;
   truly, even those who stand upright are | but a breath.
  7 'We walk about | like a shadow
   and in vain we | are in turmoil;
   we heap up riches and cannot tell | who will gather them.

4 *8* 'And now, what | is my hope?
    Truly my hope is e | ven in you.
  9 'Deliver me from all | my transgressions
    and do not make me the taunt | of the fool.'
  10 I fell silent and did not o | pen my mouth,
    for surely it | was your doing.

5 *11* Take a | way your plague from me;
    I am consumed by the blows | of your hand.
  12 With rebukes for | sin you punish us;
    like a moth you con | sume our beauty;
    truly, everyone is | but a breath.

6 *13* Hear my prayer, O Lord, and give ear | to my cry;
    hold not your peace | at my tears.
  14 For I am but a stran | ger with you,
    a wayfarer, as all my | forebears were.
  15 Turn your gaze from me, that I | may be glad again,
    before I go my way and | am no more.

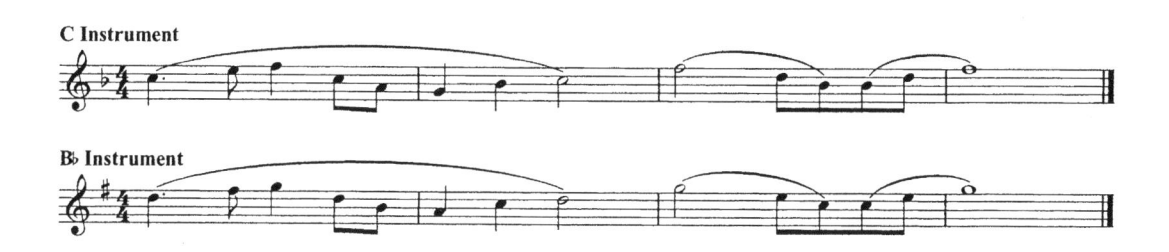

C Instrument

B♭ Instrument

Psalm 40

PRINCIPAL SERVICE
2 Epiphany A (vs. 1-12)

2ND SERVICE
2 Advent B (vs. 10-19)
3 Lent A
3 before Advent C

3RD SERVICE
6 Easter C (vs. 1-9)

Alan Rees

Response
v. 17   Let all who seek you rejoice in you and be glad.

Verse

* *Omit in verses 5 and 6*   G.N.

1   *1* I waited patiently | for the Lord;
      he inclined to me and | heard my cry.
     2 He brought me out of the roaring pit, out of the | mire and clay;
      he set my feet upon a rock and made my | footing sure.

2   *3* He has put a new song in my mouth, a song of praise | to our God;
      many shall see and fear and put their trust | in the Lord.
     4 Blessed is the one who trusts | in the Lord,
      who does not turn to the proud that fol | low a lie.

3   *5* Great are the wonders you have done, O | Lord my God.
      How great | your designs for us!
      There is none that can | be compared with you.
     6 If I were to proclaim them and tell of them
        they would be more than I am able | to express.

4   *7* Sacrifice and offering you do | not desire
      but my ears | you have opened;
     8 Burnt offering and sacrifice for sin you have | not required;
      then said I: | 'Lo, I come.

5   *9* 'In the scroll of the book | it is written of me
      that I should do your will, | O my God;
      I delight to do it: your law is with | in my heart.'

6 ₁₀ I have declared your righteousness in the great | congregation;
    behold, I did not re | strain my lips,
    and that, O | Lord, you know.

7 ₁₁ Your righteousness I have not hidden | in my heart;
    I have spoken of your faithfulness and | your salvation;
    I have not concealed your loving-kindness and truth
        from the great | congregation.
  ₁₂ Do not withhold your compassion from me, O Lord;
    let your love and your faithfulness al | ways preserve me,

8 ₁₃ For innumerable troubles have come about me;
    my sins have overtaken me so that I can | not look up;
  they are more in number than the hairs of my head,
    and | my heart fails me.
  ₁₄ Be pleased, O Lord, | to deliver me;
    O Lord, make | haste to help me.

9 ₁₅ Let them be ashamed and altogether dismayed
    who seek after my life | to destroy it;
  let them be driven back and put to shame who | wish me evil.
  ₁₆ Let those who heap in | sults upon me
  be desolate because | of their shame.

10 ₁₇ Let all who seek you rejoice in you | and be glad;
    let those who love your salvation say always, 'The | Lord is great.'
  ₁₈ Though I am poor and needy, | the Lord cares for me.
  ₁₉ You are my helper and my deliverer; O my God, make | no delay.

Psalm 41

PRINCIPAL SERVICE
Proper 3 B

2ND SERVICE
Monday of Holy Week ABC
Proper 5 A

3RD SERVICE
Proper 4 C

Response   Gerry Fitzpatrick

v. 1a Blessed are those who consider the poor.

Verse

C.M.

1 *1* Blessed are those who consider the | poor and needy;
    the Lord will deliver them in the | time of trouble.
 2 The Lord preserves them and restores their life,
    that they may be happy | in the land;
    he will not hand them over to the will | of their enemies.
 3 The Lord sustains them | on their sickbed;
    their sickness, Lord, you | will remove.

2 *4* And so I said, 'Lord, be merci | ful to me;
    heal me, for I have | sinned against you.'
 5 My enemies speak e | vil about me,
    asking when I shall die and | my name perish.
 6 If they come to see me, they utter empty words;
    their heart | gathers mischief;
    when they go out, they tell | it abroad.

3 *7* All my enemies whisper together against me,
    against me they | devise evil,
 8 Saying that a deadly thing has laid hold on me,
    and that I will not rise again from | where I lie.
 9 Even my bosom friend, whom I trusted,
    who ate | of my bread,
    has lifted up his | heel against me.
 10 But you, O Lord, be merci | ful to me
    and raise me up, that I | may reward them.

4 *11* By this I know | that you favour me,
     that my enemy does not | triumph over me.
  12 Because of my integrity | you uphold me
     and will set me before your | face for ever.
  13 Blessed be the Lord | God of Israel,
     from everlasting to everlasting. Amen | and Amen.

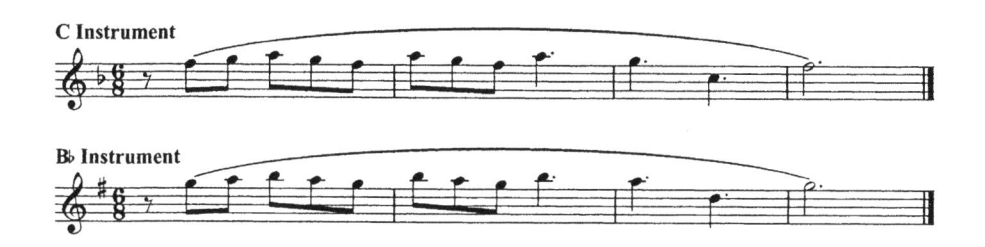

Psalm 42

Where appropriate, this Psalm may be sung with Psalm 43

PRINCIPAL SERVICE	2ND SERVICE	3RD SERVICE
Proper 7 C	Proper 6 A	Presentation ABC
Also: Easter Vigil ABC		Maundy Thursday ABC
		Corpus Christi ABC
		Proper 6 B

Richard Lloyd

Response

cf. v.14 Put your trust in God, for he is our help and indeed our God.

Verse

K.D.

1 ₁ As the deer longs | for the water brooks,
　 so longs my soul for | you, O God.
　₂ My soul is athirst for God, even for the | living God;
　 when shall I come before the pre | sence of God?

2 ₃ My tears have been my bread | day and night,
　　 while all day long they say to me, 'Where is | now your God?'
　₄ Now when I think on these things, I pour | out my soul:
　 how I went with the multitude and led the procession to the | house of God,
　₅ With the voice of praise and thanksgiving, among those | who kept holy day.

3 ₆ Why are you so full of heaviness, | O my soul,
　 and why are you so disquie | ted within me?
　₇ O put your trust in God; for I will yet | give him thanks,
　 who is the help of my countenance, | and my God.

4 ₈ My soul is hea | vy within me;
　 therefore I | will remember you
　 from the land of Jordan, | and from Hermon
　 and the | hill of Mizar.

5 *9* Deep calls to deep in the thunder | of your waterfalls;
   all your breakers and waves | have gone over me.
  10 The Lord will grant his loving-kindness | in the daytime;
   through the night his song will be with me, a prayer to the God | of my life.

6 *11* I say to God my rock, 'Why have | you forgotten me,
   and why go I so heavily, while the ene | my oppresses me?'
  12 As they crush my bones, my e | nemies mock me;
   while all day long they say to me, 'Where is | now your God?'

7 *13* Why are you so full of heaviness, | O my soul,
   and why are you so disquie | ted within me?
  14 O put your trust in God; for I will yet | give him thanks,
   who is the help of my countenance, | and my God.

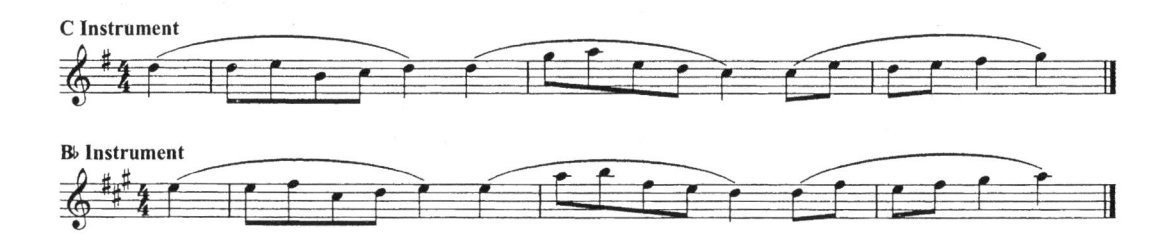

Psalm 43

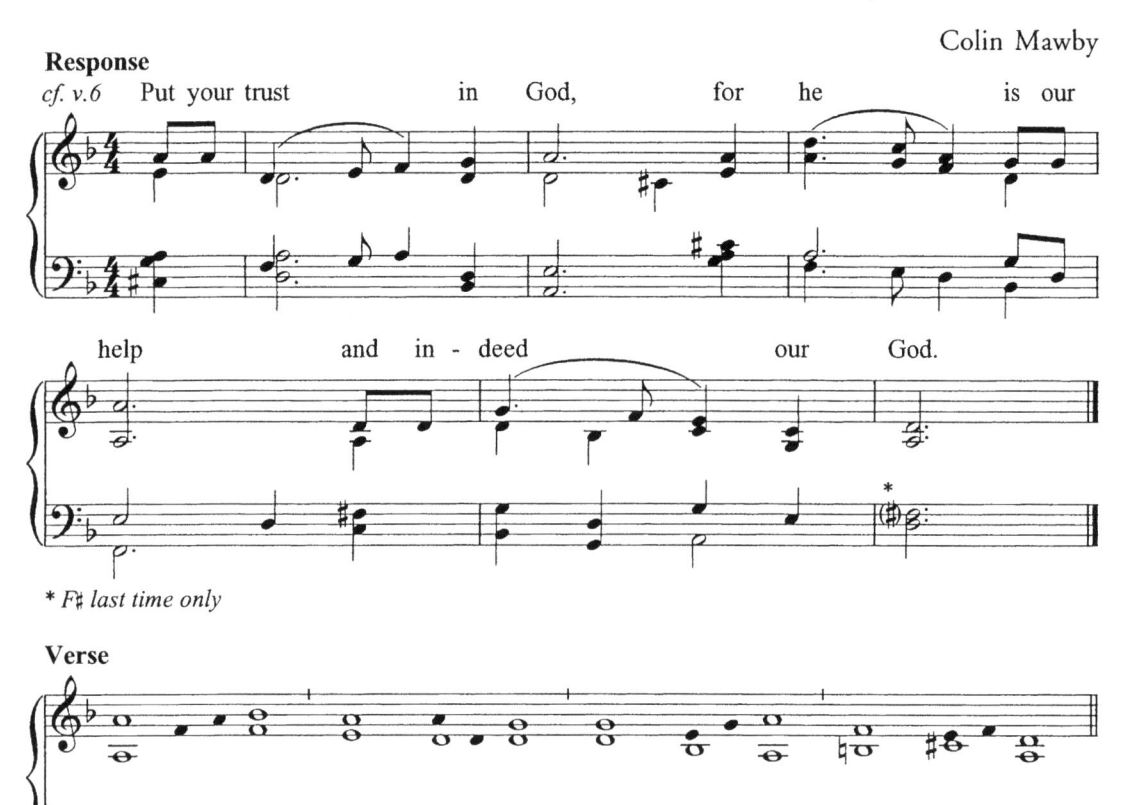

Where appropriate, this Psalm may be sung with Psalm 42

PRINCIPAL SERVICE
Proper 7 C
4 before Advent A
Also: Easter Vigil ABC

2ND SERVICE
Proper 6 A

3RD SERVICE
Presentation ABC
Maundy Thursday ABC
Corpus Christi ABC
Proper 6 B

Colin Mawby

Response

cf. v.6 Put your trust in God, for he is our help and indeed our God.

* F♮ last time only

Verse

C.M.

1 *1* Give judgement for me, O God,
    and defend my cause against an un | godly people;
   deliver me from the deceitful | and the wicked.
  2 For you are the God of my refuge;
    why have you cast | me from you,
   and why go I so heavily, while the ene | my oppresses me?

2 *3* O send out your light and your truth, that | they may lead me,
    and bring me to your holy hill and | to your dwelling,
  4 That I may go to the altar of God,
    to the God of my | joy and gladness;
   and on the lyre I will give thanks to you, O | God my God.

3 ⁵Why are you so full of heaviness, | O my soul,
and why are you so disquie | ted within me?
⁶O put your trust in God; for I will yet | give him thanks,
who is the help of my countenance, | and my God.

Psalm 44

PRINCIPAL SERVICE

2ND SERVICE
Proper 5 C (vs. 1-9)

3RD SERVICE
1 Advent ABC
5 Easter B (vs. 16-27)

Keith Duke

Response
v. 27b Re-deem us for the sake of your stead-fast love.

Verse

T.B.

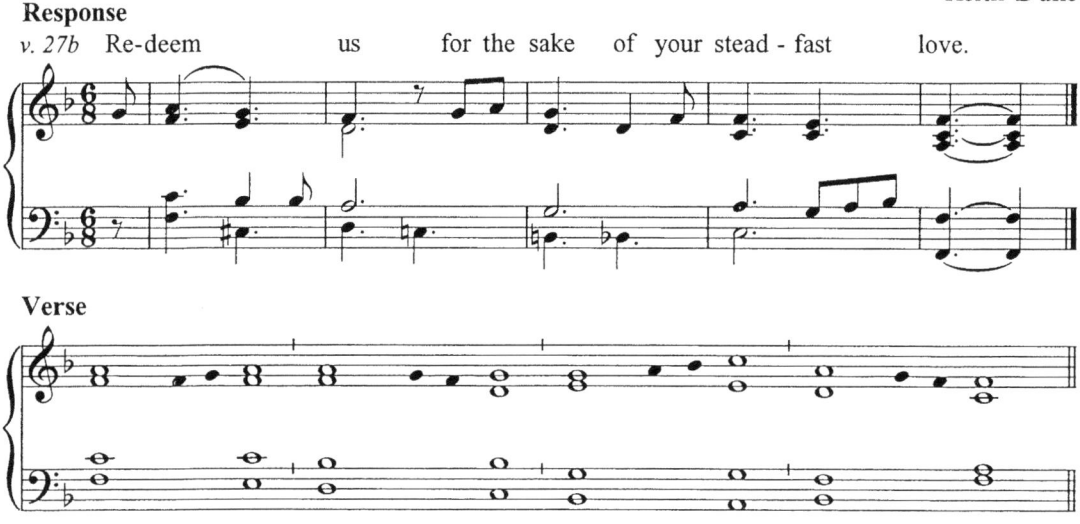

1 *1* We have heard with our ears, O God, our fore | bears have told us,
  all that you did in their days, in | time of old;
  2 How with your hand you drove out nations and plan | ted us in,
  and broke the power of peoples and | set us free.

2 *3* For not by their own sword did our ancestors | take the land
  nor did their | own arm save them,
  4 But your right hand, your arm, and the light | of your countenance,
  because | you were gracious to them.

3 *5* You are my King | and my God,
  who commanded salva | tion for Jacob.
  6 Through you we drove | back our adversaries;
  through your name we trod | down our foes.

4 *7* For I did not trust in my bow; it was not my own | sword that saved me;
  8 It was you that saved us from our enemies and put our adversa | ries to shame.
  9 We gloried in God all | the day long,
  and were ever prais | ing your name.

5 *10* But now you have rejected us and brought | us to shame,
  and go not out | with our armies.
  11 You have made us turn our backs | on our enemies,
  and our enemies | have despoiled us.

6 *12* You have made us like sheep | to be slaughtered,
  and have scattered us a | mong the nations.
  13 You have sold your people | for a pittance
  and made no profit | on their sale.

7 *14* You have made us the taunt | of our neighbours,
   the scorn and derision of those that are | round about us.
 15 You have made us a byword a | mong the nations;
   among the peoples they | wag their heads.

8 *16* My confusion is dai | ly before me,
   and shame has co | vered my face,
 17 At the taunts of the slanderer | and reviler,
   at the sight of the enemy | and avenger.

9 *18* All this has come upon us, though we have not for | gotten you
   and have not played false | to your covenant.
 19 Our hearts have | not turned back,
   nor our steps gone out | of your way,

10 *20* Yet you have crushed us in the | haunt of jackals,
   and covered us with the sha | dow of death.
 21 If we have forgotten the name | of our God,
   or stretched out our hands to | any strange god,

11 *22* Will not God | search it out?
   For he knows the secrets | of the heart.
 23 But for your sake are we killed all | the day long,
   and are counted as sheep | for the slaughter.

12 *24* Rise up! Why | sleep, O Lord?
   Awake, and do not reject | us for ever.
 25 Why do you | hide your face
   and forget our grief | and oppression?

13 *26* Our soul is bowed down | to the dust;
   our belly cleaves | to the earth.
 27 Rise up, O | Lord, to help us
   and redeem us for the sake of your | steadfast love.

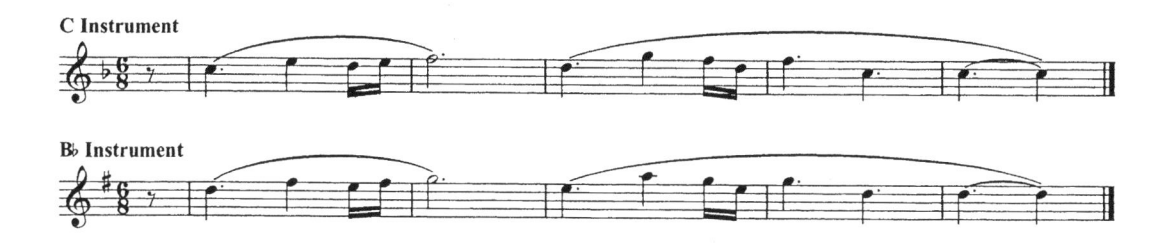

Psalm 45

PRINCIPAL SERVICE
Proper 9 A (vs. 10-17)
Proper 17 B (vs. 1-8a)

2ND SERVICE
6 Easter B

3RD SERVICE
Proper 5 C
Proper 6 A

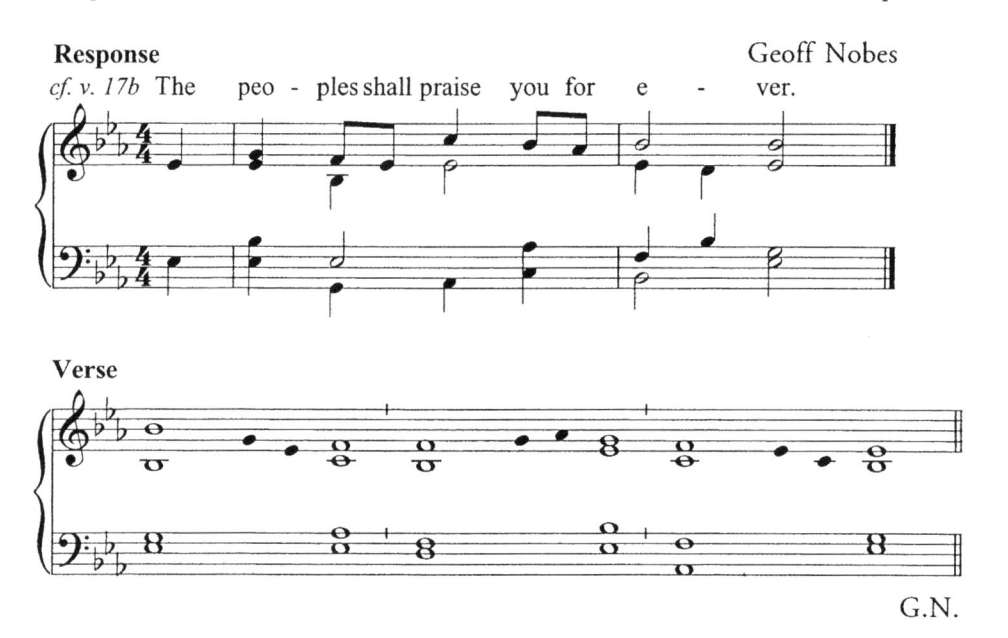

Response   Geoff Nobes

cf. v. 17b The peoples shall praise you for ever.

Verse

G.N.

1 *1* My heart is astir with | gracious words;
   as I make my song | for the king,
   my tongue is the pen of a | ready writer.

2 *2* You are the fairest of men; full of grace | are your lips,
   for God has blest | you for ever.
  3 Gird your sword upon your thigh, O mighty one;
    gird on your majes | ty and glory.

3 *4* Ride on and prosper in the cause of truth
    and for the sake of humili | ty and righteousness.
  5 Your right hand will teach you ter | rible things;
    your arrows will be sharp in the heart of the king's enemies,
    so that peoples | fall beneath you.

4 *6* Your throne is God's throne, for ever;
    the sceptre of your kingdom is the scep | tre of righteousness.
  7 You love righteousness and | hate iniquity;
    therefore God, your God, has anointed you
    with the oil of gladness a | bove your fellows.

5 *8* All your garments are fragrant with myrrh, a | loes and cassia;
    from ivory palaces the music of strings | makes you glad.
  9 Kings' daughters are among your honourable women;
    at your right hand stands the queen in | gold of Ophir.

6 *10* Hear, O daughter; consider and in | cline your ear;
　　forget your own people and your | father's house.
　11 So shall the king have pleasure in your beauty;
　　he is your lord, so | do him honour.

7 *12* The people of Tyre shall | bring you gifts;
　　the richest of the people shall | seek your favour.
　13 The king's daughter is all glorious within;
　　her clothing is embroidered | cloth of gold.

8 *14* She shall be brought to the king in rai | ment of needlework;
　　after her the virgins that are | her companions.
　15 With joy and gladness shall they be brought
　　and enter into the palace | of the king.

9 *16* 'Instead of your fathers you | shall have sons,
　　whom you shall make princes over | all the land.
　17 'I will make your name to be remembered through all generations;
　　therefore shall the peoples praise you for e | ver and ever.'

Psalm 46

PRINCIPAL SERVICE
Proper 4 A
Christ the King C

Also: Easter Vigil ABC

2ND SERVICE
Baptism ABC
Proper 7 A
3 before Advent B

3RD SERVICE
3 Lent A

Richard Lloyd

Response

v. 7 The Lord of hosts is with us; the God of Jacob is our stronghold.

Verse

C.M.

1 1 God is our re | fuge and strength,
    a very present | help in trouble;
   2 Therefore we will not fear, though the | earth be moved,
    and though the mountains tremble in the heart | of the sea;
   3 Though the waters | rage and swell,
    and though the mountains quake at the to | wering seas.

2 4 There is a river whose streams make glad the ci | ty of God,
    the holy place of the dwelling of | the Most High.
   5 God is in the midst of her; therefore shall she not | be removed;
    God shall help her at the | break of day.
   6 The nations are in uproar and the kingdoms are shaken,
    but God utters his voice and the earth shall | melt away.
   7 The Lord of hosts is with us; the God of Jacob | is our stronghold.

3 8 Come and behold the works of the Lord,
    what destruction he has wrought up | on the earth.
   9 He makes wars to cease in | all the world;
    he shatters the bow and snaps the spear
    and burns the chariots | in the fire.
   10 'Be still, and know that | I am God;
    I will be exalted among the nations; I will be exalted | in the earth.'
   11 The Lord of hosts is with us; the God of Jacob | is our stronghold.

C Instrument

B♭ Instrument

Psalm 47

PRINCIPAL SERVICE
Ascension ABC

2ND SERVICE
Baptism ABC
7 Easter A

3RD SERVICE

Response
cf. vs. 6 and 7

Alan Rees

Sing prai - ses to God, the King of all the earth.

Verse

S.L.

1 *1* Clap your hands together, | all you peoples;
   O sing to God with | shouts of joy.
   2 For the Lord Most High is | to be feared;
   he is the great King over | all the earth.

2 *3* He subdued the | peoples under us
   and the nations un | der our feet.
   4 He has chosen our heri | tage for us,
   the pride of Jacob, | whom he loves.

3 *5* God has gone up with a | merry noise,
   the Lord with the sound | of the trumpet.
   6 O sing praises to | God, sing praises;
   sing praises to our | King, sing praises.

4 *7* For God is the King of | all the earth;
   sing praises with | all your skill.
   8 God reigns o | ver the nations;
   God has taken his seat upon his | holy throne.

5 *9* The nobles of the peoples are ga | thered together
   with the people of the | God of Abraham.
   10 For the powers of the earth be | long to God
   and he is very high | ly exalted.

C Instrument

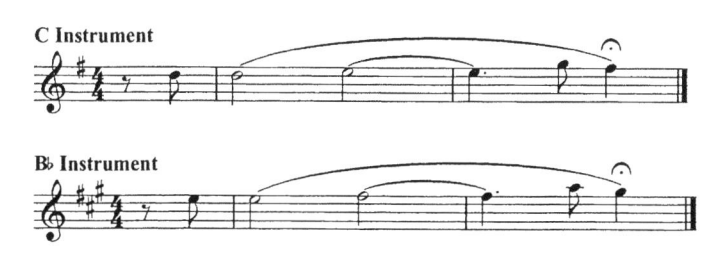

B♭ Instrument

Psalm 48

PRINCIPAL SERVICE
4 Epiphany C
Proper 9 B
Also: Evening Prayer: Pentecost ABC

2ND SERVICE
3 Easter A
Proper 7 A

3RD SERVICE
Presentation ABC
Proper 7 B
Dedication ABC

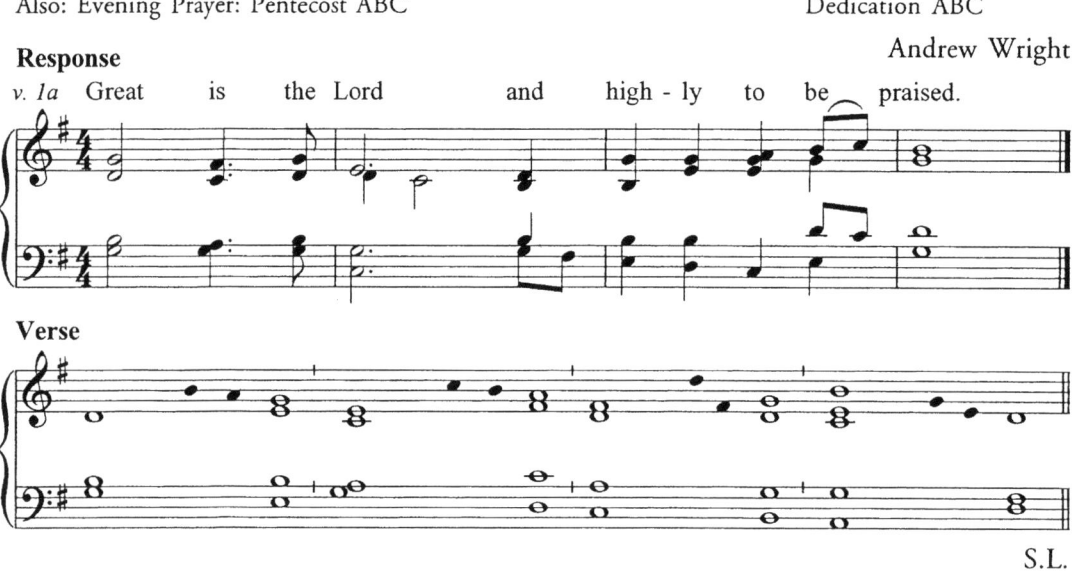

Response — Andrew Wright

v. 1a Great is the Lord and high-ly to be praised.

Verse

S.L.

1. *1* Great is the Lord and highly to be praised, in the city | of our God.
   2 His holy mountain is fair and lifted high, the joy of | all the earth.
   3 On Mount Zion, the divine dwelling place, stands the city of | the great king.
   4 In her palaces God has shown himself to be | a sure refuge.

2. *5* For behold, the kings of the earth assembled and swept for | ward together.
   6 They saw, and were dumbfounded; dismayed, they | fled in terror.
   7 Trembling seized them there; they writhed like a wo | man in labour,
   as when the east wind shatters the | ships of Tarshish.

3. *8* As we had heard, so | have we seen
   in the city of the | Lord of hosts,
   the city | of our God:
   God has established | her for ever.

4. *9* We have waited on your loving-kindness, O God, in the midst | of your temple.
   10 As with your name, O God, so your praise reaches to the ends | of the earth;
   your right hand is | full of justice.
   11 Let Mount Zion rejoice and the daughters of Judah be glad,
   because of your judge | ments, O Lord.

5 *12* Walk about Zion and go round about her; count | all her towers;
    consider well her bulwarks; pass | through her citadels,
      13 That you may tell those who come after that such is our God for e | ver and ever.
    It is he that shall be our guide for | evermore.

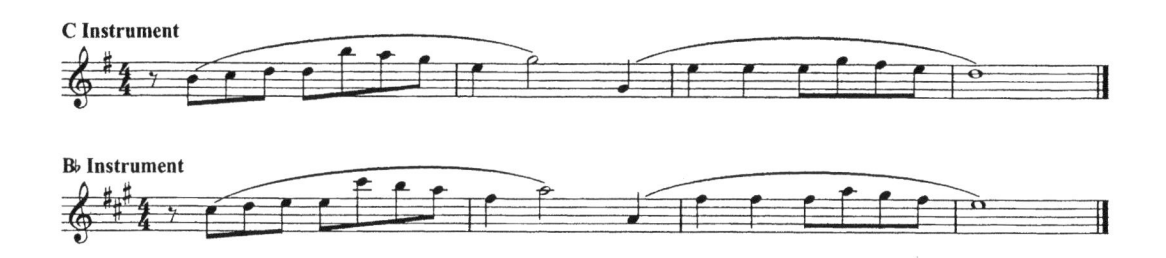

Psalm 49

PRINCIPAL SERVICE
Proper 13 C (related) (vs. 1-12 or 1-9)

2ND SERVICE
Proper 7 B

3RD SERVICE
Proper 6 C
Proper 7 A

Andrew Moore

Response
v. 16 God shall ransom my soul from the grasp of death.

Verse

* Omit in verse 5

G.N.

1 1 Hear this, | all you peoples;
   listen, all you that dwell | in the world,
   2 You of low or | high degree,
   both rich and | poor together.

2 3 My mouth shall | speak of wisdom
   and my heart shall meditate on | understanding.
   4 I will incline my ear | to a parable;
   I will unfold my riddle | with the lyre.

3 5 Why should I fear in | evil days,
   when the malice of my | foes surrounds me,
   6 Such as trust | in their goods
   and glory in the abundance | of their riches?

4 7 For no one can indeed ran | som another
   or pay to God the price | of deliverance.
   8 To ransom a soul is too costly;
   there is no price | one could pay for it,
   9 So that they might live for ever,
   and never | see the grave.

5 10 For we see that the | wise die also;
   with the foolish and igno | rant they perish
   and leave their rich | es to others.

6 *11* Their tomb is their home for ever,
  their dwelling through all | generations,
  though they call their lands after | their own names.
 12 Those who have honour, but lack | understanding,
  are like the | beasts that perish.

7 *13* Such is the way of those who boast | in themselves,
  the end of those who delight in | their own words.
 14 Like a flock of sheep they are destined to die; death | is their shepherd;
  they go down straight | to the Pit.

8 *15* Their beauty shall | waste away,
  and the land of the dead shall | be their dwelling.
 16 But God shall ran | som my soul;
  from the grasp of death | will he take me.

9 *17* Be not afraid if some grow rich and the glory of their | house increases,
 18 For they will carry nothing away when they die,
  nor will their glory | follow after them.
 19 Though they count themselves happy | while they live
  and praise you for | your success,

10 *20* They shall enter the company | of their ancestors
  who will nevermore | see the light.
 21 Those who have honour, but lack | understanding,
  are like the | beasts that perish.

Psalm 50

PRINCIPAL SERVICE
1 before Lent B (vs. 1-6)
Proper 5 A (related) (vs. 7-15)
Proper 14 C (vs. 1-7)

2ND SERVICE
3 Advent C (vs. 1-6)
1 Lent A (vs. 1-15)
Proper 7 C
Proper 8 A (vs. 1-15)

3RD SERVICE
3 Advent B (vs. 1-16)
1 Lent C (vs. 1-15)

Gerry Fitzpatrick

Response

v. 6 Let the hea-vens de-clare his right-eous-ness, for God him-self is judge.

Verse

T.B.

1 *1* The Lord, the most mighty | God, has spoken
   and called the world from the rising of the sun | to its setting.
   2 Out of Zion, perfect in beauty, | God shines forth;
   our God comes and will | not keep silence.

2 *3* Consuming fire goes | out before him
   and a mighty tempest | stirs about him.
   4 He calls the hea | ven above,
   and the earth, that he may | judge his people:

3 *5* 'Gather to | me my faithful,
   who have sealed my cove | nant with sacrifice.'
   6 Let the heavens de | clare his righteousness,
   for God him | self is judge.

4 *7* Hear, O my people, and | I will speak:
   'I will testify against you, O Israel; for I am | God, your God.
   8 'I will not reprove you | for your sacrifices,
   for your burnt offerings are al | ways before me.

5 *9* 'I will take no bull out of your house, nor he-goat out | of your folds,
   10 'For all the beasts of the forest are mine, the cattle upon a | thousand hills.
   11 'I know every bird | of the mountains
   and the insect of the | field is mine.

6 *12* 'If I were hungry, I | would not tell you,
　　for the whole world is mine and | all that fills it.
　13 'Do you think I eat the | flesh of bulls,
　　or drink the | blood of goats?

7 *14* 'Offer to God a sacrifice | of thanksgiving
　　and fulfil your vows to | God Most High.
　15 'Call upon me in the | day of trouble;
　　I will deliver you and | you shall honour me.'

8 *16* But to the wicked, says God: 'Why do you recite my statutes
　　and take my covenant u | pon your lips,
　17 'Since you refuse to be disciplined and have cast my | words behind you?
　18 'When you saw a thief, | you made friends with him
　　and you threw in your lot | with adulterers.

9 *19* 'You have loosed your | lips for evil
　　and harnessed your tongue | to deceit.
　20 'You sit and speak evil | of your brother;
　　you slander your own | mother's son.

10 *21* 'These things have you done, and should | I keep silence?
　　Did you think that I am even such a one | as yourself?
　22 'But no, I | must reprove you,
　　and set before your eyes the things that | you have done.

11 *23* 'You that forget God, consi | der this well,
　　lest I tear you apart and there is none | to deliver you.
　24 'Whoever offers me the sacrifice of thanks | giving honours me
　　and to those who keep my way will I show the salva | tion of God.'

Psalm 51

PRINCIPAL SERVICE
Ash Wednesday ABC (vs. 1-18)
5 Lent B (vs. 1-13)
Proper 13 B (vs. 1-13)
Proper 19 C (related) (vs. 1-11)

2ND SERVICE

3RD SERVICE

Response Alan Rees

v. 11 Make me a clean heart, O God, and re-new a right spi-rit with-in me.

Verse

C.M.

1   *1* Have mercy on me, O God, in | your great goodness;
       according to the abundance of your compassion blot out | my offences.
    2 Wash me thoroughly | from my wickedness
       and cleanse me | from my sin.

2   *3* For I acknowledge my faults and my sin is e | ver before me.
    4 Against you only have I sinned and done what is evil | in your sight,
    5 So that you are justified | in your sentence
       and righteous | in your judgement.

3   *6* I have been wicked even | from my birth,
       a sinner when my mo | ther conceived me.
    7 Behold, you desire truth | deep within me
       and shall make me understand wisdom in the depths | of my heart.

4   *8* Purge me with hyssop and I | shall be clean;
       wash me and I shall be whi | ter than snow.
    9 Make me hear of | joy and gladness,
       that the bones you have broken | may rejoice.

5   *10* Turn your face | from my sins
       and blot out all | my misdeeds.
    11 Make me a clean | heart, O God,
       and renew a right spi | rit within me.

6 _12_ Cast me not away | from your presence
and take not your holy | spirit from me.
  _13_ Give me again the joy of | your salvation
and sustain me with your | gracious spirit;

7 _14_ Then shall I teach your ways | to the wicked
and sinners | shall return to you.
  _15_ Deliver me from my guilt, O God, the God of | my salvation,
and my tongue shall sing | of your righteousness.

8 _16_ O Lord, open my lips and my mouth shall pro | claim your praise.
  _17_ For you desire no sacrifice, else | I would give it;
you take no delight | in burnt offerings.
  _18_ The sacrifice of God is a broken spirit;
a broken and contrite heart, O God, you will | not despise.

9 _19_ O be favourable and gra | cious to Zion;
build up the walls | of Jerusalem.
  _20_ Then you will accept sacrifices offered in righteousness,
the burnt offerings | and oblations;
then shall they offer up bulls | on your altar.

Psalm 52

PRINCIPAL SERVICE
Proper 11 C

2ND SERVICE
Proper 8 B
Proper 6 C

3RD SERVICE
Proper 8 A

Andrew Wright

Response
v. 8b I trust in the good-ness of God for e - ver.

Verse

* *Omit in verse 3*
K.D.

1 *1* Why do you glory in e | vil, you tyrant,
 while the goodness of God en | dures continually?
 2 You plot destruction, | you deceiver;
 your tongue is like a | sharpened razor.

2 *3* You love evil ra | ther than good,
 falsehood rather than the | word of truth.
 4 You love all | words that hurt,
 O you de | ceitful tongue.

3 *5* Therefore God shall utterly | bring you down;
 he shall take you and pluck you out | of your tent
 and root you out of the land | of the living.

4 *6* The righteous shall see | this and tremble;
 they shall laugh you to | scorn, and say:
 7 'This is the one who did not take God | for a refuge,
 but trusted in great riches and relied | upon wickedness.'

5 *8* But I am like a spreading olive tree in the | house of God;
 I trust in the goodness of God for e | ver and ever.
 9 I will always give thanks to you for what | you have done;
 I will hope in your name, for your faithful | ones delight in it.

C Instrument

B♭ Instrument

Psalm 53

PRINCIPAL SERVICE

2ND SERVICE
Proper 8 B
Proper 6 C

3RD SERVICE
Proper 8 A

Geoff Nobes

Response

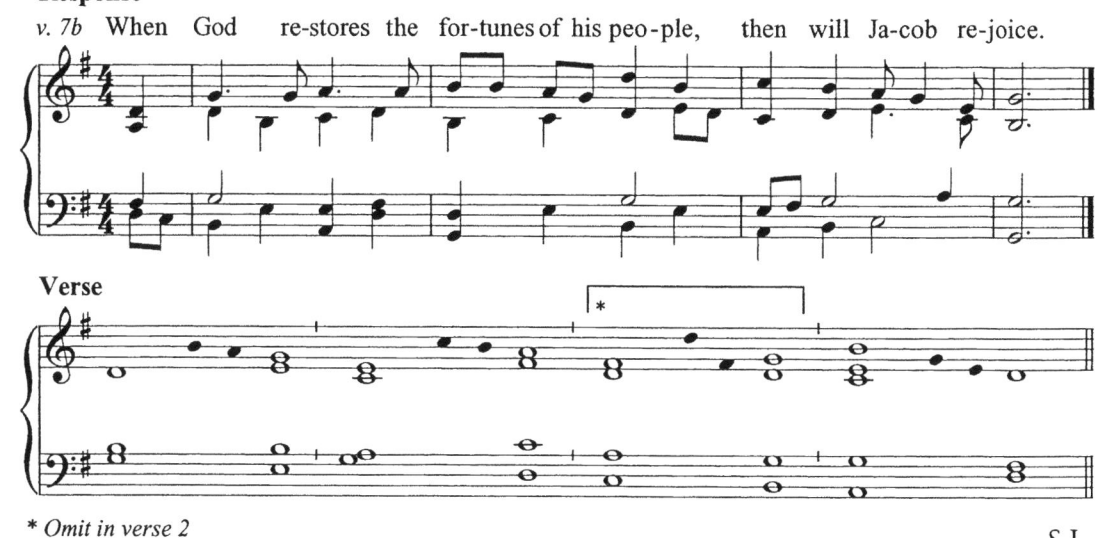

v. 7b When God re-stores the for-tunes of his peo-ple, then will Ja-cob re-joice.

Verse

* *Omit in verse 2*

S.L.

1 *1* The fool has said in his heart, 'There | is no God.'
   Corrupt are they, and abominable in their wickedness;
      there is no one | that does good.
   2 God has looked down from heaven upon the chil | dren of earth,
      to see if there is anyone who is wise and seeks | after God.

2 *3* They are all gone out | of the way;
   all alike have be | come corrupt;
   there is no one that does good, | no not one.

3 *4* Have they no knowledge, those | evildoers,
   who eat up my people as if they ate bread,
      and do not call | upon God?
   5 There shall they be in great fear, such fear as | never was;
      for God will scatter the bones of | the ungodly.

4 *6* They will be | put to shame,
   because God | has rejected them.
   7 O that Israel's salvation would come | out of Zion!
   When God restores the fortunes of his people
      then will Jacob rejoice and Isra | el be glad.

C Instrument

B♭ Instrument

New Psalms for Common Worship

Psalm 54

PRINCIPAL SERVICE
Proper 20 B (related)

2ND SERVICE

3RD SERVICE

Colin Mawby

Response

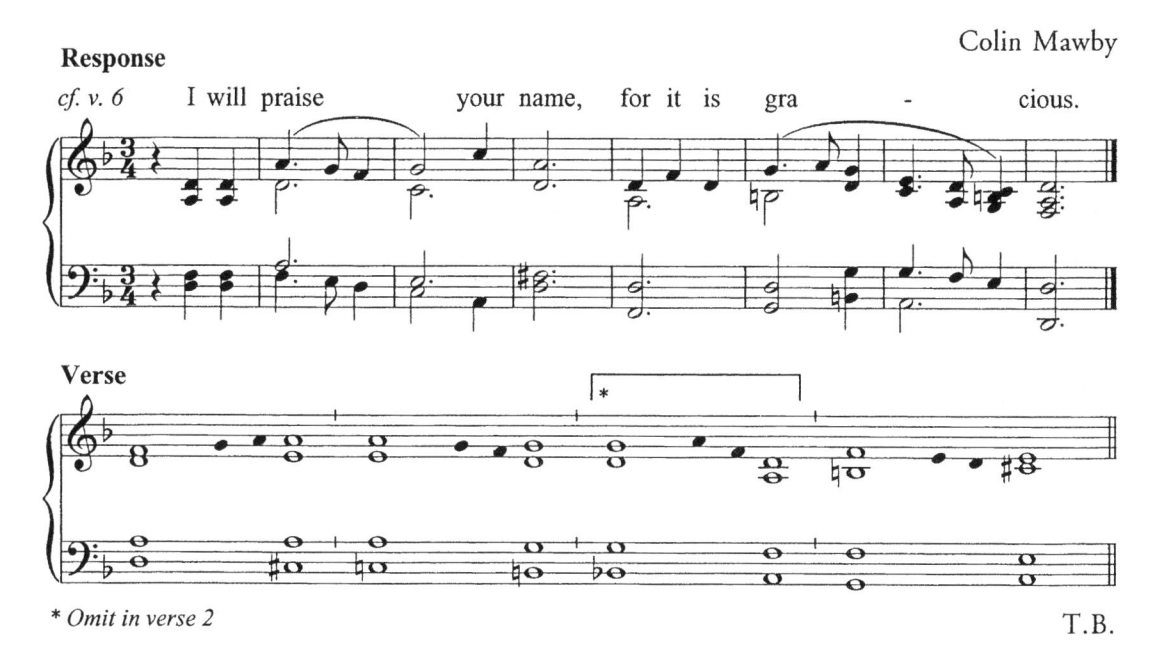

cf. v. 6 I will praise your name, for it is gracious.

Verse

* Omit in verse 2

T.B.

1 ₁ Save me, O God, | by your name
   and vindicate me | by your power.
   ₂ Hear my | prayer, O God;
   give heed to the words | of my mouth.

2 ₃ For strangers have risen | up against me,
   and the ruthless seek af | ter my life;
   they have not set | God before them.

3 ₄ Behold, God | is my helper;
   it is the Lord who up | holds my life.
   ₅ May evil rebound on those who | lie in wait for me;
   destroy them | in your faithfulness.

4 ₆ An offering of a free heart | will I give you
   and praise your name, O Lord, for | it is gracious.
   ₇ For he has delivered me out of | all my trouble,
   and my eye has seen the downfall | of my enemies.

C Instrument

B♭ Instrument

Psalm 55

Verses 25 and 26 are omitted

PRINCIPAL SERVICE   2ND SERVICE   3RD SERVICE
Tuesday of Holy Week ABC
  (vs. 13-24)
Proper 7 C
  (vs. 1-16, 18-21)
Proper 9 A (vs. 1-17, 20-24)

Simon Lesley

Response

cf v. 18 I will call up-on the Lord, and he will de-li-ver me.

Verse

* *Omit in verses 9 and 13*   K.D.

1 *1* Hear my | prayer, O God;
　　hide not yourself from | my petition.
　2 Give heed to | me and answer me;
　　I am restless in | my complaining.

2 *3* I am alarmed at the voice | of the enemy
　　and at the clamour | of the wicked;
　4 For they would bring down e | vil upon me
　　and are set against | me in fury.

3 *5* My heart is disquie | ted within me,
　　and the terrors of death have fal | len upon me.
　6 Fearfulness and trembling are | come upon me,
　　and a horrible dread has | overwhelmed me.

4 *7* And I said: 'O that I had wings | like a dove,
　　for then would I fly away and | be at rest.
　8 'Then would I flee | far away
　　and make my lodging | in the wilderness.

5 *9* 'I would make haste | to escape
　　from the stormy | wind and tempest.'
　10 Confuse their tongues, O Lord, | and divide them,
　　for I have seen violence and strife | in the city.

6 *11* Day and night they go about | on her walls;
   mischief and trouble are | in her midst.
  12 Wickedness walks | in her streets;
   oppression and guile never | leave her squares.

7 *13* For it was not an open enemy | that reviled me,
   for then I | could have borne it;
  14 Nor was it my adversary that puffed himself | up against me,
   for then I would have | hid myself from him.

8 *15* But it was even you, one | like myself,
   my companion and my own famil | iar friend.
  16 We took sweet coun | sel together
   and walked with the multitude in the | house of God.

9 *17* Let death come sudden | ly upon them;
   let them go down alive | to the Pit;
   for wickedness inhabits their dwellings, their | very hearts.

10 *18* As for me, I will call | upon God
   and the Lord | will deliver me.
  19 In the evening and morning and at noonday
   I will pray and make my | supplication,
   and he shall | hear my voice.

11 *20* He shall redeem my soul in peace
   from the battle | waged against me,
   for many have | come upon me.
  21 God, who is enthroned of old,
   will hear and | bring them down;
   they will not repent, for they have no | fear of God.

12 *22* My companion stretched out his hands a | gainst his friend
   and has bro | ken his covenant;
  23 His speech was softer than butter, though war was | in her heart;
   his words were smoother than oil, yet are they | naked swords.

13 *24* Cast your burden u | pon the Lord
   and he will | sustain you,
   and will not let the righteous | fall for ever.

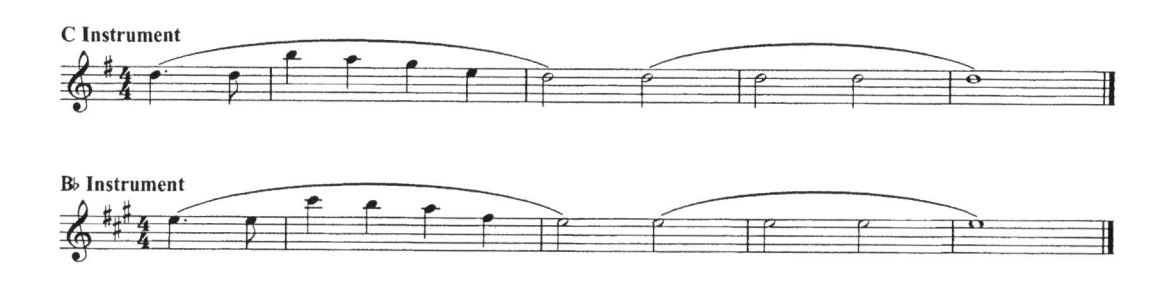

Psalm 56

PRINCIPAL SERVICE

2ND SERVICE
Proper 9 A

3RD SERVICE
Proper 8 B

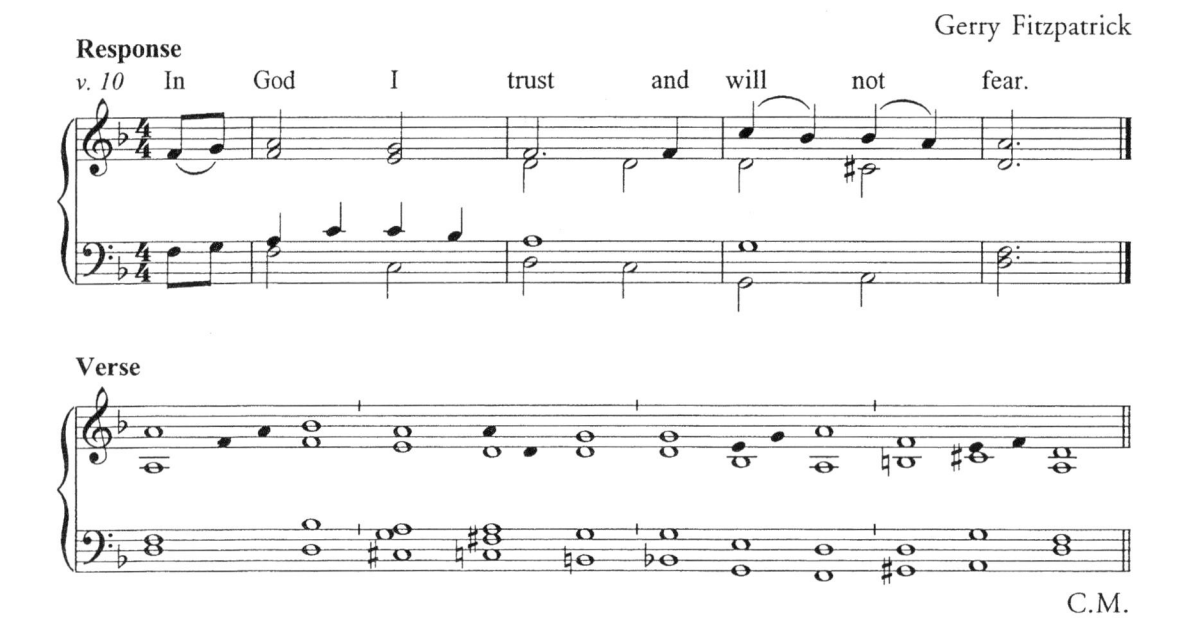

Gerry Fitzpatrick

Response
v. 10 In God I trust and will not fear.

Verse

C.M.

1 *1* Have mercy on me, O God, for they | trample over me;
   all day long they assault | and oppress me.
   2 My adversaries trample over me all | the day long;
   many are they that make proud | war against me.

2 *3* In the day of my fear I put my | trust in you,
   in God whose | word I praise.
   4 In God I trust, and | will not fear,
   for what can flesh | do to me?

3 *5* All day long they wound | me with words;
   their every thought is to | do me evil.
   6 They stir up trouble; they | lie in wait;
   marking my steps, they | seek my life.

4 *7* Shall they escape for | all their wickedness?
   In anger, O God, cast the | peoples down.
   8 You have counted up my groaning; put my tears in | to your bottle;
   are they not written | in your book?

5 *9* Then shall my enemies turn back on the day when I | call upon you;
   this I know, for God is | on my side.
   10 In God whose word I praise, in the Lord whose | word I praise,
   in God I trust and will not fear: what can flesh | do to me?

6 *11* To you, O God, will I ful | fil my vows;
    to you will I present my offer | ings of thanks,
  12 For you will deliver my soul from death and my | feet from falling,
    that I may walk before God in the light | of the living.

Psalm 57

PRINCIPAL SERVICE

2ND SERVICE
Proper 7 C
Proper 9 A

3RD SERVICE
Proper 9 B

Richard Lloyd

Response
cf. v. 2a In the shadow of your wings I take refuge, O Lord.

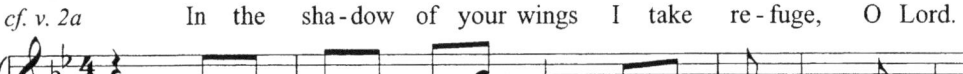

Verse

S.L.

1 *1* Be merciful to me, O | God, be merciful to me,
   for my soul takes re | fuge in you;
  2 In the shadow of your wings will | I take refuge
   until the storm of destruction | has passed by.

2 *3* I will call upon the | Most High God,
   the God who fulfils his | purpose for me.
  4 He will send from heaven and save me
    and rebuke those that would tram | ple upon me;
   God will send forth his love | and his faithfulness.

3 *5* I lie in the | midst of lions,
   people whose teeth are spears and arrows, and their | tongue a sharp sword.
  6 Be exalted, O God, a | bove the heavens,
   and your glory over | all the earth.

4 *7* They have laid a net for my feet; my soul | is pressed down;
   they have dug a pit before me and will fall into | it themselves.
  8 My heart is ready, O God, my | heart is ready;
   I will sing and | give you praise.

5 *9* Awake, my soul; awake, | harp and lyre,
   that I may awa | ken the dawn.
  10 I will give you thanks, O Lord, a | mong the peoples;
   I will sing praise to you a | mong the nations.

6 *11* For your loving-kindness is as high | as the heavens,
    and your faithfulness reaches | to the clouds.
  12 Be exalted, O God, a | bove the heavens,
    and your glory over | all the earth.

C Instrument

B♭ Instrument

Psalm 58 is omitted

New Psalms for Common Worship

Psalm 59

Verses 7 - 17 are omitted
PRINCIPAL SERVICE   2ND SERVICE   3RD SERVICE
                          Proper 8 C

Andrew Wright

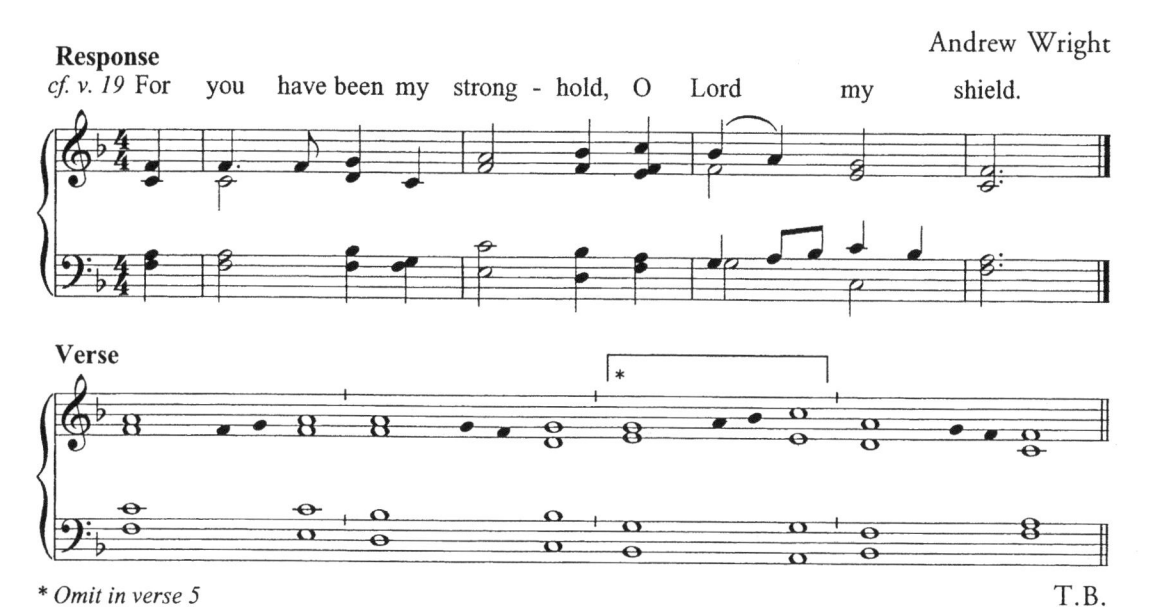

Response
cf. v. 19 For you have been my strong-hold, O Lord my shield.

Verse

* Omit in verse 5   T.B.

1 *1* Rescue me from my enemies, | O my God;
      set me high above those that rise | up against me.
   2 Save me from the | evildoers
      and from murderous | foes deliver me.

2 *3* For see how they lie in wait | for my soul
      and the mighty stir up trou | ble against me.
   4 Not for any fault or sin of | mine, O Lord;
      for no offence, they run and prepare them | selves for war.

3 *5* Rouse yourself, come to my | aid and see;
      for you are the Lord of hosts, the | God of Israel.
   6 Awake, and judge | all the nations;
      show no mercy to the | evil traitors.

4 *18* Yet will I sing | of your strength
      and every morning praise your | steadfast love;
   19 For you have | been my stronghold,
      my refuge in the day | of my trouble.

5 *20* To you, O my strength, | will I sing;
      for you, O God, | are my refuge,
      my God of | steadfast love.

C Instrument

B♭ Instrument

Psalm 60

PRINCIPAL SERVICE   2ND SERVICE   3RD SERVICE
Proper 8 C
Proper 10 A

Keith Duke

Response

cf. v. 1 Re-store us, O God, O re-store us to your-self a - gain.

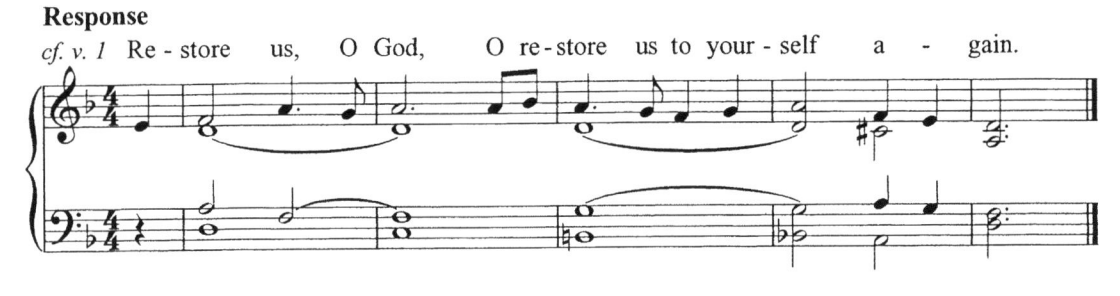

Verse

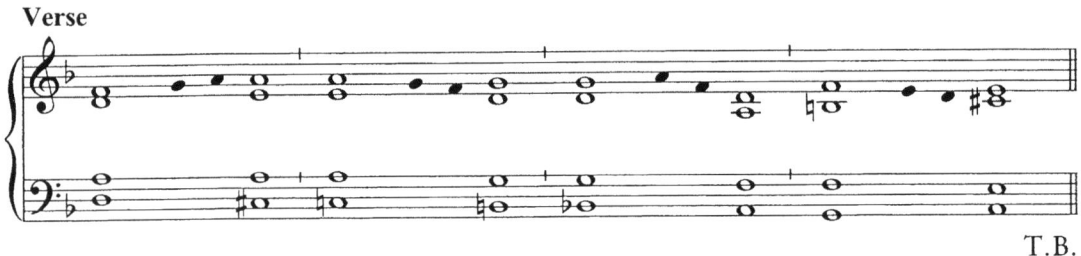

T.B.

1 *1* O God, you have cast us | off and broken us;
    you have been angry; restore us to your | self again.
  2 You have shaken the earth and torn | it apart;
    heal its wounds, | for it trembles.

2 *3* You have made your people drink | bitter things;
    we reel from the deadly wine | you have given us.
  4 You have made those who fear | you to flee,
    to escape from the range | of the bow.

3 *5* That your beloved may | be delivered,
    save us by your right | hand and answer us.
  6 God has spoken | in his holiness:
    'I will triumph and divide Shechem,
      and share out the val | ley of Succoth.

4 *7* 'Gilead is mine and Manas | seh is mine;
    Ephraim is my helmet and Ju | dah my sceptre.
  8 'Moab shall be my washpot; over Edom will I | cast my sandal;
    across Philistia will I | shout in triumph.'

5 *9* Who will lead me into | the strong city?
    Who will bring me | into Edom?
  10 Have you not cast us | off, O God?
    Will you no longer go forth | with our troops?

6 *11* Grant us your help a | gainst the enemy,
    for earthly help | is in vain.
 12 Through God will we | do great acts,
    for it is he that shall tread | down our enemies.

New Psalms for Common Worship

Psalm 61

PRINCIPAL SERVICE   2ND SERVICE   3RD SERVICE
Palm Sunday ABC

Richard Lloyd

Response

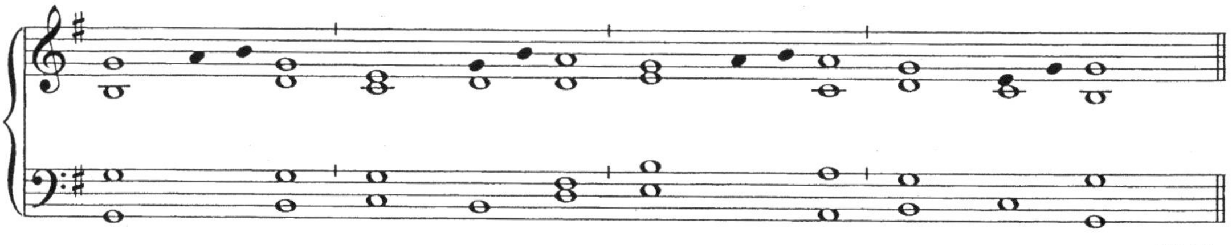

cf. v. 4b Un-der co-ver of your wings   I take re-fuge, O Lord.

Verse

K.D.

1   1 Hear my crying, O God, and listen | to my prayer.
     2 From the end of the earth I call to you with | fainting heart;
       O set me on the rock that is hig | her than I.
     3 For you are my refuge, a strong tower a | gainst the enemy.

2   4 Let me dwell in your | tent for ever
       and take refuge under the cover | of your wings.
     5 For you, O God, will | hear my vows;
       you will grant the request of those who | fear your name.

3   6 You will add length of days to the life | of the king,
       that his years may endure throughout all | generations.
     7 May he sit enthroned before God for ever;
       may steadfast love and | truth watch over him.
     8 So will I always sing praise to your name,
       and day by day ful | fil my vows.

C Instrument

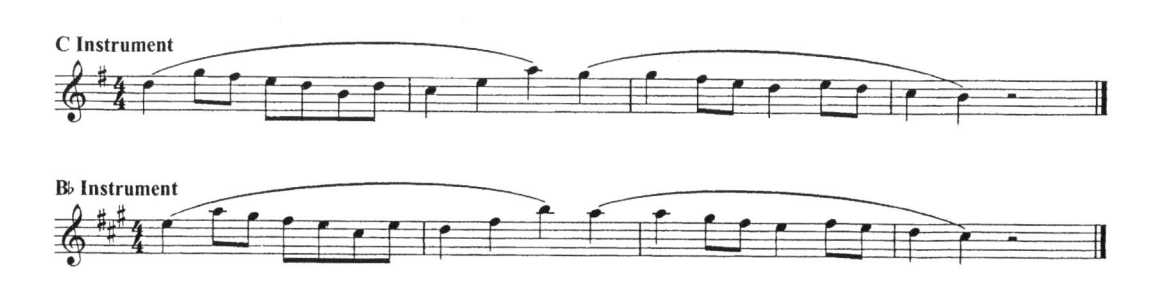

B♭ Instrument

Psalm 62

PRINCIPAL SERVICE
3 before Advent B (vs. 5-12)

2ND SERVICE
3 Advent C

3RD SERVICE
3 Advent B
Palm Sunday ABC

Simon Lesley

Response

v. 1 On God alone my soul waits in still - ness.

Verse

S.L.

1. *1* On God alone my soul in | stillness waits;
   from him comes | my salvation.
   2 He alone is my rock and | my salvation,
   my stronghold, so that I shall ne | ver be shaken.

2. *3* How long will all of you assail me | to destroy me,
   as you would a tottering wall or a | leaning fence?
   4 They plot only to thrust me down from my place of honour;
   lies are their | chief delight;
   they bless with their mouth, but in their | heart they curse.

3. *5* Wait on God alone in stillness, | O my soul;
   for in him | is my hope.
   6 He alone is my rock and | my salvation,
   my stronghold, so that I shall | not be shaken.

4. *7* In God is my strength | and my glory;
   God is my strong rock; in him | is my refuge.
   8 Put your trust in him al | ways, my people;
   pour out your hearts before him, for God | is our refuge.

5. *9* The peoples are but a breath, the whole human race | a deceit;
   on the scales they are altogether ligh | ter than air.
   10 Put no trust in oppression; in robbery take no | empty pride;
   though wealth increase, set not your | heart upon it.

6 *11* God spoke once, and twice have I | heard the same,
that power be | longs to God.
12 Steadfast love belongs to | you, O Lord,
for you repay everyone according | to their deeds.

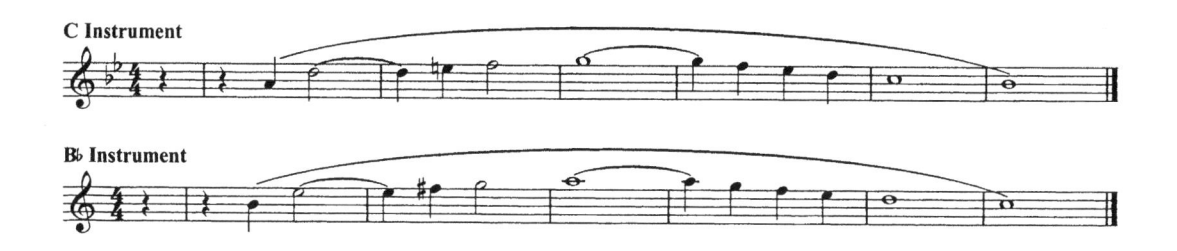

Psalm 63

PRINCIPAL SERVICE
3 Lent C (vs. 1-9)

2ND SERVICE
Proper 9 B
Proper 10 A

3RD SERVICE

Response
cf. vs. 1 and 2

Andrew Moore

My soul is a-thirst for you as in a dry and thirs-ty land.

Verse

C.M.

1 *1* O God, you are my God; eager | ly I seek you;
   my soul | is athirst for you.
 2 My flesh also | faints for you,
   as in a dry and thirsty land where there | is no water.
 3 So would I gaze upon you in your | holy place,
   that I might behold your power | and your glory.

2 *4* Your loving-kindness is better than | life itself
   and so my | lips shall praise you.
 5 I will bless you as long | as I live
   and lift up my hands | in your name.
 6 My soul shall be satisfied, as with mar | row and fatness,
   and my mouth shall praise you with | joyful lips,

3 *7* When I remember you u | pon my bed
   and meditate on you in the watches | of the night.
 8 For you have | been my helper
   and under the shadow of your wings will | I rejoice.
 9 My soul | clings to you;
   your right hand shall | hold me fast.

4 10 But those who seek my soul | to destroy it
   shall go down to the depths | of the earth;
 11 Let them fall by the edge | of the sword
   and become a por | tion for jackals.
 12 But the king shall rejoice in God;
   all those who swear by him | shall be glad,
   for the mouth of those who speak lies | shall be stopped.

Psalm 64

PRINCIPAL SERVICE

2ND SERVICE
Proper 9 B

3RD SERVICE
Proper 8 C
Proper 10 A

Gerry Fitzpatrick

Response

v. 10a The righteous shall rejoice in the Lord and put their trust in him.

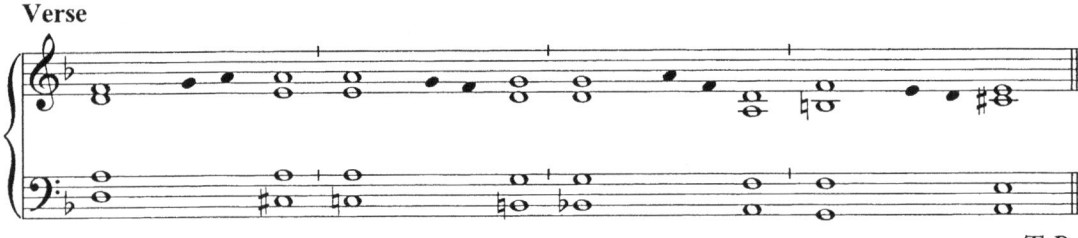

Verse

T.B.

1 ₁ Hear my voice, O God, in | my complaint;
  preserve my life from fear | of the enemy.
  ₂ Hide me from the conspiracy | of the wicked,
  from the gathering of | evildoers.

2 ₃ They sharpen their tongue | like a sword
  and aim their bitter | words like arrows,
  ₄ That they may shoot at the blameless from | hiding places;
  suddenly they shoot, and | are not seen.

3 ₅ They hold fast to their | evil course;
  they talk of laying snares, saying, | 'Who will see us?'
  ₆ They search out wickedness and lay a | cunning trap,
  for deep are the inward thoughts | of the heart.

4 ₇ But God will shoot at them with | his swift arrow,
  and suddenly they | shall be wounded.
  ₈ Their own tongues shall | make them fall,
  and all who see them shall wag their | heads in scorn.

5 *9* All peoples shall fear and tell what | God has done,
   and they will ponder | all his works.
 10 The righteous shall rejoice in the Lord
   and | put their trust in him,
   and all that are true of heart | shall exult.

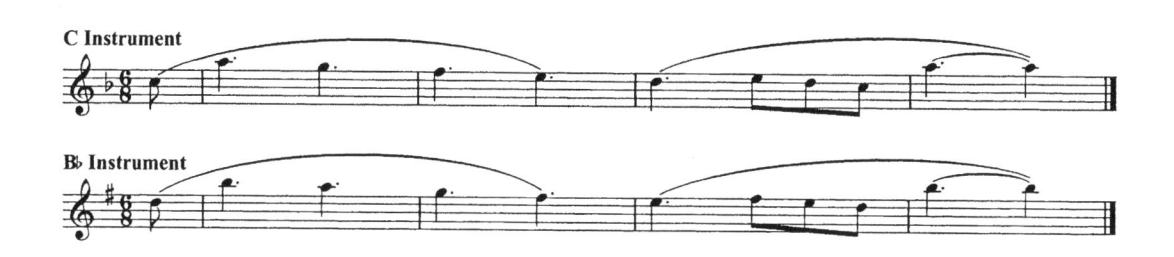

Psalm 65

PRINCIPAL SERVICE
2 before Lent C
Proper 10 A (related) (vs. 8-13 or 1-7)
Proper 25 C (vs. 1-7)

2ND SERVICE
2 before Lent B
Proper 9 C

3RD SERVICE
Proper 10 A
Proper 10 B

Colin Mawby

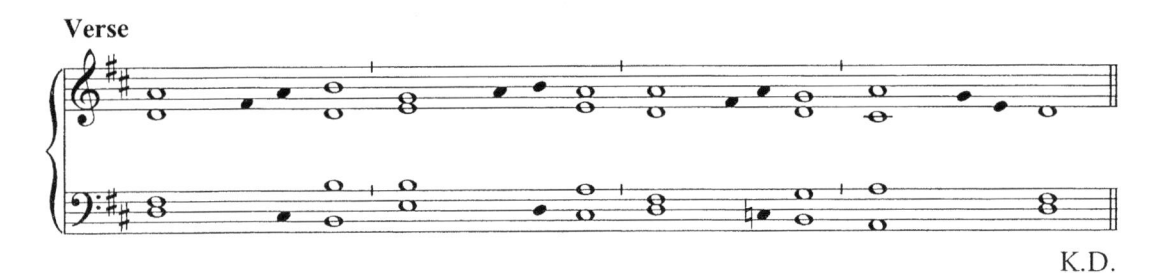

Response

cf. v. 3a Happy are they whom you choose to dwell in your courts.

Verse

K.D.

1 *1* Praise is due to you, O | God, in Zion;
   to you that answer prayer shall | vows be paid.
   2 To you shall all flesh come to con | fess their sins;
   when our misdeeds prevail against us,
      you will purge | them away.

2 *3* Happy are they | whom you choose
   and draw to your | courts to dwell there.
   We shall be satisfied with the blessings | of your house,
   even of your | holy temple.

3 *4* With wonders you will answer us in your righteousness,
      O God of | our salvation,
   O hope of all the ends of the earth and of the | farthest seas.
   5 In your strength you set | fast the mountains
   and are girded a | bout with might.

4 *6* You still the raging of the seas, the roaring | of their waves
   and the clamour | of the peoples.
   7 Those who dwell at the ends of the earth
      tremble | at your marvels;
   the gates of the morning and evening | sing your praise.

5 *8* You visit the | earth and water it;
   you make it | very plenteous.
  9 The river of God is | full of water;
   you prepare grain for your people,
    for so you provide | for the earth.

6 *10* You drench the furrows and smooth | out the ridges;
   you soften the ground with showers and | bless its increase.
  11 You crown the year | with your goodness,
   and your paths over | flow with plenty.

7 *12* May the pastures of the wilderness | flow with goodness
   and the hills be gir | ded with joy.
  13 May the meadows be clothed with | flocks of sheep
   and the valleys stand so thick with corn
    that they shall | laugh and sing.

Psalm 66

PRINCIPAL SERVICE
6 Easter A (vs. 7-18)
Proper 9 C (related) (vs. 1-8)
Proper 23 C (vs. 1-11)

2ND SERVICE
Easter Day C
Proper 10 B (vs. 1-6)

3RD SERVICE
Easter Day A (vs. 1-11)
Easter Day B (vs. 1-11)

Geoff Nobes

Response

v. 1a O be joyful in God, all the earth, sing the glory of his name.

Verse

C.M.

1 *1* Be joyful in God, | all the earth;
   sing the glory of his name; sing the glory | of his praise.
   2 Say to God, 'How awesome | are your deeds!
   Because of your great strength
   your enemies shall | bow before you.

2 *3* 'All the | earth shall worship you,
   sing to you, sing praise | to your name.'
   4 Come now and behold the | works of God,
   how wonderful he is in his deal | ings with humankind.

3 *5* He turned the sea in | to dry land;
   the river they passed through on foot;
   there | we rejoiced in him.
   6 In his might he rules for ever;
   his eyes keep watch o | ver the nations;
   let no rebel rise | up against him.

4 *7* Bless our God, | O you peoples;
   make the voice of his praise | to be heard,
   8 Who holds our | souls in life
   and suffers not our | feet to slip.

5 9 For you, O God, have proved us;
   you have tried us as sil | ver is tried.
  10 You brought us into the snare;
   you laid heavy burdens u | pon our backs.
  11 You let enemies ride over our heads;
   we went through | fire and water;
   but you brought us out into a | place of liberty.

6 12 I will come into your house with burnt offerings
   and will pay | you my vows,
   which my lips uttered
   and my mouth promised when I | was in trouble.
  13 I will offer you fat burnt sacrifices
   with the | smoke of rams;
   I will sacrifice ox | en and goats.

7 14 Come and listen, all you who fear God,
   and I will tell you what he has done | for my soul.
  15 I called out to him with my mouth
   and his praise was | on my tongue.
  16 If I had nursed evil | in my heart,
   the Lord would | not have heard me,

8 17 But in truth | God has heard me;
   he has heeded the voice | of my prayer.
  18 Blessed be God, who has not rejec | ted my prayer,
   nor withheld his loving mer | cy from me.

New Psalms for Common Worship

Psalm 67

PRINCIPAL SERVICE
6 Easter C
Proper 15 A (related)

2ND SERVICE
Pentecost A
Proper 11 A

3RD SERVICE
2 before Lent B
Proper 11 B

John McCann

Response

v. 3 Let the peo-ples praise you, O God, let all the peo-ples praise you.

Verse

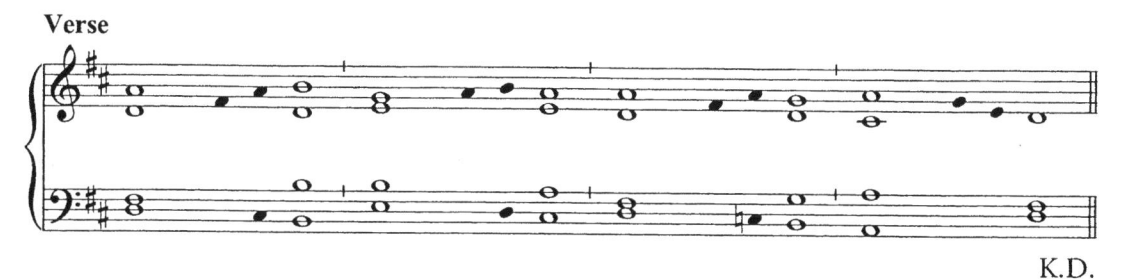

K.D.

1 1 God be gracious to us and bless us
    and make his face to | shine upon us,
   2 That your way may be known upon earth,
    your saving power a | mong all nations.
   3 Let the peoples praise | you, O God;
    let all the | peoples praise you.

2 4 O let the nations rejoice | and be glad,
    for you will judge the peoples righteously
    and govern the nations | upon earth.
   5 Let the peoples praise | you, O God;
    let all the | peoples praise you.

3 6 Then shall the earth bring | forth her increase,
    and God, our own | God, will bless us.
   7 God | will bless us,
    and all the ends of the | earth shall fear him.

C Instrument

B♭ Instrument

Psalm 68

Verses 20 - 35 are omitted

PRINCIPAL SERVICE
7 Easter A (vs. 1-10)

2ND SERVICE
3 Advent B (vs. 1-19)
7 Easter C (vs. 1-13, 18-19)

3RD SERVICE
3 Advent A (vs. 1-19)

Simon Lesley

Response
cf v. 19a Our God is a God of sal-va-tion.

Verse

* *Omit in verse 6*

S.L.

1 *1* Let God arise and let his ene | mies be scattered;
    let those that hate him | flee before him.
   2 As the smoke vanishes, so may they va | nish away;
    as wax melts at the fire,
    so let the wicked perish at the pre | sence of God.

2 *3* But let the righteous be glad and rejoice | before God;
    let them make mer | ry with gladness.
   4 Sing to God, sing praises to his name;
    exalt him who rides | on the clouds.
    The Lord is his name; re | joice before him.

3 *5* Father of the fatherless, defen | der of widows,
    God in his holy | habitation!
   6 God gives the solitary a home
    and brings forth prisoners to | songs of welcome,
    but the rebellious inhabit a | burning desert.

4 *7* O God, when you went forth be | fore your people,
    when you marched | through the wilderness,
   8 The earth shook and the heavens dropped down rain,
    at the presence of God, the | Lord of Sinai,
    at the presence of God, the | God of Israel.

5 *9* You sent down a gracious | rain, O God;
    you refreshed your inheritance when | it was weary.
   10 Your people | came to dwell there;
    in your goodness, O God, you provide | for the poor.

6 *11* The Lord gave the word;
  great was the company of women who | bore the tidings:
  'Kings and their armies they | flee, they flee!'
  and women at home are divid | ing the spoil.

7 *12* Though you stayed a | mong the sheepfolds,
  see now a dove's wings covered with silver
  and its feathers | with green gold.
 13 When the Almighty scat | tered the kings,
  it was like snowflakes fal | ling on Zalmon.

8 *14* You mighty mountain, great moun | tain of Bashan!
  You towering mountain, great moun | tain of Bashan!
 15 Why look with envy, you towering mountains,
  at the mount which God has desired | for his dwelling,
  the place where the Lord will | dwell for ever?

9 *16* The chariots of God are twice ten thousand,
  even thousands | upon thousands;
  the Lord is among them, the Lord of Sinai in | holy power.
 17 You have gone up on high and led capti | vity captive;
  you have received tribute, even from those who rebelled,
  that you may reign as | Lord and God.

10 *18* Blessed be the Lord who bears our burdens | day by day,
  for God is | our salvation.
 19 God is for us the God of | our salvation;
  God is the Lord who can deli | ver from death.

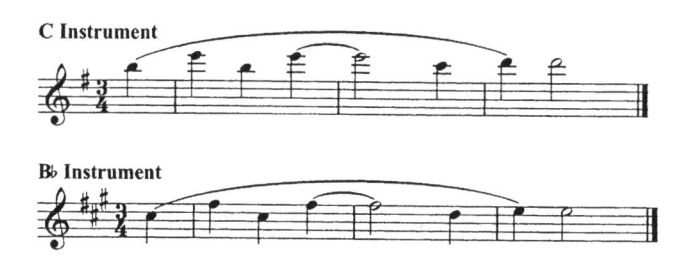

Psalm 69

PRINCIPAL SERVICE
Proper 7 A (related) (vs. 14-20)

2ND SERVICE
Palm Sunday BC (vs. 1-20)

3RD SERVICE
Good Friday ABC

Colin Mawby

Response
cf. v. 35

The Lord listens to the needy and his own he does not despise.

Verse

C.M.

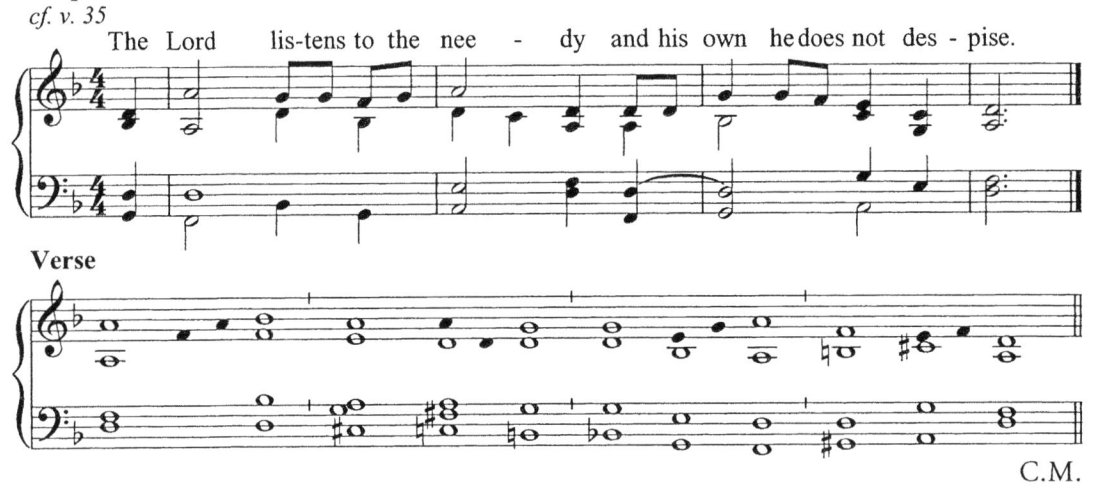

1 *1* Save | me, O God,
   for the waters have come up,
   even | to my neck.
  2 I sink in deep mire where there | is no foothold;
   I have come into deep waters
   and the | flood sweeps over me.

2 *3* I have grown weary with crying;
   my | throat is raw;
   my eyes have failed from looking
   so long | for my God.
  4 Those who hate me without | any cause
   are more than the hairs | of my head;

3 *5* Those who would destroy | me are mighty;
   my enemies accuse me falsely:
   must I now give back what I | never stole?
  6 O God, you | know my foolishness,
   and my faults are not hid | den from you.

4 *7* Let not those who hope in you
   be put to shame through me,
   Lord | God of hosts;
   let not those who seek you be disgraced
   because of me, O | God of Israel.
  8 For your sake have I suf | fered reproach;
   shame has co | vered my face.

5 *9* I have become a stranger | to my kindred,
   an alien to my | mother's children.
  10 Zeal for your house has eat | en me up;
   the scorn of those who scorn you
   has fal | len upon me.

6 *11* I humbled myself with fasting,
   but that was turned to | my reproach.
  12 I put on sackcloth also
   and became a by | word among them.
  13 Those who sit at the gate
   mur | mur against me,
   and the drunkards make | songs about me.

7 *14* But as for me,
   I make my prayer to | you, O Lord;
   at an acceptable | time, O God.
  15 Answer me, O God, in the
   abundance | of your mercy
   and with your | sure salvation.

8 *16* Draw me out of the mire, | that I sink not;
   let me be rescued from those who hate me
   and out of | the deep waters.
  17 Let not the water flood drown me,
   neither the deep swal | low me up;
   let not the Pit shut its | mouth upon me.

9 *18* Answer me, Lord, for your
   loving-kind | ness is good;
   turn to me in the multitude | of your mercies.
  19 Hide not your face from your servant;
   be swift to answer me, for I | am in trouble.
  20 Draw near to my soul and redeem me;
   deliver me because | of my enemies.

10 *21* You know my reproach,
   my shame and | my dishonour;
   my adversaries are all | in your sight.
  22 Reproach has bro | ken my heart;
   I am | full of heaviness.

11 I looked for some to have pity, but | there was no one,
    neither found I a | ny to comfort me.
 23 They gave me | gall to eat,
    and when I was thirsty, they gave me vine | gar to drink.

12 24 Let the table before them | be a trap
    and their sacred | feasts a snare.
 25 Let their eyes be darkened, that they | cannot see,
    and give them continual trembling | in their loins.

13 26 Pour out your indigna | tion upon them,
    and let the heat of your anger | overtake them.
 27 Let their | camp be desolate,
    and let there be no one to dwell | in their tents.

14 28 For they persecute the one whom | you have stricken,
    and increase the sorrows of him whom | you have pierced.
 29 Lay to their charge guilt upon guilt,
    and let them not receive your | vindication.
 30 Let them be wiped out of the book of the living
    and not be written a | mong the righteous.

15 31 As for me, I am poor | and in misery;
    your saving help, O God, will | lift me up.
 32 I will praise the name of God | with a song;
    I will proclaim his greatness | with thanksgiving.

16 33 This will please the Lord more than an offer | ing of oxen,
    more than bulls with | horns and hooves.
 34 The humble shall see | and be glad;
    you who seek God, your | heart shall live.

17 35 For the Lord listens | to the needy,
    and his own who are imprisoned he does | not despise.
 36 Let the heavens and | the earth praise him,
    the seas and | all that moves in them;

18 37 For God will save Zion and rebuild the ci | ties of Judah;
    they shall live there and have it | in possession.
 38 The children of his servants | shall inherit it,
    and they that love his name shall | dwell therein.

C Instrument

B♭ Instrument

New Psalms for Common Worship

Psalm 70

PRINCIPAL SERVICE
3 before Advent A
Wednesday of Holy Week ABC

2ND SERVICE
Proper 9 C
Proper 11 A

3RD SERVICE
Proper 11 B

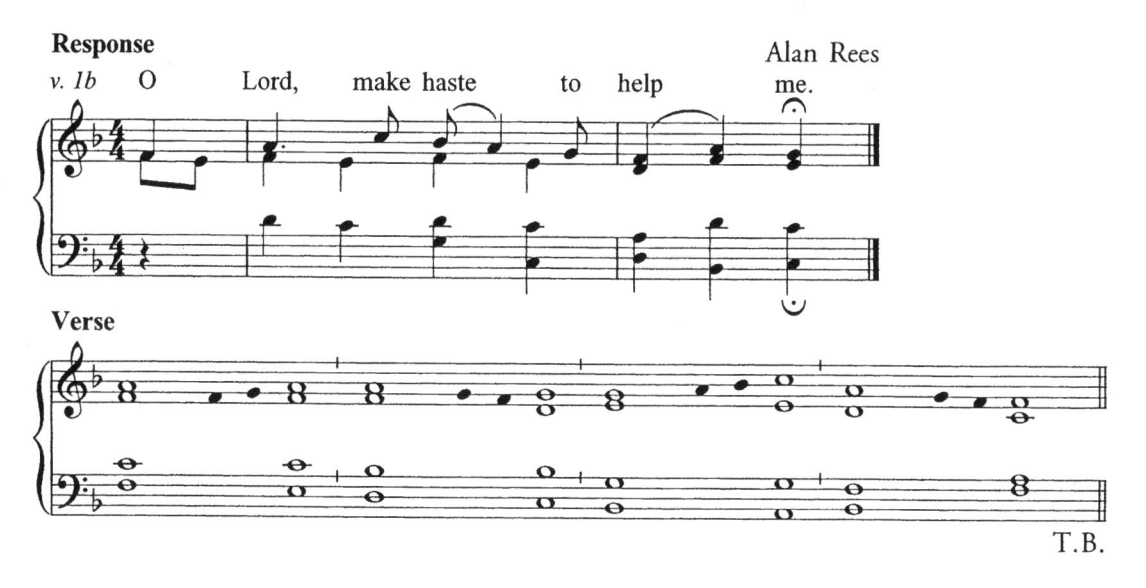

Response
v. 1b O Lord, make haste to help me.

Alan Rees

Verse

T.B.

1 *1* O God, make | speed to save me;
   O Lord, make | haste to help me.
 2 Let those who seek my life
   be put to shame | and confusion;
   let them be turned back and disgraced
   who | wish me evil.

2 *3* Let those who mock | and deride me
   turn back because | of their shame.
 4 But let all who seek you rejoice | and be glad in you;
   let those who love your salvation say always,
   'Great | is the Lord!'

3 *5* As for me, I am | poor and needy;
   come to me quick | ly, O God.
 6 You are my help and | my deliverer;
   O Lord, do | not delay.

C Instrument

B♭ Instrument

Psalm 71

PRINCIPAL SERVICE
Tuesday of Holy Week ABC (vs. 1-9)
Proper 16 C (vs. 1-6)

2ND SERVICE

3RD SERVICE
4 Epiphany ABC
(vs. 1-6, 14-17)
Proper 11 A

Geoff Nobes

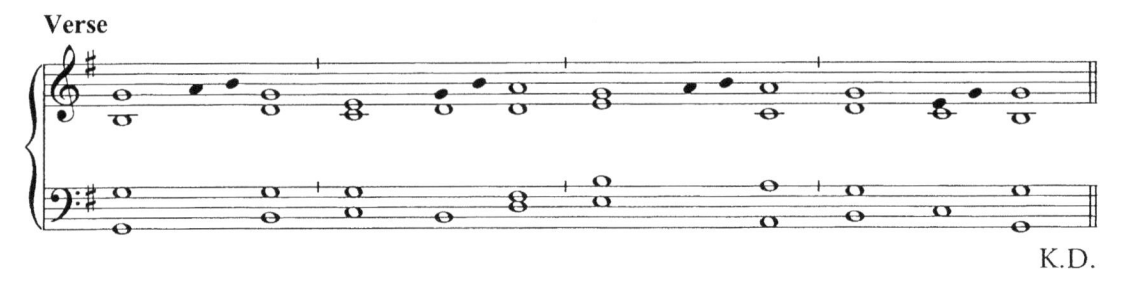

Response

cf. v. 5 You, O Lord, are my con-fi-dence and hope.

Verse

K.D.

1 *1* In you, O Lord, do | I seek refuge;
　　let me never be | put to shame.
　2 In your righteousness, deliver me and | set me free;
　　incline your ear to | me and save me.

2 *3* Be for me a stronghold to which I may e | ver resort;
　　send out to save me, for you are my rock | and my fortress.
　4 Deliver me, my God, from the hand | of the wicked,
　　from the grasp of the evildoer and | the oppressor.

3 *5* For you are my hope, | O Lord God,
　　my confidence, even | from my youth.
　6 Upon you have I leaned from my birth,
　　when you drew me from my | mother's womb;
　　my praise shall be al | ways of you.

4 *7* I have become a portent to many,
　　but you are my refuge | and my strength.
　8 Let my mouth be full of your praise
　　and your glory all | the day long.
　9 Do not cast me away in the time | of old age;
　　forsake me not when | my strength fails.

5 *10* For my enemies are talk | ing against me,
　　and those who lie in wait for my life take coun | sel together.
　11 They say, 'God | has forsaken him;
　　pursue him and take him,
　　because there is none | to deliver him.'

6 *12* O God, | be not far from me;
   come quickly to help me, | O my God.
  13 Let those who are against me
   be put to shame | and disgrace;
   let those who seek to do me evil
   be covered with scorn | and reproach.

7 *14* But as for me I will | hope continually
   and will praise you | more and more.
  15 My mouth shall tell of your righteousness
   and salvation all | the day long,
   for I know no end | of the telling.

8 *16* I will begin with the mighty works of | the Lord God;
   I will recall your righteousness, | yours alone.
  17 O God, you have taught me since | I was young,
   and to this day I tell of your won | derful works.

9 *18* Forsake me not, O God,
   when I am old | and grey-headed,
   till I make known your deeds to the next generation
   and your power to all that | are to come.
  19 Your righteousness, O God, reaches | to the heavens;
   in the great things you have done, who is like | you, O God?

10 *20* What troubles and adversities | you have shown me,
   and yet you will turn | and refresh me
   and bring me from the deep of the | earth again.
  21 Increase my honour; turn a | gain and comfort me.

11 *22* Therefore will I praise you u | pon the harp
   for your faithfulness, | O my God;
   I will sing to you | with the lyre,
   O Holy | One of Israel.

12 *23* My lips will sing out | as I play to you,
   and so will my soul, which you | have redeemed.
  24 My tongue also will tell of your righteousness all | the day long,
   for they shall be shamed and disgraced
   who sought to | do me evil.

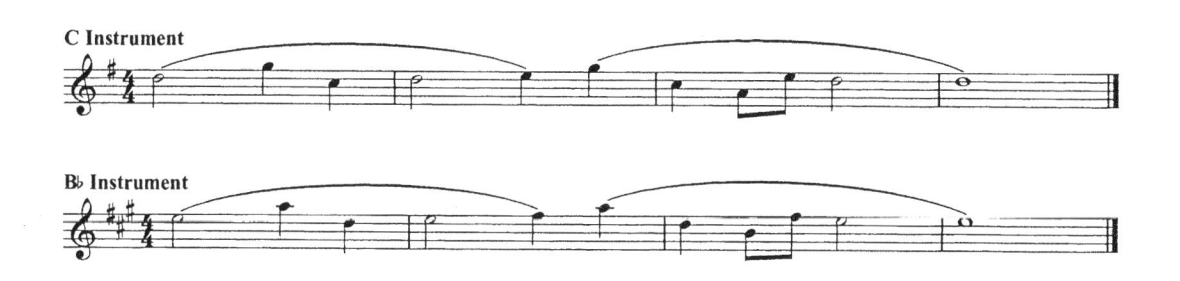

Psalm 72

PRINCIPAL SERVICE
2 Advent A (vs. 1-7)
Epiphany ABC (vs. 10-15 or 1-9)

2ND SERVICE
Christ the King BC (vs. 1-7)

3RD SERVICE
1 before Lent A

John McCann

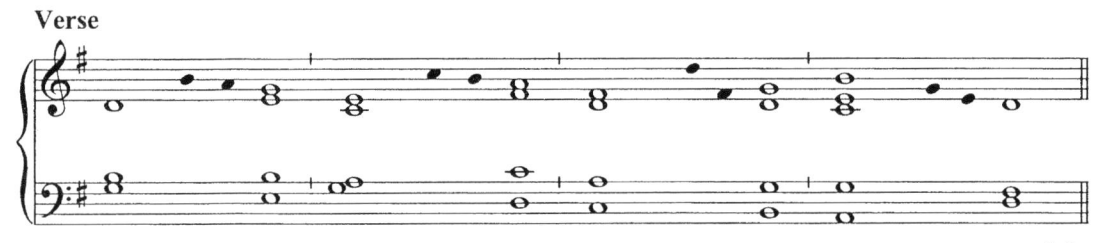

Response

v. 17c May all nations be blest in him.

Verse

S.L.

1 *1* Give the king your judgements, O God,
   and your righteousness to the son | of a king.
   2 Then shall he judge your people righteously
   and your | poor with justice.
   3 May the mountains | bring forth peace,
   and the little hills righteousness | for the people.

2 *4* May he defend the poor a | mong the people,
   deliver the children of the needy and crush | the oppressor.
   5 May he live as long as the sun and | moon endure,
   from one generation | to another.

3 *6* May he come down like rain u | pon the mown grass,
   like the showers that wa | ter the earth.
   7 In his time shall right | eousness flourish,
   and abundance of peace till the moon shall | be no more.

4 *8* May his dominion extend from | sea to sea
   and from the River to the ends | of the earth.
   9 May his foes | kneel before him
   and his enemies | lick the dust.

5 *10* The kings of Tarshish and of the isles | shall pay tribute;
   the kings of Sheba and Seba | shall bring gifts.
   11 All kings shall fall | down before him;
   all nations shall | do him service.

6 *12* For he shall deliver the poor | that cry out,
    the needy and those who | have no helper.
  13 He shall have pity on the | weak and poor;
    he shall preserve the lives | of the needy.

7 *14* He shall redeem their lives from oppres | sion and violence,
    and dear shall their blood be | in his sight.
  15 Long may he live;
    unto him may be given | gold from Sheba;
    may prayer be made for him continually
    and may they bless him all | the day long.

8 *16* May there be abundance of grain | on the earth,
    standing thick u | pon the hilltops;
    may its fruit flou | rish like Lebanon
    and its grain grow like the grass | of the field.

9 *17* May his name re | main for ever
    and be established as long as the | sun endures;
    may all nations be | blest in him
    and | call him blessed.

10 *18* Blessed be the Lord, the | God of Israel,
    who alone does won | derful things.
  19 And blessed be his glorious | name for ever.
    May all the earth be filled with his glory.
    A | men. Amen.

C Instrument

B♭ Instrument

Psalm 73

Verses 4-15 are omitted
PRINCIPAL SERVICE

2ND SERVICE
Trinity C (vs. 1-3, 16-28)
Proper 11 B (vs. 21-28)

3RD SERVICE
6 Easter A (vs. 21-28)

Keith Duke

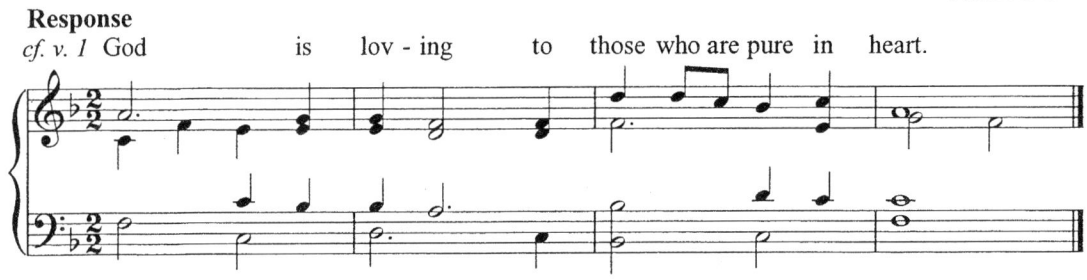

Response
cf. v. 1 God is lov-ing to those who are pure in heart.

Verse

C.M.

1 *1* Truly, God is lov | ing to Israel,
  to those who are | pure in heart.
  2 Nevertheless, my feet were | almost gone;
  my steps had | well-nigh slipped.
  3 For I was envious | of the proud;
  I saw the wicked in | such prosperity;

2 *16* Then thought I to understand this,
  but it | was too hard for me,
  17 Until I entered the sanctuary of God
  and understood the end | of the wicked:
  18 How you set them in slippery places;
  you cast them down | to destruction.
  19 How suddenly do they come to destruction,
  perish and come to a | fearful end!
  20 As with a dream when | one awakes,
  so, Lord, when you arise you will des | pise their image.

3 *21* When my heart became embittered
   and I was pierced | to the quick,
  22 I was but foolish and ignorant;
   I was like a brute beast | in your presence.
  23 Yet I am always with you;
   you hold me by | my right hand.
  24 You will guide me with your counsel
   and afterwards receive | me with glory.
  25 Whom have I in hea | ven but you?
   And there is nothing upon earth that I desire
   in compari | son with you.

4 *26* Though my flesh and | my heart fail me,
   God is the strength of my heart and my por | tion for ever.
  27 Truly, those who forsake | you will perish;
   you will put to silence the faithless | who betray you.
  28 But it is good for me to draw | near to God;
   in the Lord God have I made my refuge,
   that I may tell of | all your works.

Psalm 74

PRINCIPAL SERVICE

2ND SERVICE
Proper 12 b (vs. 11-16)

3RD SERVICE
2 Lent A
Proper 9 C

Richard Lloyd

Response
v. 21a Arise, O God, maintain your own cause.

Verse

T.B.

1 *1* O God, why have you utter | ly disowned us?
   Why does your anger burn
   against the sheep | of your pasture?
  2 Remember your congregation that you pur | chased of old,
   the tribe you redeemed for your own possession,
   and Mount Zion | where you dwelt.

2 *3* Hasten your steps towards the | endless ruins,
   where the enemy has laid waste | all your sanctuary.
  4 Your adversaries roared in the place | of your worship;
   they set up their banners as to | kens of victory.

3 *5* Like men brandishing axes on high in a thic | ket of trees,
   all her carved work they smashed down with hat | chet and hammer.
  6 They set fire to your | holy place;
   they defiled the dwelling place of your name
   and razed it | to the ground.

4 *7* They said in their heart, 'Let us make havoc of them | altogether,'
   and they burned down all the sanctuaries of God | in the land.
  8 There are no signs to see, not one | prophet left,
   not one among us who | knows how long.

5 *9* How long, O God, will the adver | sary scoff?
   Shall the enemy blaspheme your | name for ever?
  10 Why have you with | held your hand
   and hidden your right hand | in your bosom?

6 *11* Yet God is my king | from of old,
   who did deeds of salvation in the midst | of the earth.
  12 It was you that divided the sea | by your might
   and shattered the heads of the dragons | on the waters;

7 *13* You alone crushed the heads | of Leviathan
   and gave him to the beasts of the de | sert for food.
  14 You cleft the rock for foun | tain and flood;
   you dried up ever- | flowing rivers.

8 *15* Yours is the day, yours al | so the night;
   you established the moon | and the sun.
  16 You set all the bounds | of the earth;
   you fashioned both sum | mer and winter.

9 *17* Remember now, Lord, how the e | nemy scoffed,
   how a foolish people des | pised your name.
  18 Do not give to wild beasts the soul | of your turtle dove;
   forget not the lives of your | poor for ever.

10 *19* Look upon your creation, for the earth is | full of darkness,
   full of the | haunts of violence.
  20 Let not the oppressed turn a | way ashamed,
   but let the poor and needy | praise your name.

11 *21* Arise, O God, maintain | your own cause;
   remember how fools revile you all | the day long.
  22 Forget not the clamour | of your adversaries,
   the tumult of your enemies that as | cends continually.

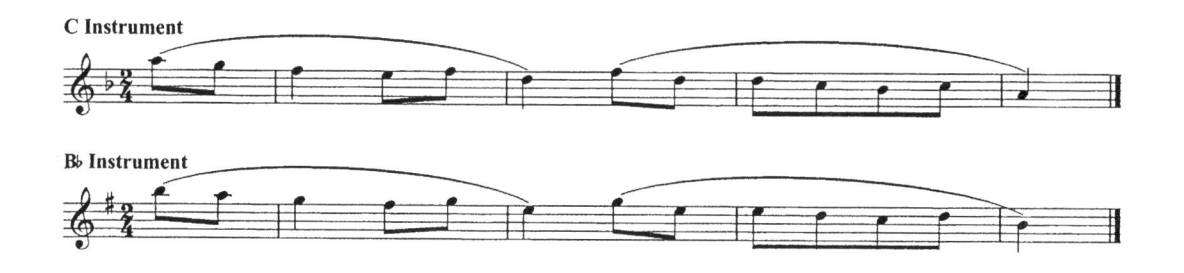

Psalm 75

PRINCIPAL SERVICE   2ND SERVICE   3RD SERVICE
                                  2 Advent C   Proper 12 B
                                  Proper 12 A

Response   John McCann

cf. v.1 We give thanks to you, O God.

Verse

                                                                          S.L.

1 *1* We give you | thanks, O God,
      we give you thanks, for your | name is near,
      as your wonderful | deeds declare.

2 *2* 'I will seize the appointed time;
      I, the Lord, will | judge with equity.
   3 'Though the earth reels and | all that dwell in her,
      it is I that hold her | pillars steady.

3 *4* 'To the boasters I say, | 'Boast no longer,'
      and to the wicked, 'Do not lift up your horn.
   5 'Do not lift up your | horn on high;
      do not speak with | a stiff neck.'

4 *6* For neither from the east nor | from the west,
      nor yet from the wilderness comes | exaltation.
   7 But God alone is judge;
      he puts down one and raises | up another.

5 *8* For in the hand of the Lord there is a cup,
      well mixed and full of | foaming wine.
   9 He pours it out for all the wicked | of the earth;
      they shall drink it, and | drain the dregs.

6 *10* But I will rejoice for ever
      and make music to the | God of Jacob.
   11 All the horns of the wicked | will I break,
      but the horns of the righteous shall | be exalted.

C Instrument

B♭ Instrument

Psalm 76

PRINCIPAL SERVICE

2ND SERVICE
2 Advent C
Proper 12 A

3RD SERVICE
7 Easter B
Proper 10 C

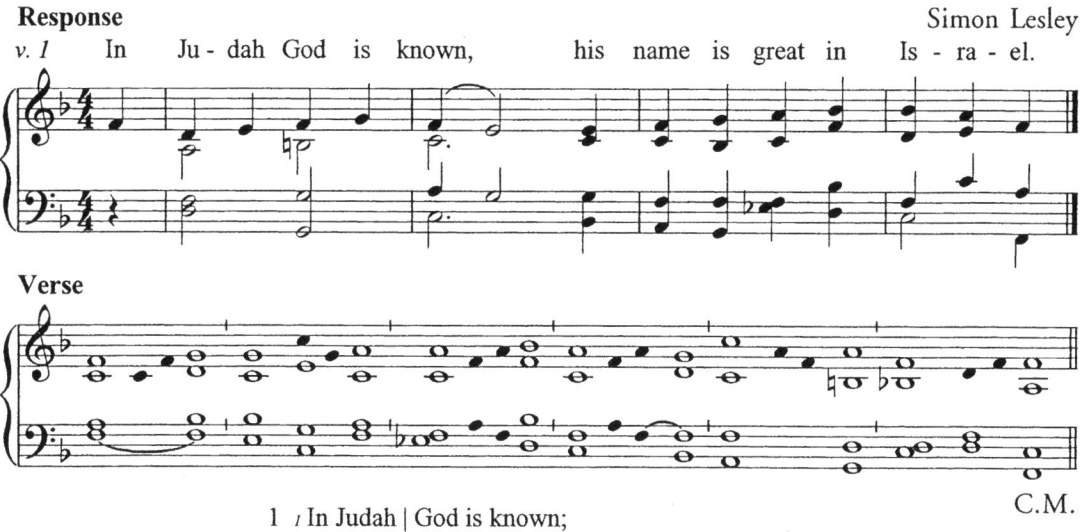

Response   Simon Lesley

v. 1 In Judah God is known, his name is great in Israel.

Verse

C.M.

1 *1* In Judah | God is known;
    his name is | great in Israel.
  2 At Salem | is his tabernacle,
    and his dwelling | place in Zion.
  3 There broke he the flashing arrows | of the bow,
    the shield, the sword and the wea | pons of war.

2 *4* In the light of splendour | you appeared,
    glorious from the e | ternal mountains.
  5 The boastful were plundered; they have | slept their sleep;
    none of the warriors can | lift their hand.
  6 At your rebuke, O | God of Jacob,
    both horse and chari | ot fell stunned.

3 *7* Terrible are | you in majesty:
    who can stand before your face when | you are angry?
  8 You caused your judgement to be | heard from heaven;
    the earth trembled | and was still,
  9 When God a | rose to judgement,
    to save all the meek | upon earth.

4 *10* You crushed the wrath | of the peoples
    and bridled the | wrathful remnant.
  11 Make a vow to the Lord your | God and keep it;
    let all who are round about him bring gifts
    to him that is worthy | to be feared.
  12 He breaks down the spi | rit of princes
    and strikes terror in the kings | of the earth.

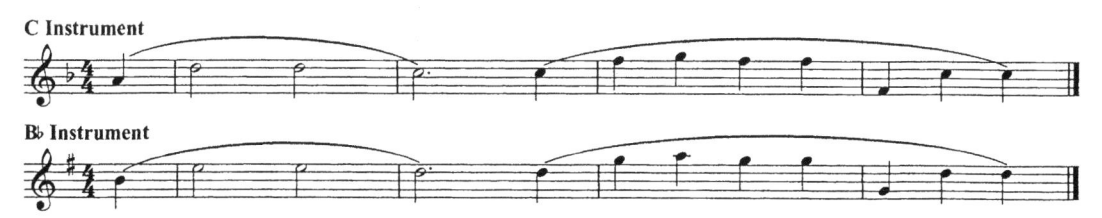

C Instrument

B♭ Instrument

Psalm 77

PRINCIPAL SERVICE
Proper 8 C (vs. 11-20)

2ND SERVICE
Proper 10 C (vs. 1-13)

3RD SERVICE
1 Lent B
3 Easter B (vs. 11-20)
Proper 12 A

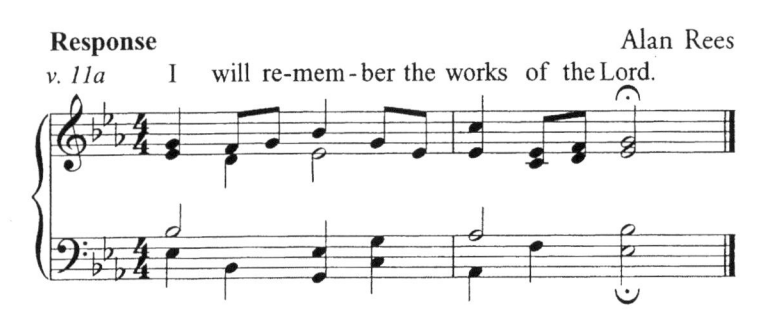

Response — Alan Rees
v. 11a I will remember the works of the Lord.

Verse

G.N.

1 *1* I cry aloud to God;
   I cry aloud to God and | he will hear me.
   2 In the day of my trouble I have | sought the Lord;
   by night my hand is stretched out and | does not tire;
   my soul re | fuses comfort.

2 *3* I think upon God | and I groan;
   I ponder, and my | spirit faints.
   4 You will not let my | eyelids close;
   I am so troubled that I | cannot speak.

3 *5* I consider the days of old;
   I remember the | years long past;
   6 I commune with my heart in the night;
   my spirit searches for | understanding.
   7 Will the Lord cast us | off for ever?
   Will he no more show | us his favour?

4 *8* Has his loving mercy clean gone for ever?
   Has his promise come to an end for | evermore?
   9 Has God forgotten | to be gracious?
   Has he shut up his compassion | in displeasure?
   10 And I said, 'My grief is this: that the right hand
   of the Most High has | lost its strength.'

5 ⁱ¹ I will remember the works | of the Lord
    and call to mind your wonders | of old time.
  ¹² I will meditate on all your works
    and ponder your | mighty deeds.
  ¹³ Your way, O God, is holy;
    who is so great a god | as our God?

6 ¹⁴ You are the God | who worked wonders
    and declared your power a | mong the peoples.
  ¹⁵ With a mighty arm you re | deemed your people,
    the children of Ja | cob and Joseph.

7 ¹⁶ The waters saw you, O God;
    the waters saw you and | were afraid;
    the depths al | so were troubled.
  ¹⁷ The clouds poured out water; | the skies thundered;
    your arrows flashed on | ev'ry side;

8 ¹⁸ The voice of your thunder was in the whirlwind;
    your lightnings lit | up the ground;
    the earth trem | bled and shook.
  ¹⁹ Your way was in the sea, and your paths in the great waters,
    but your footsteps | were not known.
  ²⁰ You led your people like sheep
    by the hand of Mo | ses and Aaron.

C Instrument

B♭ Instrument

Psalm 78

Verses 8-22 and 30-72 are omitted

PRINCIPAL SERVICE   2ND SERVICE   3RD SERVICE
Proper 13 B (related) (vs. 23-29)
Proper 21 A (vs. 1-7)

Gerry Fitzpatrick

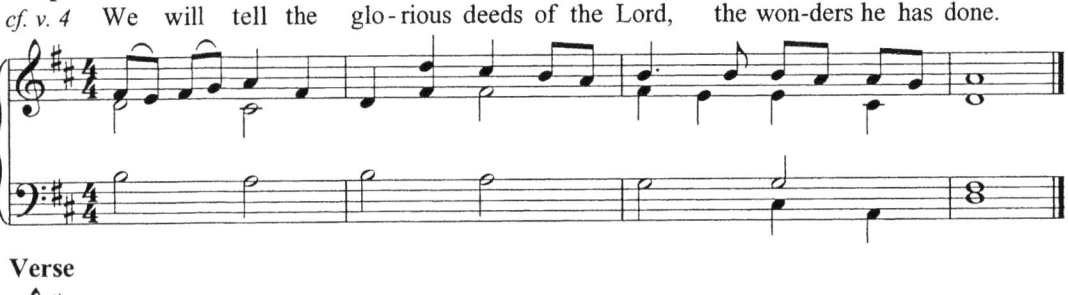

Response

cf. v. 4 We will tell the glorious deeds of the Lord, the wonders he has done.

Verse

K.D.

1. *1* Hear my teaching, O my people;
    incline your ears to the words | of my mouth.
   2 I will open my mouth | in a parable;
    I will pour forth mysteries | from of old,
   3 Such as we have heard and known,
    which our fore | bears have told us.

2. *4* We will not hide from their children,
    but will recount to genera | tions to come,
    the praises of the Lord and his power
    and the wonderful works | he has done.
   5 He laid a solemn charge on Jacob
    and made it a | law in Israel,
    which he commanded them to | teach their children,

3. *6* That the generations to come might know,
    and the children | yet unborn,
    that they in turn might tell it | to their children;
   7 So that they might put their | trust in God
    and not forget the deeds of God,
    but keep | his commandments,

4 23 So he commanded the | clouds above
  and opened the | doors of heaven.
  24 He rained down upon them man | na to eat
  and gave them the | grain of heaven.

5 25 So mortals ate the | bread of angels;
  he sent them | food in plenty.
  26 He caused the east wind to blow | in the heavens
  and led out the south wind | by his might.

6 27 He rained flesh upon them as | thick as dust
  and winged fowl like the sand | of the sea.
  28 He let it fall in the midst of their camp
  and round a | bout their tents.
  29 So they ate and were well filled,
  for he gave them what | they desired.

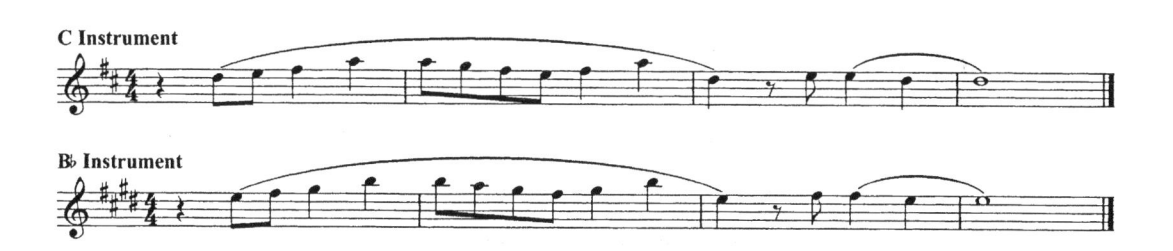

C Instrument

B♭ Instrument

Psalm 79

Verses 10-14 are omitted
PRINCIPAL SERVICE
Proper 20 C (vs. 1-9)

2ND SERVICE

3RD SERVICE

Geoff Nobes

Response
cf. v. 9 Help us, O God, for the glory of your name.

Verse

Omit in verse 3

C.M.

1. 1 O God, the heathen have come in | to your heritage;
    your holy temple have | they defiled
    and made Jerusalem a | heap of stones.
   2 The dead bodies of your servants | they have given
    to be food for the birds | of the air,
    and the flesh of your faithful to the beasts | of the field.

2. 3 Their blood have they shed like water
    on every side | of Jerusalem,
    and there was no | one to bury them.
   4 We have become the taunt | of our neighbours,
    the scorn and derision of those that are | round about us.
   5 Lord, how long will you be an | gry, for ever?
    How long will your jealous fury | blaze like fire?

3. 6 Pour out your wrath u | pon the nations
    that | have not known you,
    and upon the kingdoms that have not called u | pon your name.
   7 For they have de | voured Jacob
    and laid | waste his dwelling place.

4 ₈ Remember not against us our | former sins;
    let your compassion make | haste to meet us,
    for we are brought | very low.
  ₉ Help us, O God of | our salvation,
    for the glory | of your name;
    deliver us, and wipe away our sins for | your name's sake.

Psalm 80

PRINCIPAL SERVICE
1 Advent B (vs. 1-8)
4 Advent A (vs. 1-8)
4 Advent C (vs. 1-8)
Proper 15 C (vs. 9-20)
Proper 22 A (related) (vs. 8-16)

2ND SERVICE
Palm Sunday A
Proper 13 A (vs. 1-8)

3RD SERVICE
2 Advent ABC
3 Easter C (vs. 1-8)

Colin Mawby

Response

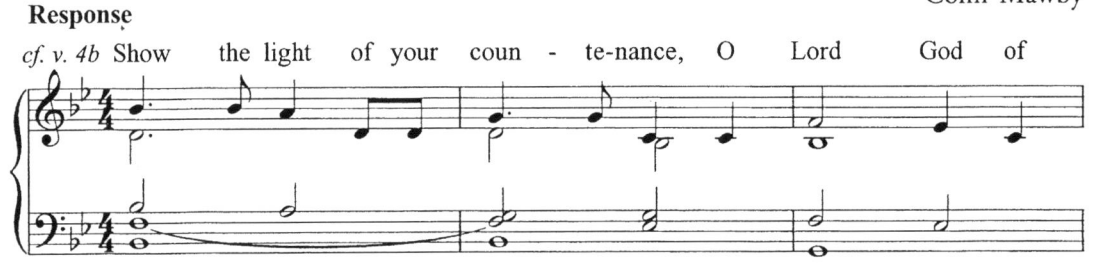

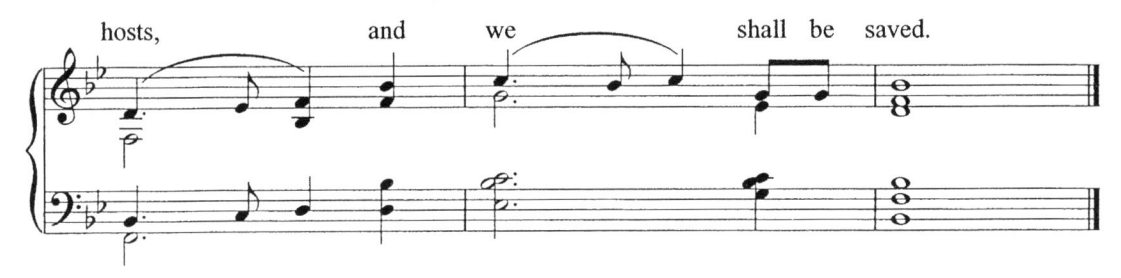

cf. v. 4b Show the light of your coun-tenance, O Lord God of hosts, and we shall be saved.

Verse

S.L.

1 *1* Hear, O Shep | herd of Israel,
   you that led Joseph | like a flock;
  2 Shine forth, you that are enthroned u | pon the cherubim,
   before Ephraim, Benjamin | and Manasseh.

2 *3* Stir up your | mighty strength
   and come to | our salvation.
  4 Turn us a | gain, O God;
   show the light of your countenance,
   and we | shall be saved.

3 *5* O Lord | God of hosts,
   how long will you be angry at your | people's prayer?
  6 You feed them with the | bread of tears;
   you give them abundance of | tears to drink.

4 ⁷You have made us the derision | of our neighbours,
and our enemies laugh | us to scorn.
⁸ Turn us again, O | God of hosts;
show the light of your countenance, and we | shall be saved.

5 ⁹You brought a vine | out of Egypt;
you drove out the na | tions and planted it.
¹⁰ You made | room around it,
and when it had taken root, it | filled the land.

6 ¹¹The hills were covered | with its shadow
and the cedars of God | by its boughs.
¹² It stretched out its branches | to the Sea
and its tendrils | to the River.

7 ¹³Why then have you broken | down its wall,
so that all who pass by pluck | off its grapes?
¹⁴ The wild boar out of the wood | tears it off,
and all the insects of the | field devour it.

8 ¹⁵Turn again, O | God of hosts,
look down from heaven | and behold;
¹⁶ Cherish this vine which your right | hand has planted,
and the branch that you made so strong | for yourself.

9 ¹⁷Let those who burnt it with fire, who | cut it down,
perish at the rebuke | of your countenance.
¹⁸ Let your hand be upon the man at | your right hand,
the son of man you made so strong | for yourself.

10 ¹⁹And so will we | not go back from you;
give us life, and we shall call u | pon your name.
²⁰ Turn us again, O Lord | God of hosts;
show the light of your countenance, and we | shall be saved.

Psalm 81

PRINCIPAL SERVICE
Proper 4 B (related) (vs. 1-10)
Proper 17 C (vs. 1-10)

2ND SERVICE
4 Easter B (vs. 8-16)
Proper 11 C

3RD SERVICE
2 Easter A (vs. 1-10)

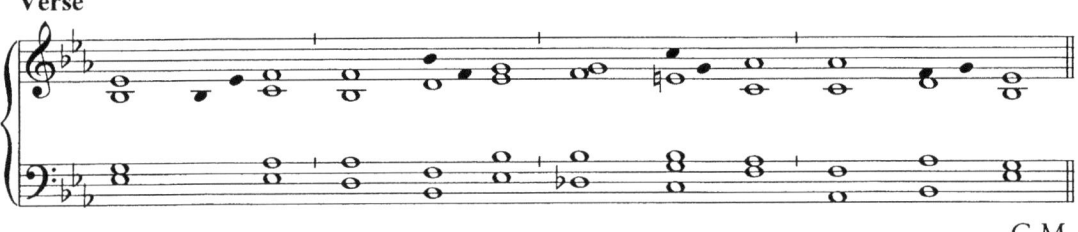

Richard Lloyd

Response
v. 1b Shout for joy to the God of Ja - cob.

Verse

C.M.

1 *1* Sing merrily to | God our strength,
   shout for joy to the | God of Jacob.
  2 Take up the song and | sound the timbrel,
   the tuneful lyre | with the harp.

2 *3* Blow the trumpet at | the new moon,
   as at the full moon, upon our | solemn feast day.
  4 For this is a statute for Israel,
   a law of the | God of Jacob,
  5 The charge he laid on the people of Joseph,
   when they came out of the | land of Egypt.

3 *6* I heard a voice I did not | know, that said:
   'I eased their shoulder from the burden;
   their hands were set free from bear | ing the load.
  7 'You called upon me in trouble and | I delivered you;
   I answered you from the secret place of thunder
   and proved you at the waters of | Meribah.

4 *8* 'Hear, O my people, and I will admonish you:
   O Israel, if you | would but listen to me!
  9 'There shall be no strange god among you;
   you shall not worship a | foreign god.
  10 'I am the Lord your God,
   who brought you up from the | land of Egypt;
   open your mouth wide and | I shall fill it.'

5 *11* But my people would not | hear my voice
   and Israel would | not obey me.
   12 So I sent them away in the stubbornness | of their hearts,
   and let them walk after | their own counsels.

6 *13* O that my peo | ple would listen to me,
   that Israel would walk | in my ways!
   14 Then I should soon put | down their enemies
   and turn my hand a | gainst their adversaries.

7 *15* Those who hate the Lord would be hum | bled before him,
   and their punishment would | last for ever.
   16 But Israel would I feed with the | finest wheat
   and with honey from the rock | would I satisfy them.

C Instrument

B♭ Instrument

New Psalms for Common Worship

Psalm 82

PRINCIPAL SERVICE
Proper 10 C
Proper 15 C (related)

2ND SERVICE
3 before Advent A
3 before Advent B

3RD SERVICE
Proper 11 C

Keith Duke

Response
v. 8 A-rise, O God and judge the earth.

Verse

T.B.

1 *1* God has taken his stand in the council of heaven;
   in the midst of the gods | he gives judgement:
  2 'How long will you judge unjustly
   and show such favour | to the wicked?
  3 'You were to judge the weak | and the orphan;
   defend the right of the hum | ble and needy;

2 *4* 'Rescue the weak | and the poor;
   deliver them from the hand | of the wicked.
  5 'They have no knowledge or wisdom;
   they walk on | still in darkness:
   all the foundations of the | earth are shaken.

3 *6* 'Therefore I say that though you are gods
   and all of you children of | the Most High,
  7 'Nevertheless, you shall die like mortals
   and fall like one | of their princes.'
  8 Arise, O God and | judge the earth,
   for it is you that shall take all nations for | your possession.

Psalm 83 is omitted

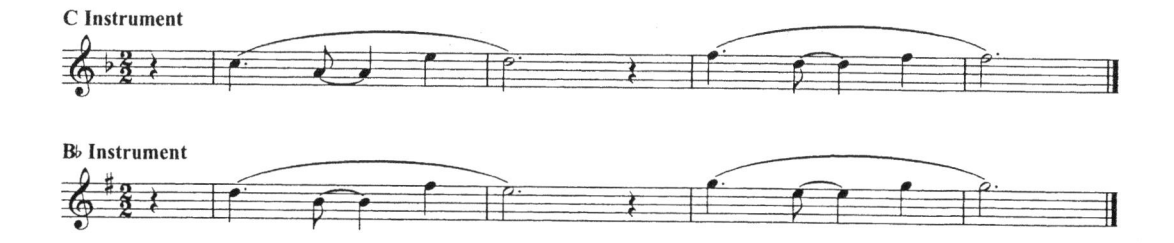

C Instrument

B♭ Instrument

Psalm 84

PRINCIPAL SERVICE
Proper 16 B
Proper 25 C (related) (vs. 1-6)

2ND SERVICE
1 before Lent A
All Saints ABC

3RD SERVICE
4 Lent C

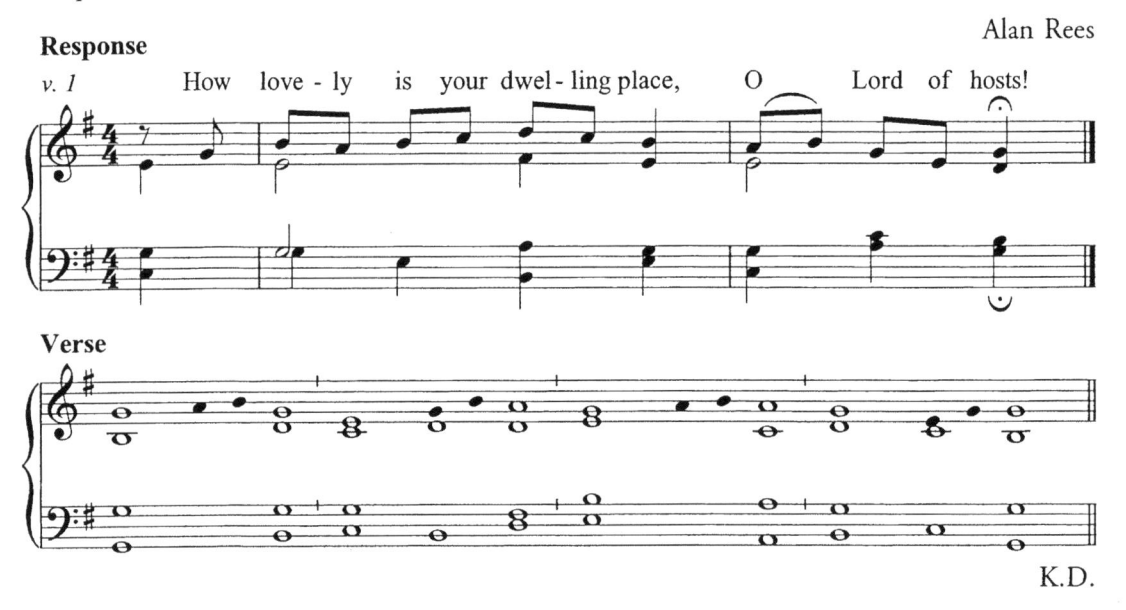

Alan Rees

Response

v. 1 How lovely is your dwelling place, O Lord of hosts!

Verse

K.D.

1. *1* How lovely | is your dwelling place,
   O | Lord of hosts!
   My soul has a desire and longing to enter the courts | of the Lord;
   my heart and my flesh rejoice in the | living God.

2. *2* The sparrow has found | her a house
   and the swallow a nest where she may | lay her young:
   at your altars, O | Lord of hosts,
   my King | and my God.

3. *3* Blessed are they who dwell | in your house:
   they will al | ways be praising you.
   4 Blessed are those whose strength | is in you,
   in whose heart are the high |ways to Zion,

4. *5* Who going through the barren valley find | there a spring,
   and the early rains will clothe | it with blessing.
   6 They will go from | strength to strength
   and appear before | God in Zion.

5. *7* O Lord God of hosts, hear my prayer; listen, O | God of Jacob.
   8 Behold our defender, O God,
   and look upon the face of | your anointed.
   9 For one day in your courts is better | than a thousand.
   10 I would rather be a doorkeeper in the house of my God
   than dwell in the tents | of ungodliness.

6 *11* For the Lord God is both | sun and shield;
　　he will give | grace and glory;
　　no good thing shall the Lord withhold
　　from those who walk | with integrity.
　12 O Lord God of hosts,
　　blessed are those who | put their trust in you.

Psalm 85

PRINCIPAL SERVICE
2 Advent B (vs. 8-13)
Proper 10 B (related) (vs. 8-13)
Proper 12 C (vs. 1-7)
Proper 14 A (related) (vs. 8-13)
Also Evening Prayer: Christmas Eve ABC

2ND SERVICE

3RD SERVICE
4 Lent C
Proper 13 A

Response — Andrew Wright
v. 7a Show us, O Lord, your mer-cy.

Verse

C.M.

1 *1* Lord, you were gracious | to your land;
   you restored the fortunes | of Jacob.
 2 You forgave the offence | of your people
   and covered | all their sins.
 3 You laid aside | all your fury
   and turned from your wrathful | indignation.

2 *4* Restore us again, O God our Saviour,
   and let your | anger cease from us.
 5 Will you be displeased with | us for ever?
   Will you stretch out your wrath
   from one generation | to another?
 6 Will you not give us life again,
   that your people | may rejoice in you?
 7 Show us your mer | cy, O Lord,
   and grant us | your salvation.

3 *8* I will listen to what the Lord | God will say,
   for he shall speak peace to his people and to the faithful,
   that they turn not a | gain to folly.
 9 Truly, his salvation is near to | those who fear him,
   that his glory may dwell | in our land.
 10 Mercy and truth are | met together,
   righteousness and peace have | kissed each other;

4 *11* Truth shall spring up | from the earth
and righteousness look | down from heaven.
12 The Lord will indeed give all | that is good,
and our land will | yield its increase.
13 Righteousness shall | go before him
and direct his steps | in the way.

Psalm 86

PRINCIPAL SERVICE
Proper 7 A (vs. 1-10)
Proper 11 A (related) (vs. 11-17)

2ND SERVICE
3 Easter C
Proper 14 A

3RD SERVICE
5 Lent A
Trinity A (vs. 9-13)
Proper 13 B

Geoff Nobes

Response
v. 11a Teach me your way, O Lord, and I will walk in your truth.

Verse

C.M.

1 *1* Incline your ear, O | Lord, and answer me,
 for I am poor | and in misery.
 2 Preserve my soul, for | I am faithful;
 save your servant, for I | put my trust in you.

2 *3* Be merciful to me, O Lord, for you | are my God;
 I call upon you all | the day long.
 4 Gladden the soul | of your servant,
 for to you, O Lord, I lift | up my soul.

3 *5* For you, Lord, are good | and forgiving,
 abounding in steadfast love to all who | call upon you.
 6 Give ear, O Lord, | to my prayer
 and listen to the voice of my | supplication.

4 *7* In the day of my distress I will | call upon you,
 for | you will answer me.
 8 Among the gods there is none like | you, O Lord,
 nor any | works like yours.

5 *9* All nations you have made shall come and worship | you, O Lord,
 and shall glori | fy your name.
 10 For you are great and do won | derful things;
 you a | lone are God.

6 *11* Teach me your | way, O Lord,
    and I will walk | in your truth;
    knit my | heart to you,
    that I may | fear your name.

7 *12* I will thank you, O Lord my God, with | all my heart,
    and glorify your name for | evermore;
  13 For great is your steadfast | love towards me,
    for you have delivered my soul from the depths | of the grave.

8 *14* O God, the proud rise up against me
    and a ruthless horde seek af | ter my life;
    they have not set you be | fore their eyes.
  15 But you, Lord, are gracious and full | of compassion,
    slow to anger and full of kind | ness and truth.

9 *16* Turn to me and have mer | cy upon me;
    give your strength to your servant
    and save the child | of your handmaid.
  17 Show me a token of your favour,
    that those who hate me may see it and | be ashamed;
    because you, O Lord, have | helped and comforted me.

New Psalms for Common Worship

Psalm 87

PRINCIPAL SERVICE

2ND SERVICE
6 Easter A

3RD SERVICE
2 Christmas ABC
Pentecost A
4 before Advent C

Response Andrew Wright

cf. v. 2 Glorious things are spoken of you, O city of God.

Verse

G.N.

1 *1* His foundation is on the | holy mountains.
  The Lord loves the gates of Zion
  more than all the dwel | lings of Jacob.
  2 Glorious things are spoken of you,
  Zion, city | of our God.

2 *3* I record Egypt and Babylon as | those who know me;
  behold Philistia, Tyre and | Ethiopia:
  in Zion | were they born.

3 *4* And of Zion it | shall be said,
  'Each | one was born in her,
  and the Most High himself | has established her.'

4 *5* The Lord will record as he writes | up the peoples,
  'This one al | so was born there.'
  6 And as they dance they shall sing,
  'All my fresh springs | are in you.'

C Instrument

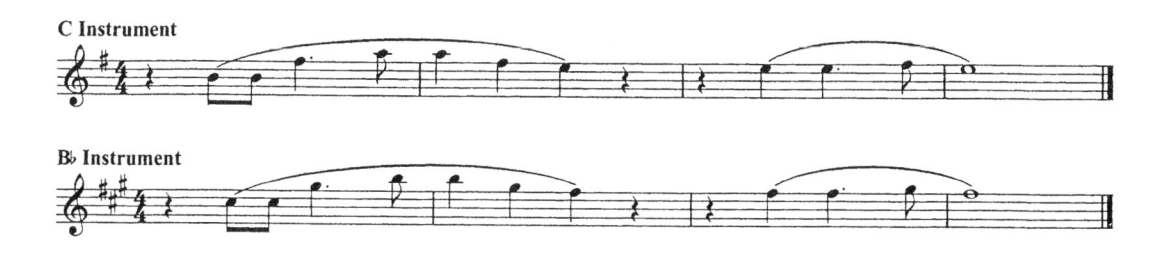

B♭ Instrument

Psalm 88

PRINCIPAL SERVICE

2ND SERVICE
Proper 12 C (vs. 1-11)
Proper 13 B (vs. 1-11)

3RD SERVICE
Wednesday of
   Holy Week ABC
Proper 14 A

Simon Lesley

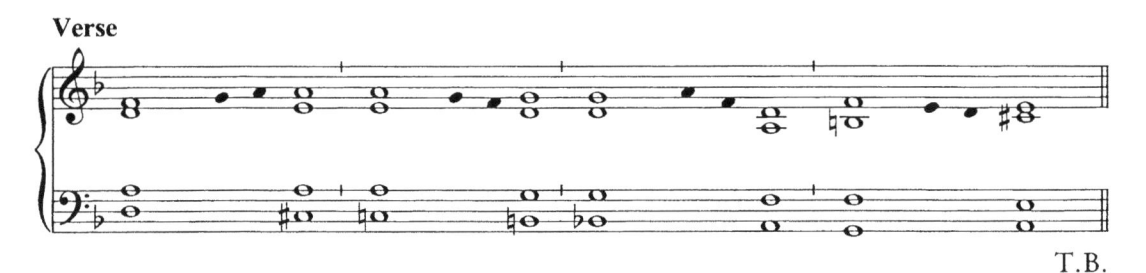

Response

cf. v. 15 I cry out to you, O Lord, and my prayer shall come be-fore you.

Verse

T.B.

1   *1* O Lord, God of | my salvation,
       I have cried day and | night before you.
    2 Let my prayer come in | to your presence;
       incline your ear | to my cry.

2   *3* For my soul is | full of troubles;
       my life draws near to the | land of death.
    4 I am counted as one gone down | to the Pit;
       I am like one that | has no strength,

3   *5* Lost a | mong the dead,
       like the slain who lie | in the grave,
    6 Whom you remem | ber no more,
       for they are cut off | from your hand.

4   *7* You have laid me in the | lowest pit,
       in a place of darkness in | the abyss.
    8 Your anger lies hea | vy upon me,
       and you have afflicted me with | all your waves.

5   *9* You have put | my friends far from me
       and made me to | be abhorred by them.
    10 I am so fast in prison that I can | not get free;
       my eyes fail from | all my trouble.

6 *11* Lord, I have called dai | ly upon you;
   I have stretched | out my hands to you.
 12 Do you work wonders | for the dead?
   Will the shades stand | up and praise you?

7 *13* Shall your loving-kindness be declared | in the grave,
   your faithfulness in the land | of destruction?
 14 Shall your wonders be known | in the dark
   or your righteous deeds in the land where all | is forgotten?

8 *15* But as for me, O Lord, | I will cry to you;
   early in the morning my prayer shall | come before you.
 16 Lord, why have you rejec | ted my soul?
   Why have you hid | den your face from me?

9 *17* I have been wretched and at the point of death | from my youth;
   I suffer your terrors and am | no more seen.
 18 Your | wrath sweeps over me;
   your horrors are come | to destroy me;

10 *19* All day long they come about | me like water;
   they close me in on | ev'ry side.
 20 Lover and friend have | you put far from me
   and hid my companions out | of my sight.

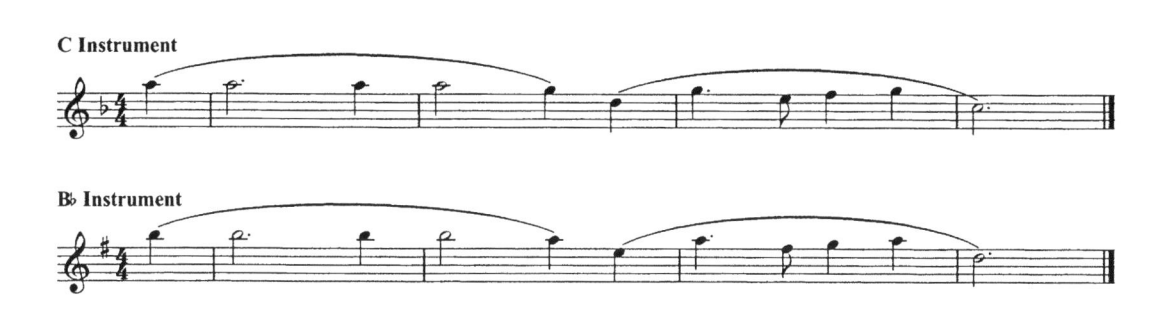

C Instrument

B♭ Instrument

Psalm 89

Verses 38-52 are omitted

PRINCIPAL SERVICE	2ND SERVICE	3RD SERVICE
4 Advent B (vs. 1-8)	1 before Lent C (vs. 5-12)	Baptism ABC (vs. 19-29)
Christmas Eve (vs. 1-2, 22-27) ABC	2 before Advent A (vs. 19-29)	
Proper 8 A (related) (vs. 8-18)		
Proper 11 B (vs. 20-37)		

Andrew Moore

Response
cf. v. 1 My soul shall pro-claim your stead-fast love, O Lord.

Verse

S.L.

1 *1* My song shall be always of the
   loving-kindness | of the Lord:
   with my mouth will I proclaim your faithfulness
   throughout all | generations.
 2 I will declare that your love is
   esta | blished for ever;
   you have set your faithfulness
   as firm | as the heavens.

2 *3* For you said: 'I have made a
   covenant | with my chosen one;
   I have sworn an oath to Da | vid my servant:
 4 'Your seed will I esta | blish for ever
   and build up your throne for all | generations.'

3 *5* The heavens praise your won | ders, O Lord,
   and your faithfulness in the
   assembly | of the holy ones;
 6 For who among the clouds
   can be compared | to the Lord?
   Who is like the Lord among the | host of heaven?

4 *7* A God feared in the council | of the holy ones,
   great and terrible above
   all those | round about him.
 8 Who is like you, Lord | God of hosts?
   Mighty Lord, your faithfulness
   is | all around you.

5 *9* You rule the raging | of the sea;
   you still its waves when | they arise.
 10 You crushed Rahab
   with a | deadly wound
   and scattered your enemies
   with your | mighty arm.

6 *11* Yours are the heavens;
   the earth al | so is yours;
   you established the world
   and | all that fills it.
 12 You created the north | and the south;
   Tabor and Hermon
   rejoice | in your name.

7 *13* You have a | mighty arm;
   strong is your hand and
   high | is your right hand.
 14 Righteousness and justice
   are the foundation | of your throne;
   steadfast love and faithfulness
   go be | fore your face.

8 *15* Happy are the people
   who know the | shout of triumph:
   they walk, O Lord, in the
   light | of your countenance.
 16 In your name they rejoice all | the day long
   and are exalted | in your righteousness.

9 ₁₇ For you are the glory | of their strength,
   and in your favour you lift | up our heads.
  ₁₈ Truly the Lord | is our shield;
   the Holy One of Israel | is our king.

10 ₁₉ You spoke once | in a vision
   and said to your | faithful people:
   'I have set a youth a | bove the mighty;
   I have raised a young man o | ver the people.

11 ₂₀ 'I have found Da | vid my servant;
   with my holy oil have | I anointed him.
  ₂₁ 'My hand shall | hold him fast
   and my | arm shall strengthen him.

12 ₂₂ 'No enemy | shall deceive him,
   nor any wicked per | son afflict him.
  ₂₃ 'I will strike down his foes be | fore his face
   and beat down | those that hate him.

13 ₂₄ 'My truth also and my steadfast love | shall be with him,
   and in my name shall his head | be exalted.
  ₂₅ 'I will set his dominion u | pon the sea
   and his right hand u | pon the rivers.

14 ₂₆ 'He shall call to me, 'You | are my Father,
   my God, and the rock of | my salvation;'
  ₂₇ 'And I will make | him my firstborn,
   the most high above the kings | of the earth.

15 ₂₈ 'The love I have pledged to him will I | keep for ever,
   and my covenant | will stand fast with him.
  ₂₉ 'His seed also will I make to en | dure for ever
   and his throne as the | days of heaven.

16 ₃₀ 'But if his children forsake my law
   and cease to walk | in my judgements,
  ₃₁ 'If they break my statutes
   and do not keep | my commandments,
  ₃₂ 'I will punish their offences | with a rod
   and their | sin with scourges.

17 ₃₃ 'But I will not take from him my | steadfast love
   nor suffer my | truth to fail.
  ₃₄ 'My covenant will | I not break
   nor alter what has gone out | of my lips.

18 ₃₅ 'Once for all have I sworn by my holiness
   that I will not prove | false to David.
  ₃₆ 'His seed shall endure for ever
   and his throne as the | sun before me;
  ₃₇ 'It shall stand fast for ever | as the moon,
   the enduring witness | in the heavens.'

Psalm 90

PRINCIPAL SERVICE
Proper 23 B (related) (vs. 13-17)
Proper 25 A (vs. 1-6)
2 before Advent A (vs. 1-8)

2ND SERVICE
Proper 15 A (vs. 1-12)

3RD SERVICE
Proper 14 B
3 before Advent C

Gerry Fitzpatrick

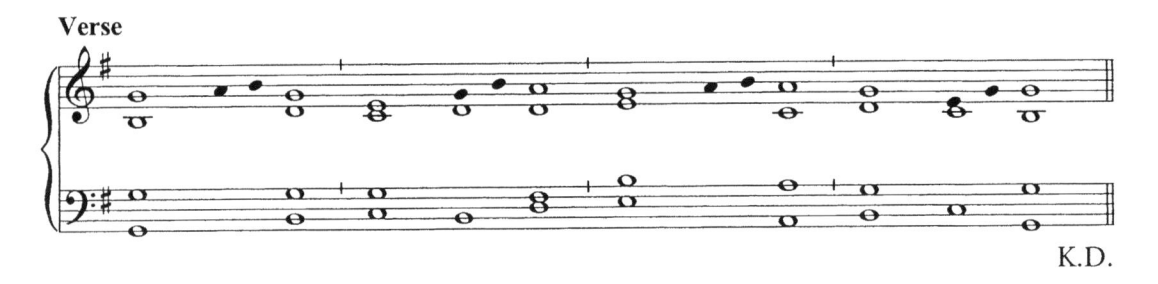

Response

cf. v. 17a May the favour of the Lord, our God, be upon us.

Verse

K.D.

1 *1* Lord, you have | been our refuge
    from one generation | to another.
   2 Before the mountains were brought forth,
    or the earth and the | world were formed,
    from everlasting to everlasting | you are God.

2 *3* You turn us back to | dust and say:
    'Turn back, O child | ren of earth.'
   4 For a thousand years in your sight are | but as yesterday,
    which passes like a watch | in the night.

3 *5* You sweep them away | like a dream;
    they fade away suddenly | like the grass.
   6 In the morning it is | green and flourishes;
    in the evening it is dried | up and withered.

4 *7* For we consume away in | your displeasure;
    we are afraid at your wrathful | indignation.
   8 You have set our mis | deeds before you
    and our secret sins in the light | of your countenance.

5 ⁹ When you are angry, all our | days are gone;
   our years come to an end | like a sigh.
  ¹⁰ The days of our life are three score years and ten,
   or if our strength endures, | even four score;
   yet the sum of them is but labour and sorrow,
   for they soon pass away and | we are gone.

6 ¹¹ Who regards the power | of your wrath
   and your indignation like | those who fear you?
  ¹² So teach us to num | ber our days
   that we may apply our | hearts to wisdom.

7 ¹³ Turn again, O Lord; how long will you delay?
   Have compassion | on your servants.
  ¹⁴ Satisfy us with your loving-kindness in the morning,
   that we may rejoice and be glad | all our days.
  ¹⁵ Give us gladness for the days you | have afflicted us,
   and for the years in which we have | seen adversity.

8 ¹⁶ Show your ser | vants your works,
   and let your glory be o | ver their children.
  ¹⁷ May the gracious favour of the Lord our God | be upon us;
   prosper our handiwork; O prosper the work | of our hands.

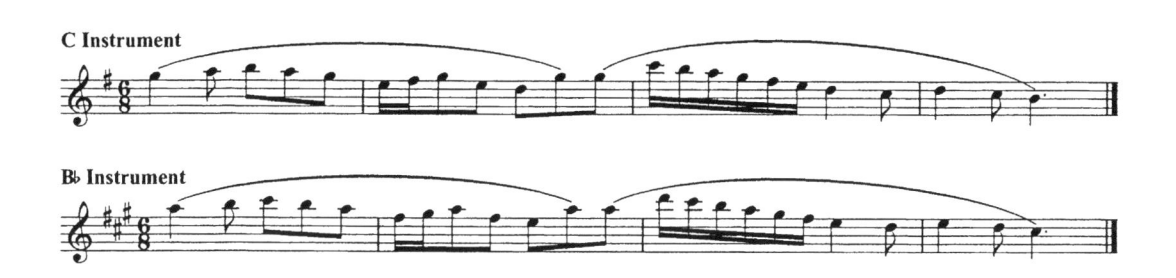

Psalm 91

PRINCIPAL SERVICE
1 Lent C (vs. 1-10)
Proper 21 C (vs. 11-16)
Proper 24 B (related) (vs. 9-16)

2ND SERVICE
Proper 14 B (vs. 1-12)

3RD SERVICE
3 before Advent A

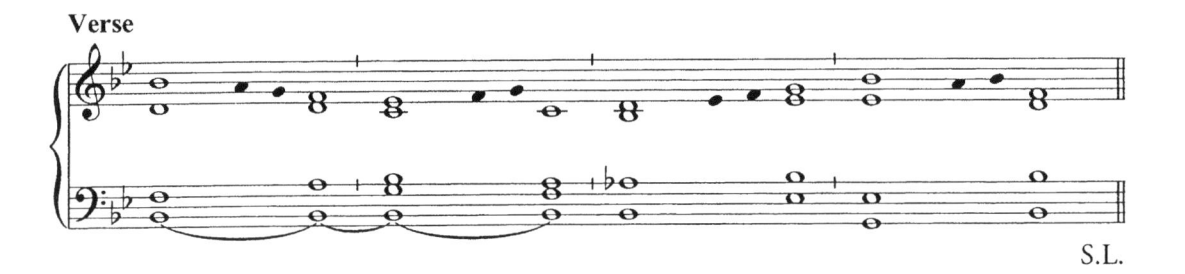

Response Simon Lesley
cf. v. 2 You are my God in whom I trust.

Verse

S.L.

1 *1* Whoever dwells in the shelter of | the Most High
   and abides under the shadow of | the Almighty,
  2 Shall say to the Lord, 'My refuge | and my stronghold,
   my God, in whom I | put my trust.'

2 *3* For he shall deliver you from the snare | of the fowler
   and from the | deadly pestilence.
  4 He shall cover you with his wings
   and you shall be safe un | der his feathers;
   his faithfulness shall be your | shield and buckler.

3 *5* You shall not be afraid of any ter | ror by night,
   nor of the arrow that | flies by day;
  6 Of the pestilence that | stalks in darkness,
   nor of the sickness that des | troys at noonday.

4 *7* Though a thousand fall at your side
   and ten thousand | at your right hand,
   yet it shall | not come near you.
  8 Your eyes have only | to behold
   to see the reward | of the wicked.

5 *9* Because you have made the | Lord your refuge
and the Most | High your stronghold,
  10 There shall no | evil happen to you,
neither shall any plague come | near your tent.

6 *11* For he shall give his angels charge | over you,
to keep you in | all your ways.
  12 They shall bear you | in their hands,
lest you dash your foot a | gainst a stone.

7 *13* You shall tread upon the li | on and adder;
the young lion and the serpent you shall trample | underfoot
  14 Because they have set their love upon me,
therefore will | I deliver them;
I will lift them up, because they | know my name.

8 *15* They will call upon me and | I will answer them;
I am with them in trouble,
I will deliver them and bring | them to honour.
  16 With long life | will I satisfy them
and show them | my salvation.

Psalm 92

PRINCIPAL SERVICE
Proper 6 B (related) (vs. 1-8)

2ND SERVICE
Proper 15 B

3RD SERVICE
Proper 15 A

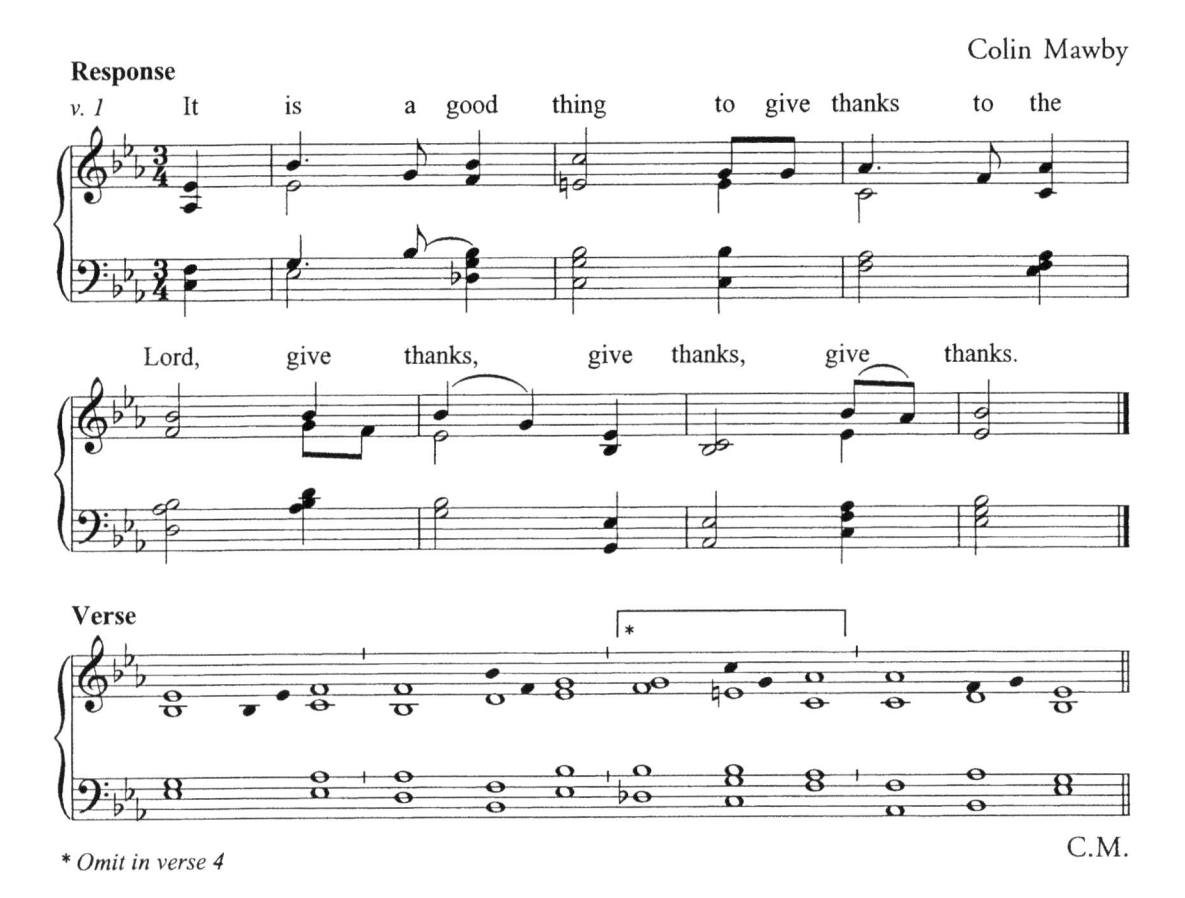

Colin Mawby

Response

v. 1 It is a good thing to give thanks to the Lord, give thanks, give thanks, give thanks.

Verse

Omit in verse 4

C.M.

1 *1* It is a good thing to give thanks to the Lord
   and to sing praises to your name, | O Most High;
 2 To tell of your love early in the morning
   and of your faithfulness | in the night-time,
 3 Upon the ten-stringed instrument, u | pon the harp,
   and to the melody | of the lyre.

2 *4* For you, Lord, have made me
   glad | by your acts,
   and I sing aloud at the works | of your hands.
 5 O Lord, how glorious | are your works!
   Your thoughts are | very deep.

3 *6* The senseless do not know,
   nor do fools | understand,
 7 That though the wicked sprout like grass
   and all the workers of ini | quity flourish,
 8 It is only to be des | troyed for ever;
   but you, O Lord,
   shall be exalted for | evermore.

4 ⁹ For lo, your ene | mies, O Lord,
    lo, your ene | mies shall perish,
    and all the workers of
        iniquity | shall be scattered.

5 ¹⁰ But my horn you have exalted
        like the horns | of wild oxen;
    I am anointed | with fresh oil.
   ¹¹ My eyes will look down | on my foes;
    my ears shall hear the ruin of the
        evildoers who rise | up against me.

6 ¹² The righteous shall
        flourish | like a palm tree,
    and shall spread abroad
        like a ce | dar of Lebanon.
   ¹³ Such as are planted in the
        house | of the Lord
    shall flourish in the
        courts | of our God.

7 ¹⁴ They shall still bear fruit | in old age;
    they shall be vigorous and | in full leaf;
   ¹⁵ That they may show that the | Lord is true;
    he is my rock, and there is
        no unrighteous | ness in him.

New Psalms for Common Worship

Psalm 93

PRINCIPAL SERVICE
Ascension ABC
Christ the King B

2ND SERVICE
Trinity A
2 before Advent C
Christ the King A

3RD SERVICE

John McCann

Response

cf. v. 1 The Lord is King, and his ap-par-el is glo-ri-ous.

Verse

S.L.

1 *1* The Lord is king and has put on glori | ous apparel;
   the Lord has put | on his glory
   and girded him | self with strength.

2 *2* He has made the whole world so sure
       that it can | not be moved.
   3 Your throne has been established | from of old;
       you are from | everlasting.

3 *4* The floods have lifted | up, O Lord,
   the floods have lifted | up their voice;
   the floods lift up their | pounding waves.

4 *5* Mightier than the thunder of | many waters,
   mightier than the breakers | of the sea,
   the Lord on | high is mightier.

5 *6* Your testimonies are | very sure;
   holiness a | dorns your house,
   O | Lord, for ever.

Psalm 94 is omitted

C Instrument

B♭ Instrument

185

Psalm 95

PRINCIPAL SERVICE
3 Lent A
Christ the King A (vs. 1-7)

2ND SERVICE
Proper 16 A
2 before Advent B

3RD SERVICE
Proper 12 C

Colin Mawby

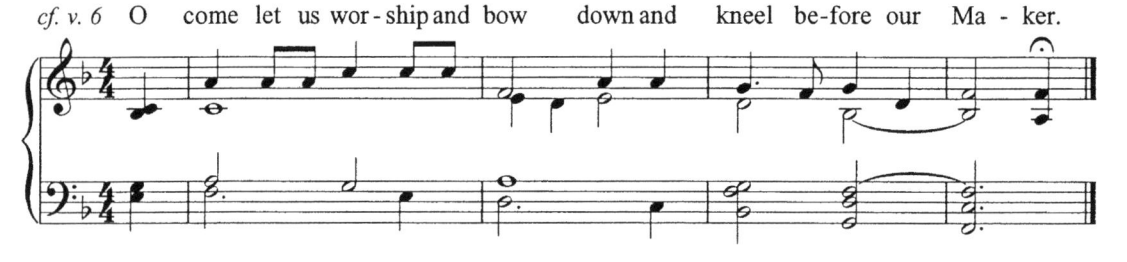

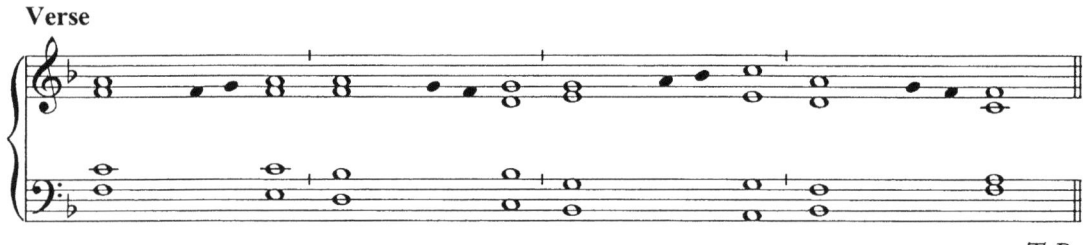

Response

cf. v. 6 O come let us wor-ship and bow down and kneel be-fore our Ma-ker.

Verse

T.B.

1 *1* O come, let us sing | to the Lord;
   let us heartily rejoice in the rock of | our salvation.
   2 Let us come into his presence | with thanksgiving
   and be glad in | him with psalms.

2 *3* For the Lord is a great God
   and a great king a | bove all gods.
   4 In his hand are the depths of the earth
   and the heights of the mountains | are his also.
   5 The sea is his, | for he made it,
   and his hands have moul | ded the dry land.

3 *6* Come, let us worship | and bow down
   and kneel before the | Lord our Maker.
   7 For he | is our God;
   we are the people of his pasture and the sheep | of his hand.

4 *8* O that today you would listen | to his voice:
   'Harden not your hearts as at Meribah,
   on that day at Massah | in the wilderness,
   9 'When your forebears tested me, and put me | to the proof,
   though they had | seen my works.

5 *10* 'Forty years long I detested that gene | ration and said,
   "This people are wayward in their hearts;
   they do not | know my ways."
 11 'So I swore | in my wrath,
   "They shall not enter in | to my rest." '

C Instrument

B♭ Instrument

Psalm 96

PRINCIPAL SERVICE
Christmas Day I
Proper 4 C
Proper 4 C (related) (vs. 1-9)
Proper 24 A (related) (vs. 1-9 or 10-13)
Also: Evening Prayer: Epiphany ABC

2ND SERVICE
2 Epiphany ABC
5 Easter B

3RD SERVICE
2 before Advent B

Richard Lloyd

Response
cf. v. 1 O sing to the Lord a new song; O sing to the Lord, all the earth.

Verse

K.D.

1 *1* Sing to the | Lord a new song;
 sing to the Lord, | all the earth.
 2 Sing to the Lord and | bless his name;
 tell out his salvation from | day to day.

2 *3* Declare his glory a | mong the nations
 and his wonders a | mong all peoples.
 4 For great is the Lord and greatly | to be praised;
 he is more to be feared | than all gods.

3 *5* For all the gods of the nations | are but idols;
 it is the Lord who | made the heavens.
 6 Honour and majesty | are before him;
 power and splendour are | in his sanctuary.

4 *7* Ascribe to the Lord, you families of the peoples;
 ascribe to the Lord hon | our and strength.
 8 Ascribe to the Lord the honour due to his name;
 bring offerings and come in | to his courts.
 9 O worship the Lord in the beau | ty of holiness;
 let the whole earth trem | ble before him.

5 *10* Tell it out among the nations that the | Lord is king.
 He has made the world so firm that it cannot be moved;
 he will judge the peo | ples with equity.
 11 Let the heavens rejoice and let the | earth be glad;
 let the sea thunder and all | that is in it;

6 *12* Let the fields be joyful and all | that is in them;
    let all the trees of the wood shout for joy be | fore the Lord.
  13 For he comes, he comes to | judge the earth;
    with righteousness he will judge the world
    and the peoples | with his truth.

Psalm 97

PRINCIPAL SERVICE
Christmas Day II
7 Easter C

2ND SERVICE
2 before Advent C
Christ the King A

3RD SERVICE

Also: Evening Prayer: Epiphany ABC;
Trinity ABC

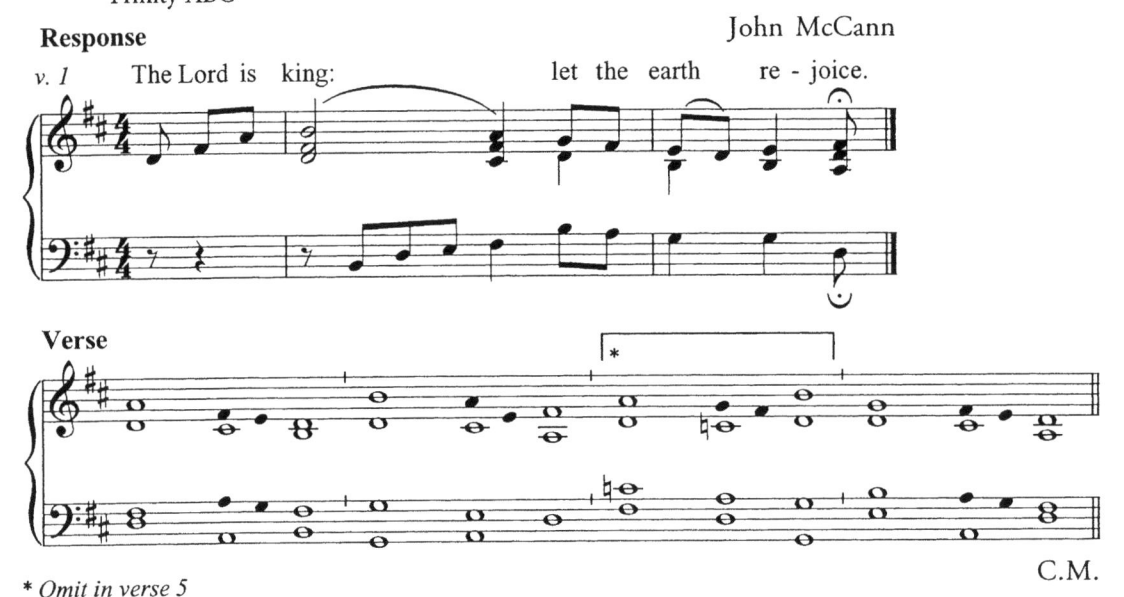

Response   John McCann

v. 1 The Lord is king: let the earth re-joice.

Verse

* *Omit in verse 5*

C.M.

1 *1* The Lord is king: let the | earth rejoice;
   let the multitude of the | isles be glad.
   2 Clouds and darkness are | round about him;
   righteousness and justice are the foundation | of his throne.

2 *3* Fire goes before him and burns up his enemies on | ev'ry side.
   4 His lightnings lit up the world; the earth saw | it and trembled.
   5 The mountains melted like wax at the presence | of the Lord,
   at the presence of the Lord of | the whole earth.

3 *6* The heavens de | clared his righteousness,
   and all the peoples have | seen his glory.
   7 Confounded be all who worship carved images
   and delight | in mere idols.
   Bow down before him, | all you gods.

4 *8* Zion heard and was glad, and the daughters of Ju | dah rejoiced,
   because of your judge | ments, O Lord.
   9 For you, Lord, are most high over | all the earth;
   you are exalted far a | bove all gods.

5 *10* The Lord loves those | who hate evil;
   he preserves the lives | of his faithful
   and delivers them from the hand | of the wicked.

6 *11* Light has sprung up | for the righteous
and joy for the | true of heart.
12 Rejoice in the | Lord, you righteous,
and give thanks to his | holy name.

Psalm 98

PRINCIPAL SERVICE
Christmas Day III
6 Easter B
2 before Advent C

2ND SERVICE
Epiphany ABC
5 Easter C

3RD SERVICE
2 before Advent A

Also: Evening Prayer: Trinity ABC;
Easter Vigil ABC

Andrew Wright

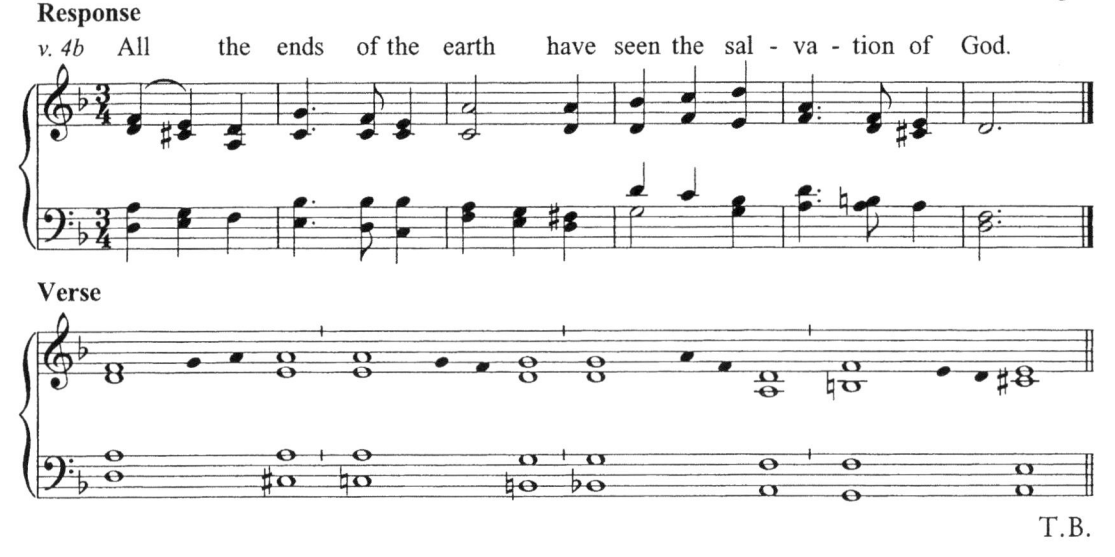

Response

v. 4b All the ends of the earth have seen the sal-va-tion of God.

Verse

T.B.

1 1 Sing to the | Lord a new song,
   for he has done mar | vellous things.
   2 His own right hand and his | holy arm
   have won for | him the victory.

2 3 The Lord has made known | his salvation;
   his deliverance has he openly shown in the sight | of the nations.
   4 He has remembered his mercy and faithfulness
   towards the | house of Israel,
   and all the ends of the earth have seen the salvation | of our God.

3 5 Sound praises to the Lord, | all the earth;
   break into singing | and make music.
   6 Make music to the Lord | with the lyre,
   with the lyre and the | voice of melody.

4 7 With trumpets and the sound | of the horn
   sound praises before the | Lord, the King.
   8 Let the sea thunder and | all that fills it,
   the world and all that | dwell upon it.

5 *9* Let the rivers | clap their hands
    and let the hills ring out together be | fore the Lord,
    for he comes to | judge the earth.
 10 In righteousness shall he judge the world
    and the peo | ples with equity.

Psalm 99

PRINCIPAL SERVICE
1 before Lent A
1 before Lent C
Proper 24 A (vs. 1-9)
Also: Evening Prayer: Christ the King ABC

2ND SERVICE
1 before Lent B

3RD SERVICE
7 Easter C

Colin Mawby

Response

v. 9b The Lord our God is ho-ly.

Verse

* Omit in verses 2 and 3   C.M.

1 *1* The Lord is king: let the | peoples tremble;
   he is enthroned above the cherubim: let | the earth shake.
   2 The Lord is | great in Zion
   and high a | bove all peoples.
   3 Let them praise your name, which is | great and awesome;
   the Lord our | God is holy.

2 *4* Mighty king, | who loves justice,
   you have e | stablished equity;
   you have executed justice and righteous | ness in Jacob.
   5 Exalt the | Lord our God;
   bow down before his footstool, for | he is holy.

3 *6* Moses and Aaron a | mong his priests
   and Samuel among those who call u | pon his name;
   they called upon the Lord | and he answered them.
   7 He spoke to them out of the pil | lar of cloud;
   they kept his testimonies and the law | that he gave them.

4 ⁸You answered them, O | Lord our God;
　you were a God | who forgave them
　and pardoned them for | their offences.
　⁹Exalt the | Lord our God
　and worship him upon his | holy hill,
　for the Lord our | God is holy.

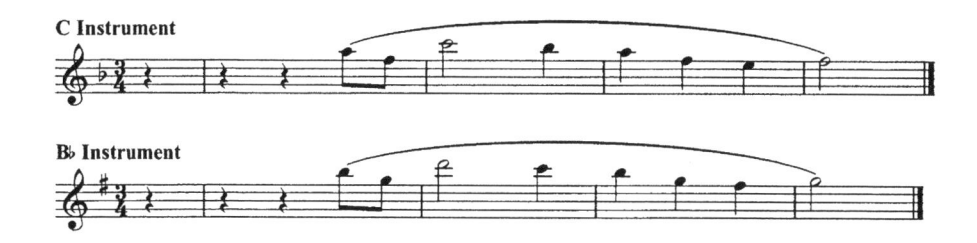

Psalm 100

PRINCIPAL SERVICE
Proper 6 A (related)
Also: Evening Prayer:
   Christ the King ABC

2ND SERVICE
Epiphany ABC
Proper 15 B

3RD SERVICE
2 before Lent A
Proper 11 C

Response   Alan Rees

cf. v. 1 O be joy-ful in the Lord, O be joy-ful, all the earth.

Verse

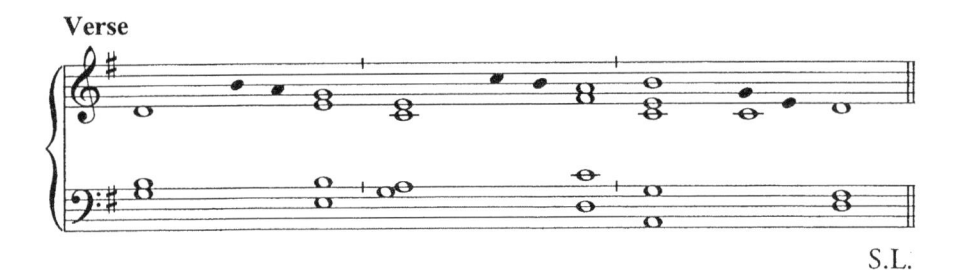

S.L.

1 *1* O be joyful in the Lord, | all the earth;
    serve the | Lord with gladness
    and come before his presence | with a song.

2 *2* Know that the | Lord is God;
    it is he that has made us and | we are his;
    we are his people and the sheep | of his pasture.

3 *3* Enter his gates | with thanksgiving
    and his | courts with praise;
    give thanks to him and | bless his name.

4 *4* For the | Lord is gracious;
    his steadfast love is | everlasting,
    and his faithfulness endures from generation to | generation.

Psalm 101 is omitted

C Instrument

B♭ Instrument

Psalm 102

Verses 19-29 are omitted

PRINCIPAL SERVICE   **2ND SERVICE**   **3RD SERVICE**

Ash Wednesday ABC (vs. 1-18)
Wednesday of
Holy Week ABC (vs. 1-18)

Andrew Moore

Response

cf. v. 1 Let my cry, let my cry, let my cry come before you, O Lord.

Verse

K.D.

1 *1* O Lord, hear my prayer
and let my crying | come before you.
 2 Hide not your face from me
in the day of | my distress.
 3 In | cline your ear to me;
when I call, make | haste to answer me,

2 *4* For my days are con | sumed in smoke
and my bones burn away
as | in a furnace.
 5 My heart is smitten down
and wi | thered like grass,
so that I forget to | eat my bread.

3 *6* From the sound of my groaning
my bones cleave fast | to my skin.
 7 I am become like a vulture in the wilderness,
like an owl that | haunts the ruins.
 8 I keep watch and am become like a sparrow
solitary u | pon the housetop.
 9 My enemies revile me all the day long,
and those who rage at me
have sworn toge | ther against me.

4 *10* I have eaten ashes for bread
and mingled my | drink with weeping,
 11 Because of your indigna | tion and wrath,
for you have taken me up and | cast me down.
 12 My days fade away like a shadow,
and I am wi | thered like grass.

5 *13* But you, O Lord, shall en | dure for ever
and your name through all | generations.
 14 You will arise and have pi | ty on Zion;
it is time to have mercy upon her;
surely the | time has come.

6 *15* For your servants love her | very stones
and feel compassion | for her dust.
 16 Then shall the nations fear your | name, O Lord,
and all the kings of the | earth your glory,

7 *17* When the Lord has | built up Zion
and shown him | self in glory;
 18 When he has turned to the
prayer | of the destitute
and has not des | pised their plea.

C Instrument

B♭ Instrument

Psalm 103

Verses 14-22 are omitted
PRINCIPAL SERVICE   2ND SERVICE   3RD SERVICE
Proper 16 C (related) (vs. 1-9)
Proper 19 A (related) (vs. 8-13)

Richard Lloyd

Response
cf. v. 13 The Lord has compassion on his children.

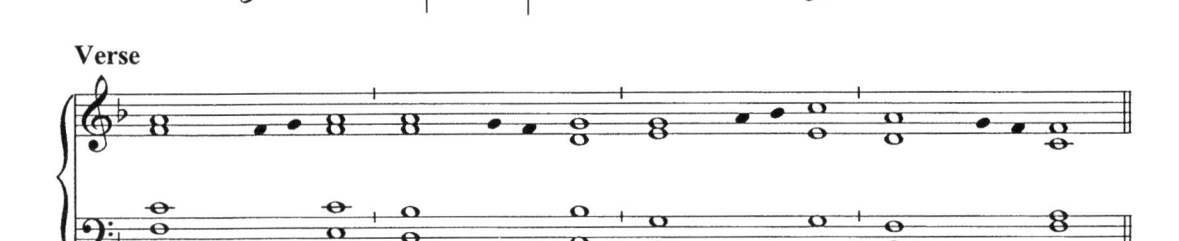

Verse

T.B.

1 *1* Bless the Lord, | O my soul,
  and all that is within me bless his | holy name.
 2 Bless the Lord, | O my soul,
  and forget not | all his benefits;

2 *3* Who forgives all your sins
  and heals all | your infirmities;
 4 Who redeems your life from the Pit
  and crowns you with faithful love | and compassion;
 5 Who satisfies you | with good things,
  so that your youth is renewed | like an eagle's.

3 *6* The Lord executes righteousness
  and judgement for all who | are oppressed.
 7 He made his ways known to Moses
  and his works to the chil | dren of Israel.
 8 The Lord is full of compassion and mercy,
  slow to anger and | of great kindness.
 9 He will not always accuse us,
  neither will he keep his an | ger for ever.

4 *10* He has not dealt with us according | to our sins,
  nor rewarded us according | to our wickedness.
 11 For as the heavens are high a | bove the earth,
  so great is his mercy upon | those who fear him.

5 *12* As far as the east is | from the west,
   so far has he | set our sins from us.
 13 As a father has compassion | on his children,
   so is the Lord merciful towards | those who fear him.

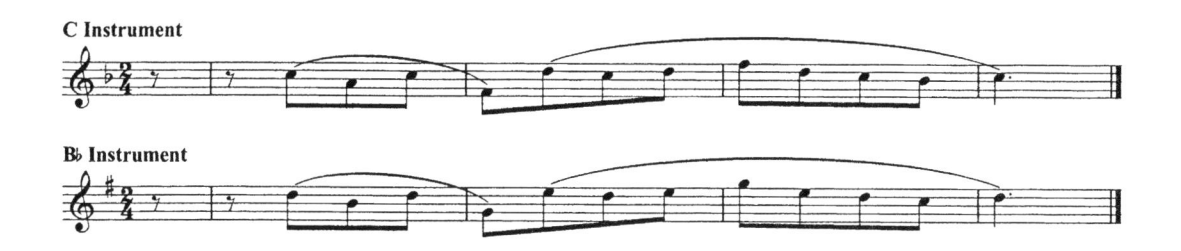

Psalm 104

PRINCIPAL SERVICE
2 before Lent B (vs. 26-37)
Pentecost ABC (vs. 26-37)
Proper 24 B (vs. 1-10)

2ND SERVICE
Trinity B (vs. 1-10)

3RD SERVICE
2 before Lent C (vs. 1-27)
6 Easter B (vs. 28-34)
7 Easter A (vs. 26-37)
Proper 16 A (vs. 1-27)

Response — Geoff Nobes

v. 1a Bless the Lord, O my soul.

Verse

G.N.

1 *1* Bless the Lord, | O my soul.
   O Lord my God, how excellent | is your greatness!
 2 You are clothed with majes | ty and honour,
   wrapped in light as | in a garment.

2 *3* You spread out the heavens | like a curtain
   and lay the beams of your dwelling place
   in the wa | ters above.
 4 You make the | clouds your chariot
   and ride on the wings | of the wind.

3 *5* You make the | winds your messengers
   and flames of | fire your servants.
 6 You laid the foundations | of the earth,
   that it never should move at | any time.

4 *7* You covered it with the deep | like a garment;
   the waters stood high a | bove the hills.
 8 At your re | buke they fled;
   at the voice of your thunder
   they has | tened away.

5 *9* They rose up to the hills and flowed
   down to the val | leys beneath,
   to the place which you | had appointed for them.
 10 You have set them their bounds t
   hat they | should not pass,
   nor turn again to co | ver the earth.

6 *11* You send the springs into the brooks,
   which run a | mong the hills.
 12 They give drink to every beast | of the field,
   and the wild asses | quench their thirst.
 13 Beside them the birds of the air make their nests
   and sing a | mong the branches.

7 *14* You water the hills from your dwel | ling on high
   the earth is filled with the fruit | of your works.
 15 You make grass to grow | for the cattle
   and plants to | meet our needs,

8 *16* Bringing forth food | from the earth
   and wine to glad | den our hearts,
 17 Oil to give us a | cheerful countenance
   and bread to streng | then our hearts.

9 *18* The trees of the Lord are | full of sap,
   the cedars of Lebanon | which he planted,
 19 In which the birds | build their nests,
   while the fir trees are a dwelling | for the stork.

10 *20* The mountains are a refuge for | the wild goats
   and the stony cliffs | for the conies.
 21 You appointed the moon to | mark the seasons,
   and the sun knows the time | for its setting.

11 ₂₂ You make darkness that it | may be night,
    in which all the beasts of the for | est creep forth.
  ₂₃ The lions roar | for their prey
    and seek their | food from God.

12 ₂₄ The sun rises and | they are gone
    to lay themselves down | in their dens.
  ₂₅ People go forth | to their work
    and to their labour un | til the evening.

13 ₂₆ O Lord, how manifold are your works!
    In wisdom you have | made them all;
    the earth is full | of your creatures.
  ₂₇ There is the sea, spread | far and wide,
    and there move creatures beyond number, both | small and great.

14 ₂₈ There go the ships, and there is | that Leviathan
    which you have made to play | in the deep.
  ₂₉ All of these | look to you
    to give them their food | in due season.

15 ₃₀ When you give it | them, they gather it;
    you open your hand and they are | filled with good.
  ₃₁ When you hide your face | they are troubled;
    when you take away their breath,
    they die and return again | to the dust.

16 ₃₂ When you send forth your spirit, they are created,
    and you renew the face | of the earth.
  ₃₃ May the glory of the Lord endure for ever;
    may the Lord rejoice | in his works;
  ₃₄ He looks on the earth | and it trembles;
    he touches the mountains | and they smoke.

17 ₃₅ I will sing to the Lord as long as I live;
    I will make music to my God while I | have my being.
  ₃₆ So shall my song please him while I rejoice | in the Lord.
  ₃₇ Let sinners be consumed out of the earth
    and the wicked | be no more.
    Bless the Lord, | O my soul.
    (Alleluia.)

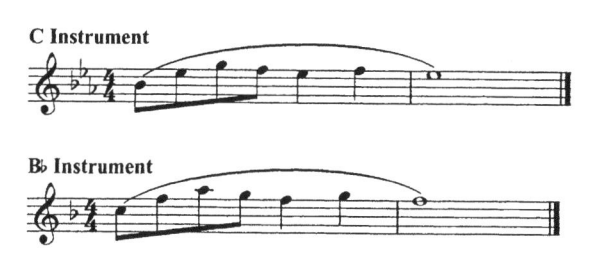

C Instrument

B♭ Instrument

Psalm 105

PRINCIPAL SERVICE
Proper 12 A (vs. 1-11)
Proper 14 A (vs. 1-6, 16-22)
Proper 17 A (vs. 1-6, 23-26)
Proper 20 A (vs. 37-45)

2ND SERVICE
Proper 17 A (vs. 1-15)

3RD SERVICE
1 Christmas AB (vs. 1-9)
1 Christmas C (vs. 1-11)
2 Lent B (vs. 1-6, 37-45)
Easter Day AB

Keith Duke

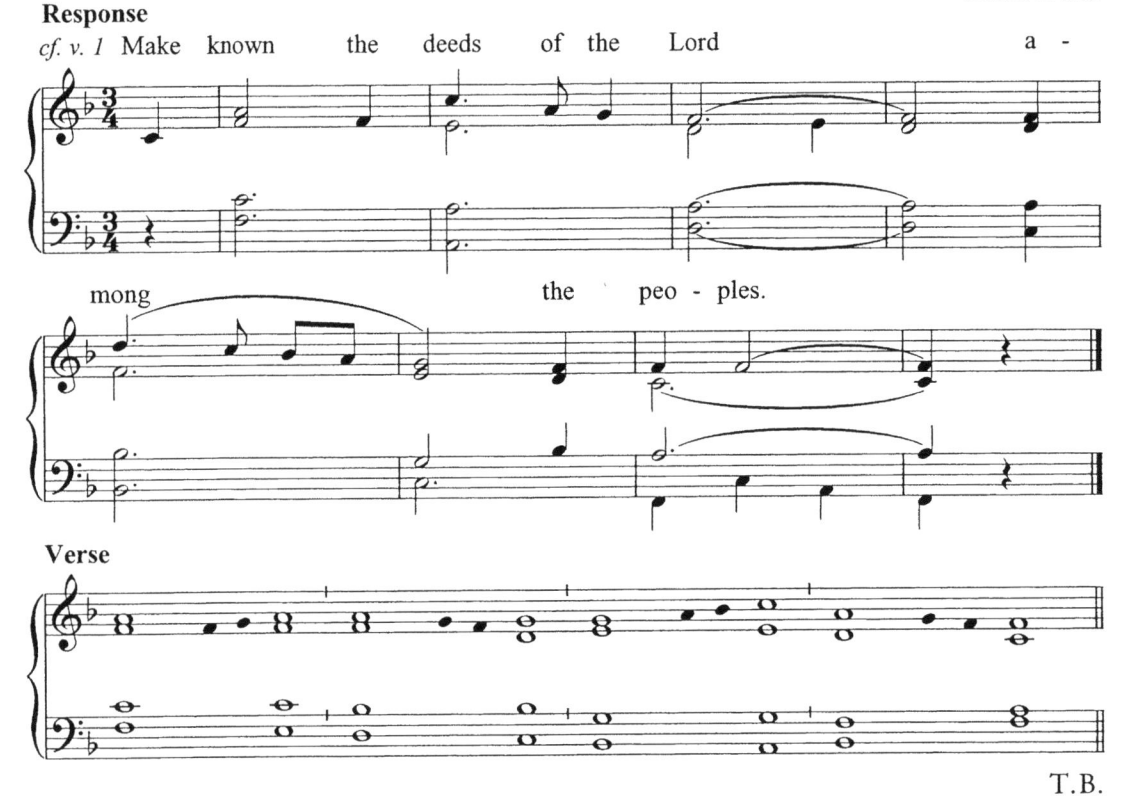

Response
cf. v. 1 Make known the deeds of the Lord among the peoples.

Verse

T.B.

1 *1* O give thanks to the Lord
   and call u | pon his name;
   make known his
   deeds a | mong the peoples.
 2 Sing to | him, sing praises,
   and tell of all his mar | vellous works.

2 *3* Rejoice in the praise of his | holy name;
   let the hearts of them rejoice
   who | seek the Lord.
 4 Seek the Lord | and his strength;
   seek his | face continually.

3 *5* Remember the marvels | he has done,
   his wonders and the
   judgements | of his mouth,
 6 O seed of Abra | ham his servant,
   O children of Ja | cob his chosen.

4 *7* He is the Lord our God;
   his judgements are in | all the earth.
 8 He has always been mindful | of his covenant,
   the promise that he made
   for a thousand | generations:
 9 The covenant he made with Abraham,
   the oath that he | swore to Isaac,

5 *10* Which he established as a sta | tute for Jacob,
   an everlasting cove | nant for Israel,
 11 Saying, 'To you will I
   give the | land of Canaan
   to be the portion of | your inheritance.'

6 *12* When they were but | few in number,
   of little account, and sojourners | in the land,
 13 Wandering from na | tion to nation,
   from one kingdom to an | other people,

7 ₁₄ He suffered no one to | do them wrong
  and rebuked even kings | for their sake,
 ₁₅ Saying, 'Touch not | my anointed
  and do my pro | phets no harm.'

8 ₁₆ Then he called down famine o | ver the land
  and broke every | staff of bread.
 ₁₇ But he had sent a | man before them,
  Joseph, who was sold | as a slave.

9 ₁₈ They shackled his | feet with fetters;
  his neck was | ringed with iron.
 ₁₉ Until all he foretold | came to pass,
  the word of | the Lord tested him.

10 ₂₀ The king sent and released him;
  the ruler of peoples | set him free.
 ₂₁ He appointed him lord of his household
  and ruler of all | he possessed,
 ₂₂ To instruct his princes | as he willed
  and to teach his coun | sellors wisdom.

11 ₂₃ Then Israel came | into Egypt;
  Jacob sojourned in the | land of Ham.
 ₂₄ And the Lord made his
  people exceed | ingly fruitful;
  he made them
  too many | for their adversaries,

12 ₂₅ Whose heart he turned,
  so that they hat | ed his people
  and dealt craftily | with his servants.
 ₂₆ Then sent he Mo | ses his servant
  and Aaron whom | he had chosen.

13 ₂₇ He showed his signs through their word
  and his wonders in the | land of Ham.
 ₂₈ He sent darkness and it grew dark;
  yet they did not | heed his words.
 ₂₉ He turned their waters into blood
  and slew | all their fish.
 ₃₀ Their land swarmed with frogs,
  even in | their kings' chambers.

14 ₃₁ He spoke the word,
  and there came | clouds of flies,
  swarms of gnats within | all their borders.
 ₃₂ He gave them hail | stones for rain
  and flames of lightning | in their land.

15 ₃₃ He blasted their vines | and their fig trees
  and shattered trees a | cross their country.
 ₃₄ He spoke the word, and the
  grass | hoppers came
  and young locusts | without number;

16 ₃₅ They ate every plant | in their land
  and devoured the fruit | of their soil.
 ₃₆ He smote all the firstborn | in their land,
  the first fruits of | all their strength.

17 ₃₇ Then he brought them out
  with sil | ver and gold;
  there was not one among
  their | tribes that stumbled.
 ₃₈ Egypt was glad at | their departing,
  for a dread of them had fal | len upon them.

18 ₃₉ He spread out a cloud | for a covering
  and a fire to light | up the night.
 ₄₀ They asked and he | brought them quails;
  he satisfied them with the | bread of heaven.

19 ₄₁ He opened the rock,
  and the wa | ters gushed out
  and ran in the dry places | like a river.
 ₄₂ For he remembered his | holy word
  and Abra | ham, his servant.

20 ₄₃ So he brought forth his people with joy,
  his chosen | ones with singing.
 ₄₄ He gave them the lands | of the nations
  and they took possession
  of the fruit | of their toil,
 ₄₅ That they might keep his statutes
  and faithfully ob | serve his laws.
  (Alleluia.)

Psalm 106

Verses 25-49 are omitted

PRINCIPAL SERVICE 2ND SERVICE 3RD SERVICE
Proper 23 A (vs. 1-5)   4 Easter A (vs. 6-24)
                          Proper 13 C (vs. 1-10)
                          Proper 15 B (vs. 1-10)

Colin Mawby

Response

v. 1 Give thanks to the Lord, for he is gra-cious.

Verse

* *Omit in verses 2, 3 and 9*   C.M.

1 *1* (Alleluia.)
   Give thanks to the Lord, for | he is gracious,
   for his faithfulness en | dures for ever.
  2 Who can express the mighty acts | of the Lord
   or show forth | all his praise?
  3 Blessed are those who observe | what is right
   and always do | what is just.

2 *4* Remember me, O Lord, in the favour you bear | for your people;
   visit me in the day of | your salvation;
  5 That I may see the prosperity | of your chosen
   and rejoice in the gladness | of your people,
   and exult with | your inheritance.

3 *6* We have sinned | like our forebears;
   we have done wrong | and dealt wickedly.
  7 In Egypt they did not consi | der your wonders,
   nor remember the abundance of your | faithful love;
   they rebelled against the Most High at | the Red Sea.

4 ⁸But he saved them | for his name's sake,
   that he might make his power | to be known.
  ⁹He rebuked the Red Sea and it | was dried up;
   so he led them through the deep as | through the wilderness.
  ¹⁰He saved them from the adver | sary's hand
   and redeemed them from the hand | of the enemy.

5 ¹¹As for those that troubled them, the waters | overwhelmed them;
   there was not one | of them left.
  ¹²Then they be | lieved his words
   and sang a | loud his praise.
  ¹³But soon they for | got his deeds
   and would not wait | for his counsel.

6 ¹⁴A craving seized them | in the wilderness,
   and they put God to the test | in the desert.
  ¹⁵He gave them | their desire,
   but sent a wasting sick | ness among them.
  ¹⁶They grew jealous of Moses | in the camp
   and of Aaron, the holy one | of the Lord.

7 ¹⁷So the earth opened and swal | lowed up Dathan
   and covered the company | of Abiram.
  ¹⁸A fire was kindled | in their company;
   the flame burnt | up the wicked.
  ¹⁹They made a | calf at Horeb
   and worshipped the | molten image;

8 ²⁰Thus they ex | changed their glory
   for the image of an ox that | feeds on hay.
  ²¹They forgot | God their saviour,
   who had done such great | things in Egypt,
  ²²Wonderful deeds in the | land of Ham
   and fearful things at | the Red Sea.

9 ²³So he would | have destroyed them,
   had not Moses his chosen stood before him | in the breach,
   to turn away his wrath | from consuming them.
  ²⁴Then they scorned the | Promised Land
   and would not be | lieve his word.

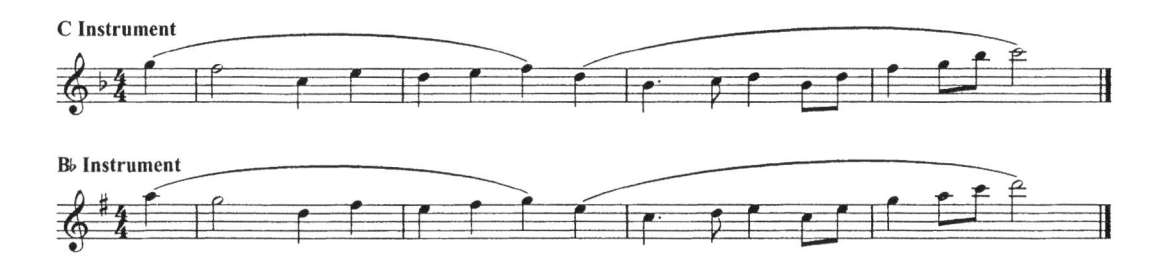

Psalm 107

Verses 33-43 are omitted

PRINCIPAL SERVICE
4 Lent B (vs. 1-9)
Proper 7 B (related) (vs. 23-32)
Proper 13 C (vs. 1-9)

2ND SERVICE
Proper 13 C (vs. 1-12)

3RD SERVICE
5 Lent B (vs. 1-22)
Proper 17 A (vs. 1-32)

Andrew Wright

Response

cf. v. 1 Give thanks to the Lord, for he is gracious.

Verse

* *Omit in verse 2*

C.M.

1 *1* O give thanks to the Lord, for | he is gracious,
    for his steadfast love en | dures for ever.
  2 Let the redeemed of the | Lord say this,
    those he redeemed from the hand | of the enemy,
  3 And gathered out of the lands
    from the east and | from the west,
    from the north and | from the south.

2 *4* Some went astray in | desert wastes
    and found no path to a ci | ty to dwell in.
  5 Hungry and thirsty,
    their soul was faint | ing within them.
  6 So they cried to the Lord | in their trouble
    and he delivered them from | their distress.

3 *7* He set their feet | on the right way
    till they came to a ci | ty to dwell in.
  8 Let them give thanks to the Lord | for his goodness
    and the wonders he does | for his children.
  9 For he satisfies the | longing soul
    and fills the hungry | soul with good.

4 *10* Some sat in darkness and in the sha | dow of death,
    bound fast in mise | ry and iron,
  11 For they had rebelled against the | words of God
    and despised the counsel of | the Most High.
  12 So he bowed down their | heart with heaviness;
    they stumbled and there was | none to help them.

5 *13* Then they cried to the Lord in their trouble,
and he delivered them from | their distress.
14 He brought them out of darkness and out of the shadow of death,
and broke their | bonds asunder.
15 Let them give thanks to the Lord | for his goodness
and the wonders he does | for his children.
16 For he has broken the | doors of bronze
and breaks the bars of i | ron in pieces.

6 *17* Some were foolish and took a re | bellious way,
and were plagued because of | their wrongdoing.
18 Their soul abhorred all man | ner of food
and drew near to the | gates of death.
19 Then they cried to the Lord | in their trouble,
and he delivered them from | their distress.

7 *20* He sent forth his | word and healed them,
and saved them | from destruction.
21 Let them give thanks to the Lord | for his goodness
and the wonders he does | for his children.
22 Let them offer him sacrifices | of thanksgiving
and tell of his acts with | shouts of joy.

8 *23* Those who go down to the | sea in ships
and ply their trade | in great waters,
24 These have seen the works | of the Lord
and his wonders | in the deep.
25 For at his word the stormy | wind arose
and lifted up the waves | of the sea.

9 *26* They were carried up to the heavens
and down again | to the deep;
their soul melted away | in their peril.
27 They reeled and staggered like a drunkard
and were | at their wits' end.
28 Then they cried to the Lord in their trouble,
and he brought them out of | their distress.
29 He made the | storm be still
and the waves of the | sea were calmed.

10 *30* Then were they glad because they | were at rest,
and he brought them to the haven | they desired.
31 Let them give thanks to the Lord | for his goodness
and the wonders he does | for his children.
32 Let them exalt him in the congregation | of the people
and praise him in the council | of the elders.

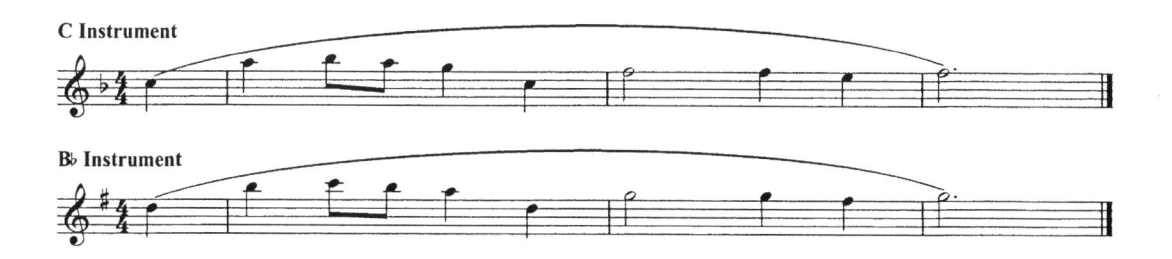

Psalm 108

PRINCIPAL SERVICE 2ND SERVICE 3RD SERVICE
Proper 14 C
Proper 18 A

Alan Rees

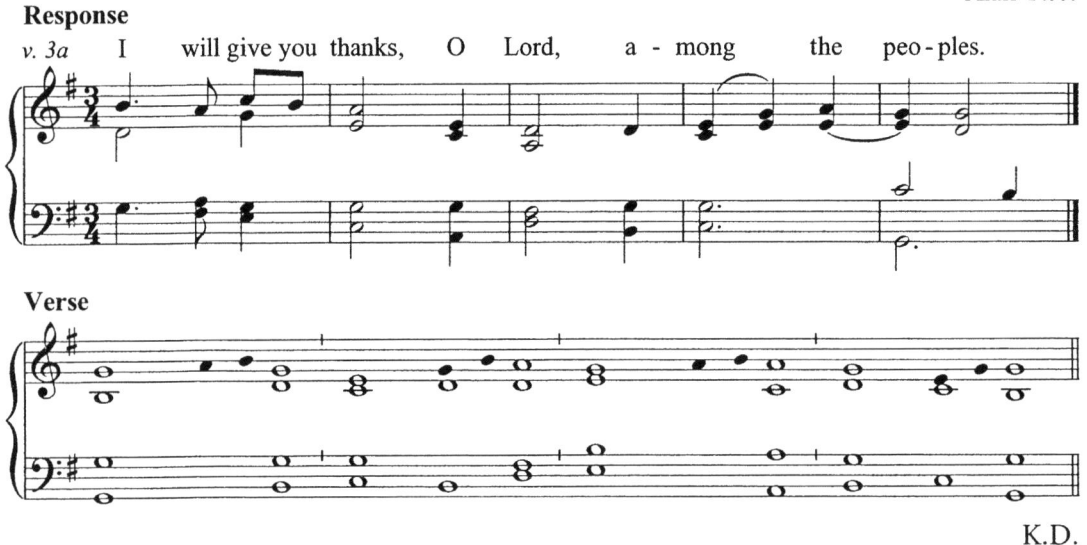

Response

v. 3a I will give you thanks, O Lord, a-mong the peo-ples.

Verse

K.D.

1 *1* My heart is ready, O God, my | heart is ready;
   I will sing and | give you praise.
   2 Awake, my soul; awake, | harp and lyre,
   that I may awa | ken the dawn.

2 *3* I will give you thanks, O Lord, a | mong the peoples;
   I will sing praise to you a | mong the nations.
   4 For your loving-kindness is as high | as the heavens
   and your faithfulness reaches | to the clouds.

3 *5* Be exalted, O God, a | bove the heavens
   and your glory over | all the earth.
   6 That your beloved may | be delivered,
   save us by your right | hand and answer me.

4 *7* God has spoken | in his holiness:
   'I will triumph and | divide Shechem
   and share out the val | ley of Succoth.
   8 'Gilead is mine and Manas | seh is mine;

5   Ephraim is my helmet and Ju | dah my sceptre.
   9 'Moab shall | be my washpot,
   over Edom will I | cast my sandal,
   across Philistia will I | shout in triumph.'

6 *10* Who will lead me into | the strong city?
   Who will bring me | into Edom?
   11 Have you not cast us | off, O God?
   Will you no longer go forth | with our troops?

7 *12* O grant us your help a | gainst the enemy,
    for earthly help | is in vain.
  13 Through God will we | do great acts,
    for it is he that shall tread | down our enemies.

Psalm 109 is omitted

New Psalms for Common Worship

Psalm 110

PRINCIPAL SERVICE

Also: Evening Prayer:
 Corpus Christi ABC

2ND SERVICE

3RD SERVICE
Christmas Day ABC
Ascension ABC
Christ the King ABC

Richard Lloyd

Response

v. 4b You are a priest for e-ver af-ter the or-der of Mel-chi-ze-dek.

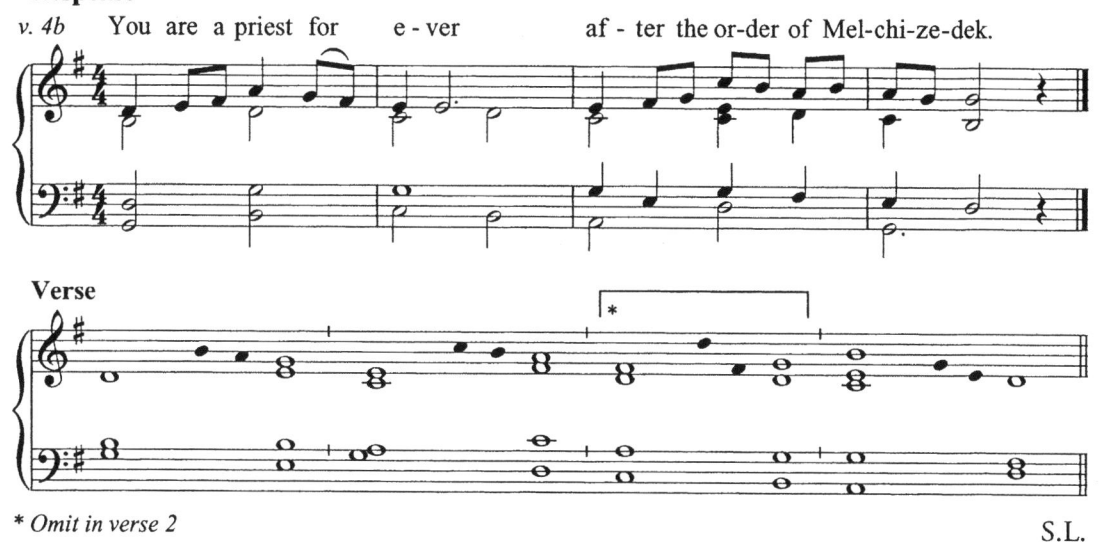

Verse

* *Omit in verse 2*

S.L.

1 *1* The Lord said to my lord, 'Sit | at my right hand,
 until I make your ene | mies your footstool.'
 2 May the Lord stretch forth the sceptre | of your power;
 rule from Zion in the midst | of your enemies.

2 *3* 'Noble are you on this day | of your birth;
 on the holy mountain, from the womb | of the dawn
 the dew of your new birth | is upon you.'

3 *4* The Lord has sworn and will | not retract:
 'You are a priest for ever after the order | of Melchizedek.'
 5 The king at your right | hand, O Lord,
 shall smite down kings in the day | of his wrath.

4 *6* In all his majesty, he shall judge a | mong the nations,
 smiting heads over | all the wide earth.
 7 He shall drink from the brook be | side the way;
 therefore shall he lift | high his head.

C Instrument

B♭ Instrument

Psalm 111

PRINCIPAL SERVICE
4 Epiphany B
Proper 15 B
Proper 23 C (related)
Also: Evening Prayer:
　　Corpus Christi ABC

2ND SERVICE
All Saints ABC
4 before Advent A

3RD SERVICE
5 Lent C

Andrew Moore

Response

v. 10a The fear of the Lord, the fear of the Lord is the beginning of wisdom.

Verse

T.B.

1 ₁ Alleluia. I will give thanks to the Lord
　　with | my whole heart,
　　　in the company of the faithful and in the | congregation.
　₂ The works of the | Lord are great,
　　　sought out by all | who delight in them.

2 ₃ His work is full of majes | ty and honour
　　　and his righteousness en | dures for ever.
　₄ He appointed a memorial for his mar | vellous deeds;
　　　the Lord is gracious and full | of compassion.

3 ₅ He gave food to | those who feared him;
　　　he is ever mindful | of his covenant.
　₆ He showed his people the power | of his works
　　　in giving them the heritage | of the nations.

4 ⁷The works of his hands are | truth and justice;
   all his command | ments are sure.
  ⁸They stand fast for e | ver and ever;
   they are done in | truth and equity.

5 ⁹He sent redemption to his people;
   he commanded his cove | nant for ever;
   holy and awesome | is his name.
  ¹⁰The fear of the Lord is the beginning of wisdom;
   a good understanding have | those who live by it;
   his praise en | dures for ever.

C Instrument

B♭ Instrument

Psalm 112

PRINCIPAL SERVICE
Proper 1 A (vs. 1-9)
Proper 17 C (related)

2ND SERVICE
All Saints ABC

3RD SERVICE
5 Lent C
4 before Advent B

Response — Gerry Fitzpatrick

v. 1a Bles-sed are those who fear the Lord.

Verse

* *Omit in verses 5 and 6* K.D.

1 1 Alleluia. Blessed are those who | fear the Lord
   and have great delight in | his commandments.
  2 Their descendants will be mighty | in the land,
   a generation of the faithful that | will be blest.

2 3 Wealth and riches will be | in their house,
   and their righteousness en | dures for ever.
  4 Light shines in the darkness | for the upright;
   gracious and full of compassion | are the righteous.

3 5 It goes well with those who are gene | rous in lending
   and order their af | fairs with justice,
  6 For they will ne | ver be shaken;
   the righteous will be held in everlast | ing remembrance.

4 7 They will not be afraid of any | evil tidings;
   their heart is steadfast, trusting | in the Lord.
  8 Their heart is sustained and | will not fear,
   until they see the downfall | of their foes.

5 9 They have given freely | to the poor;
   their righteousness stands | fast for ever;
   their head will be exal | ted with honour.

6 *10* The wicked shall see it | and be angry;
they shall gnash their teeth | in despair;
the desire of the wick | ed shall perish.

Psalm 113

PRINCIPAL SERVICE
Proper 20 C (related)

2ND SERVICE
4 Advent AB
4 Easter C

3RD SERVICE
Epiphany ABC
3 Epiphany ABC

Simon Lesley

Response

v. 1b Praise, O praise the name of the Lord.

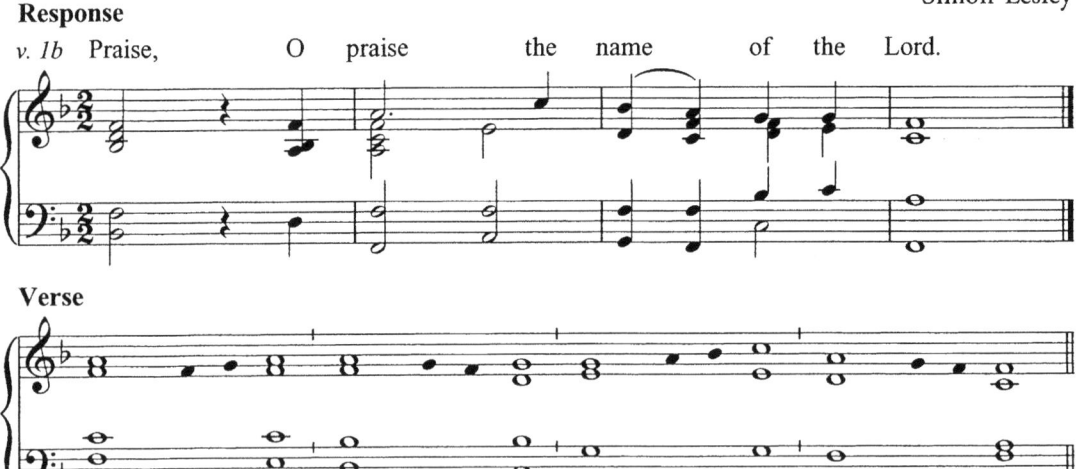

Verse

T.B.

1 *1* Alleluia. Give praise, you servants | of the Lord,
   O praise the name | of the Lord.
 2 Blessed be the name | of the Lord,
   from this time forth and for | evermore.

2 *3* From the rising of the sun | to its setting
   let the name of the | Lord be praised.
 4 The Lord is high a | bove all nations
   and his glory a | bove the heavens.

3 *5* Who is like the | Lord our God,
   that has his | throne so high,
   yet humbles himself | to behold
   the things of hea | ven and earth?

4 *6* He raises the poor | from the dust
   and lifts the needy | from the ashes,
 7 To set them with princes,
   with the princes | of his people.
 8 He gives the barren woman a place in the house
   and makes her a joyful mo | ther of children.
   Alleluia.

C Instrument

B♭ Instrument

Psalm 114

PRINCIPAL SERVICE
Proper 19 A

Also: Easter Vigil ABC

2ND SERVICE
Easter Day ABC
4 Easter C

3RD SERVICE
Easter Day C

Andrew Moore

Response

cf. v. 2 Ju-dah be-came God's sanc-tua-ry and Is-ra-el his do-mi-nion.

Verse

S.L.

1 *1* When Israel came | out of Egypt,
 the house of Jacob from a people of | a strange tongue,
 2 Judah be | came his sanctuary,
 Israel | his dominion.

2 *3* The sea saw | that, and fled;
 Jordan was | driven back.
 4 The mountains | skipped like rams,
 the little hills | like young sheep.

3 *5* What ailed you, O sea, | that you fled?
 O Jordan, that you were | driven back?
 6 You mountains, that you | skipped like rams,
 you little hills | like young sheep?

4 *7* Tremble, O earth, at the presence | of the Lord,
 at the presence of the | God of Jacob,
 8 Who turns the hard rock into a | pool of water,
 the flint-stone into a | springing well.

C Instrument

B♭ Instrument

Psalm 115

PRINCIPAL SERVICE

2ND SERVICE
Proper 18 A

3RD SERVICE
Proper 14 C
Proper 16 B

Colin Mawby

Response

cf. v. 1 Not to us, Lord, but to your name give the glo - ry.

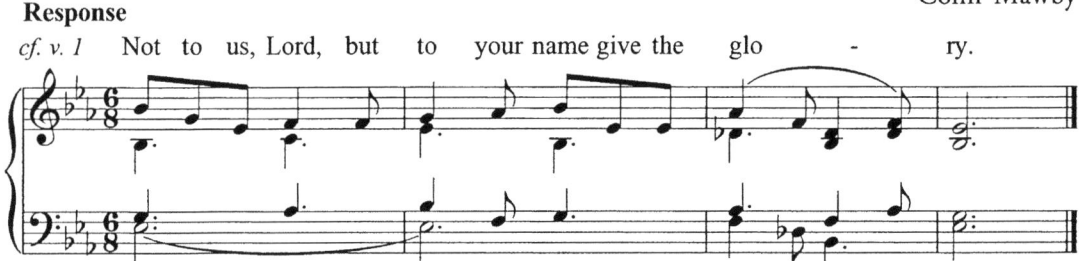

Verse

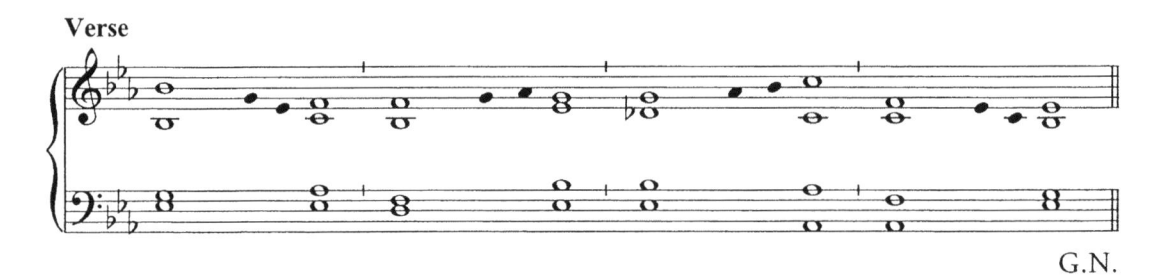

G.N.

1 *1* Not to us, Lord, not to us,
   but to your name | give the glory,
   for the sake of your loving mer | cy and truth.
  2 Why should the nations say,
   'Where is | now their God?'
  3 As for our God, he is in heaven;
   he does whate | ver he pleases.

2 *4* Their idols are sil | ver and gold,
   the work of | human hands.
  5 They have mouths, but | cannot speak;
   eyes have they, but | cannot see;

3 *6* They have ears, but | cannot hear;
   noses have they, but | cannot smell;
  7 They have hands, but cannot feel;
   feet have they, but | cannot walk;
   not a whisper do they make | from their throats.

4 *8* Those who make them shall be | come like them
   and so will all who | put their trust in them.
  9 But you, Israel, put your trust | in the Lord;
   he is their help | and their shield.

5 *10* House of Aaron, trust | in the Lord;
    he is their help | and their shield.
  11 You that fear the Lord, trust | in the Lord;
    he is their help | and their shield.

6 *12* The Lord has been mindful of us and | he will bless us;
    may he bless the | house of Israel;
    may he bless the | house of Aaron;
  13 May he bless those who fear the Lord,
    both small and | great together.

7 *14* May the Lord increase you more and more,
    you and your | children after you.
  15 May you be blest by the Lord,
    the maker of hea | ven and earth.
  16 The heavens are the heavens | of the Lord,
    but the earth he has entrusted | to his children.

8 *17* The dead do not | praise the Lord,
    nor those gone down | into silence;
  18 But we will | bless the Lord,
    from this time forth for | evermore.
    (Alleluia.)

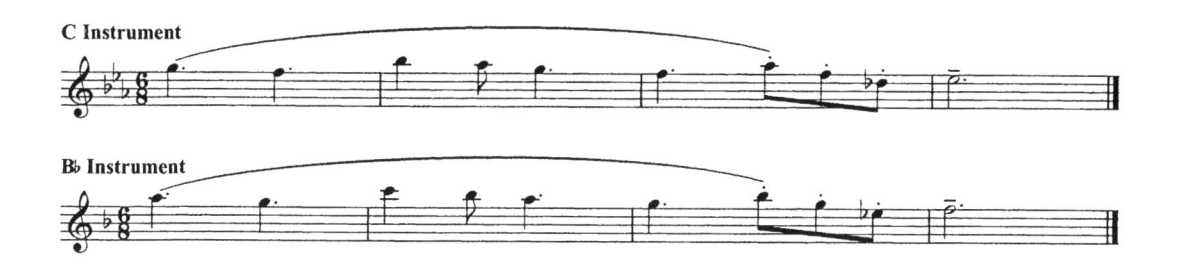

Psalm 116

PRINCIPAL SERVICE
Maundy Thursday ABC (vs. 10-17)
3 Easter A (vs. 1-8)
Corpus Christi ABC (vs. 10-17)
Proper 6 A (vs. 10-17)
Proper 19 B (related) (vs. 1-8)

2ND SERVICE
Proper 14 C
Proper 16 B (vs. 10-17)

3RD SERVICE
Easter Eve ABC

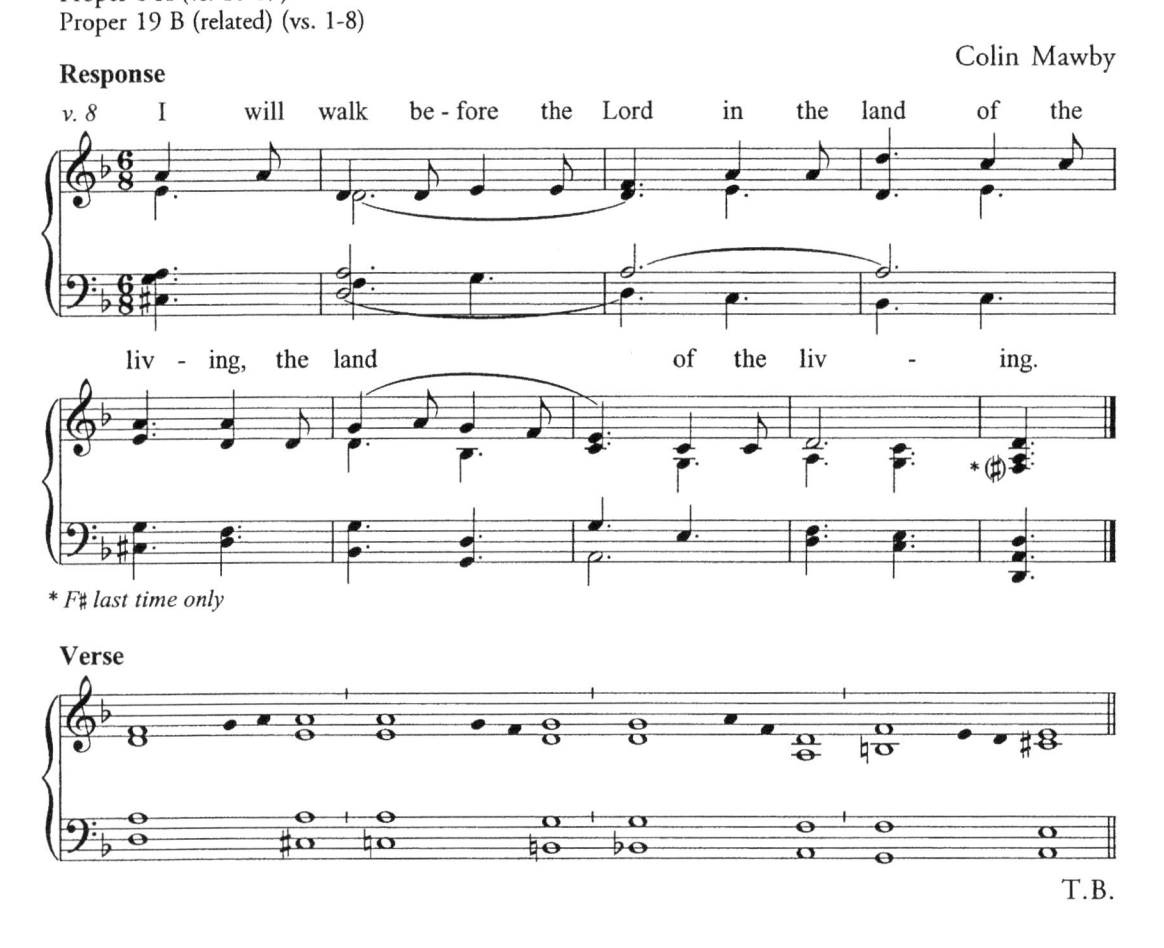

Colin Mawby

Response

v. 8 I will walk before the Lord in the land of the living, the land of the living.

* F♮ last time only

Verse

T.B.

1 ₁ I love the Lord,
   for he has heard the voice of my | supplication;
   because he inclined his ear to me
   on the | day I called to him.
   ₂ The snares of death encompassed me;
   the pains of | hell took hold of me;
   by grief and sorrow | was I held.

2 ₃ Then I called upon the name | of the Lord:
   'O Lord, I beg you, deli | ver my soul.'
   ₄ Gracious is the | Lord and righteous;
   our God is full | of compassion.

3 ₅ The Lord watches o | ver the simple;
   I was brought very low | and he saved me.
   ₆ Turn again to your rest, | O my soul,
   for the Lord has been gra | cious to you.

4 ⁷ For you have delivered my | soul from death,
 my eyes from tears and my | feet from falling.
 ⁸ I will walk be | fore the Lord
 in the land | of the living.

5 ⁹ I believed that | I should perish
 for I was | sorely troubled;
 and I said in | my alarm,
 'Everyone | is a liar.'

6 ¹⁰ How shall I re | pay the Lord
 for all the benefits | he has given to me?
 ¹¹ I will lift up the cup | of salvation
 and call upon the name | of the Lord.

7 ¹² I will fulfil my vows | to the Lord
 in the presence of | all his people.
 ¹³ Precious in the sight | of the Lord
 is the death of his | faithful servants.

8 ¹⁴ O Lord, I am your servant,
 your servant, the child | of your handmaid;
 you have freed me | from my bonds.
 ¹⁵ I will offer to you a sacrifice | of thanksgiving
 and call upon the name | of the Lord.

9 ¹⁶ I will fulfil my vows | to the Lord
 in the presence of | all his people,
 ¹⁷ In the courts of the house | of the Lord,
 in the midst of you, | O Jerusalem.
 (Alleluia.)

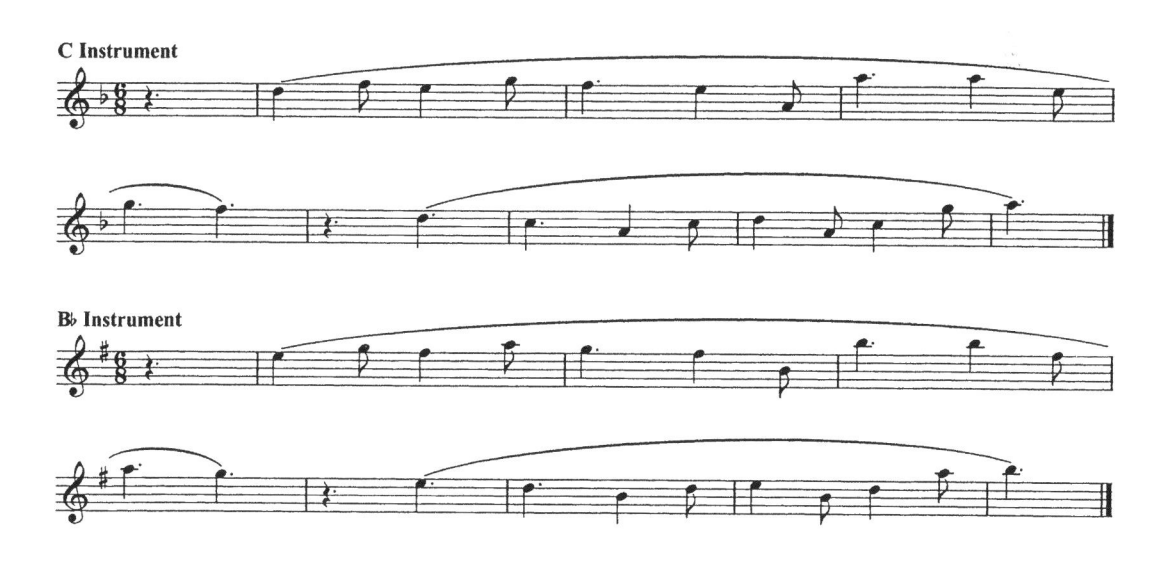

New Psalms for Common Worship

Psalm 117

PRINCIPAL SERVICE

2ND SERVICE
Easter Day ABC
All Saints ABC
4 before Advent A

3RD SERVICE
Easter Day C

John McCann

Response

v. 1 Praise the Lord, O praise the Lord, all you na-tions.

Verse

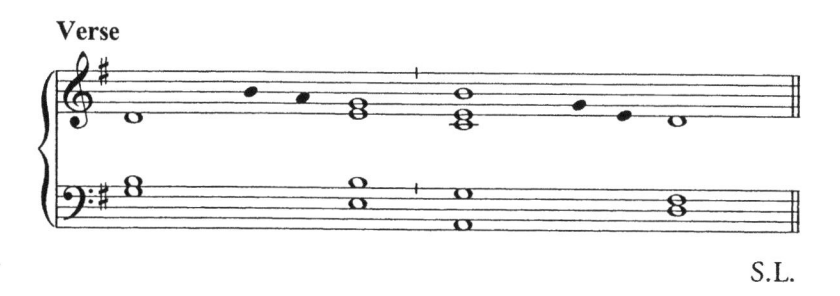

S.L.

1 *1* O praise the Lord, | all you nations;
  praise him, | all you peoples.

2 *2* For great is his steadfast | love towards us,
  and the faithfulness of the Lord en | dures for ever.
  (Alleluia.)

C Instrument

B♭ Instrument

Psalm 118

PRINCIPAL SERVICE 2ND SERVICE 3RD SERVICE
Palm Sunday:
   Liturgy of the Palms ABC (vs. 19-25)
Easter Day ABC (vs. 15-25)
2 Easter C (vs. 15-29)
Also: Evening Prayer: Presentation ABC

Alan Rees

Response
v. 1 O give thanks to the Lord for he is good.

Verse

C.M.

1 *1* O give thanks to the Lord, for he is good;
   his mercy en | dures for ever.
  2 Let Israel now proclaim,
   'His mercy en | dures for ever.'
  3 Let the house of Aaron now proclaim,
   'His mercy en | dures for ever.'
  4 Let those who fear the Lord proclaim,
   'His mercy en | dures for ever.'

2 *5* In my constraint I called to the Lord;
   the Lord answered and | set me free.
  6 The Lord is at my side; I will not fear;
   what | can flesh do to me?
  7 With the Lord at my side | as my saviour,
   I shall see the downfall | of my enemies.

3 *8* It is better to take refuge | in the Lord
   than to put any confi | dence in flesh.
  9 It is better to take refuge | in the Lord
   than to put any confi | dence in princes.

4 *10* All the nations encompassed me,
   but by the name of the Lord I | drove them back.
  11 They hemmed me in, they hemmed me in on every side,
   but by the name of the Lord I | drove them back.
  12 They swarmed about me like bees;
   they blazed like fire | among thorns,
   but by the name of the Lord I | drove them back.

5 *13* Surely, I was thrust | to the brink,
    but the Lord came | to my help.
  14 The Lord is my strength | and my song,
    and he has become | my salvation.

6 *15* Joyful shouts | of salvation
    sound from the tents | of the righteous:
  16 'The right hand of the Lord does mighty deeds;
    the right hand of the Lord | raises up;
    the right hand of the Lord does | mighty deeds.'

7 *17* I shall not | die, but live
    and declare the works | of the Lord.
  18 The Lord has pun | ished me sorely,
    but he has not given me o | ver to death.

8 *19* Open to me the | gates of righteousness,
    that I may enter and give thanks | to the Lord.
  20 This is the gate | of the Lord;
    the righteous shall | enter through it.

9 *21* I will give thanks to you, for | you have answered me
    and have become | my salvation.
  22 The stone which the buil | ders rejected
    has become the chief | cornerstone.

10 *23* This is the Lord's doing,
    and it is marvellous | in our eyes.
  24 This is the day that the Lord has made;
    we will rejoice | and be glad in it.
  25 Come, O Lord, and save | us we pray.
    Come, Lord, send us | now prosperity.

11 *26* Blessed is he who comes in the name | of the Lord;
    we bless you from the house | of the Lord.
  27 The Lord is God; he has gi | ven us light;
    link the pilgrims with cords
    right to the horns | of the altar.

12 *28* You are my God and | I will thank you;
    you are my God and I | will exalt you.
  29 O give thanks to the Lord, for | he is good;
    his mercy en | dures for ever.

Psalm 119

PRINCIPAL SERVICE
Proper 2 A (vs. 1-8)
Proper 3 A (vs. 33-40)
5 Lent B (vs. 9-16)
Proper 10 A (vs. 105-112)
Proper 12 A (related) (vs. 129-136)
Proper 18 A (related) (vs. 33-40)
Proper 24 C (vs. 97-104)
Bible Sunday A (vs. 9-16)
Bible Sunday BC (vs. 129-136)
4 before Advent B (vs. 1-8)

2ND SERVICE
1 Lent B (vs. 17-32)
1 Lent C (vs. 73-88)
Proper 15 C (vs. 17-24)
Proper 16 C (vs. 49-56)
Proper 17 B (vs. 9-16)
Proper 17 C (vs. 81-88)
Proper 18 B (vs. 49-56)
Proper 19 A (vs. 41-48)
Proper 19 B (vs. 73-80)
Proper 20 A (vs. 121-128)
Proper 20 B (vs. 137-144)
Proper 25 A (vs. 89-104)
Proper 25 B (vs. 121-136)
Proper 25 C (vs. 1-16)
Bible Sunday A (vs. 89-104)
Bible Sunday BC (vs. 1-16)

3RD SERVICE
1 Lent A (vs. 1-16)
2 Lent C (vs. 161-176)
4 Easter B (vs. 89-96)
Proper 15 C (vs. 33-48)
Proper 16 C (vs. 73-88)
Proper 17 B (vs. 17-40)
Proper 17 C (vs. 161-176)
Proper 18 A (vs. 17-32)
Proper 18 B (vs. 57-72)
Proper 19 A (vs. 65-88)
Proper 19 B (vs. 105-120)
Proper 20 A (vs. 153-176)
Proper 20 B (vs. 153-176)
Proper 25 A (vs. 137-152)
Proper 25 B (vs. 89-104)
Proper 25 C (vs. 105-128)
Bible Sunday A (vs. 137-152)
Bible Sunday B (vs. 89-104)
Bible Sunday C (vs. 105-128)

Richard Lloyd

Response
cf. v. 35 Lead me, O Lord, in the path of your com-mand-ments.

Verse

Instrumental parts will be found on page 234

K.D.

1 Aleph

1 *1* Blessed are those whose | way is pure,
who walk in the law | of the Lord.
  2 Blessed are those who | keep his testimonies
  and seek him with | their whole heart,

2 *3* Those who | do no wickedness,
but walk | in his ways.
  4 You, O | Lord, have charged
  that we should diligently
    keep | your commandments.

3 *5* O that my ways were made | so direct
that I might | keep your statutes.
  6 Then should I not be | put to shame,
  because I have regard
    for all | your commandments.

4 *7* I will thank you with an | unfeigned heart,
when I have learned
your | righteous judgements.
  8 I will | keep your statutes;
  O forsake | me not utterly.

2 Beth

5 *9* How shall young people | cleanse their way
to keep themselves according | to your word?
  10 With my whole heart | have I sought you;
  O let me not go astray
    from | your commandments.

6 *11* Your words have I hidden with | in my heart,
that I should not | sin against you.
  12 Blessed are | you, O Lord;
  O teach | me your statutes.

7 *13* With my lips have | I been telling
 of all the judgements | of your mouth.
  14 I have taken greater delight
   in the way | of your testimonies
   than in all man | ner of riches.

8 *15* I will meditate on | your commandments
 and contem | plate your ways.
  16 My delight shall be | in your statutes
   and I will not for | get your word.

3   Gimel

9 *17* O do good to your servant that | I may live,
 and so shall I | keep your word.
  18 Open my eyes, that | I may see
   the wonders | of your law.

10 *19* I am a stranger | upon earth;
 hide not your com | mandments from me.
  20 My soul is con | sumed at all times
   with fervent longing | for your judgements.

11 *21* You have re | buked the arrogant;
 cursed are those who stray
  | from your commandments.
  22 Turn from me shame | and rebuke,
   for I have | kept your testimonies.

12 *23* Rulers also sit and | speak against me,
 but your servant meditates | on your statutes.
  24 For your testimonies are | my delight;
   they are my | faithful counsellors.

4   Daleth

13 *25* My soul cleaves | to the dust;
 O give me life according | to your word.
  26 I have acknowledged my ways
   and | you have answered me;
   O teach | me your statutes.

14 *27* Make me understand the
 way of | your commandments,
 and so shall I meditate
 on your | wondrous works.
  28 My soul melts away in | tears of sorrow;
   raise me up according | to your word.

15 *29* Take from me the | way of falsehood;
 be gracious to me | through your law.
  30 I have chosen the | way of truth
   and your judgements have I | laid before me.

16 *31* I hold fast | to your testimonies;
 O Lord, let me not be | put to shame.
  32 I will run the way
   of | your commandments,
   when you have set my | heart at liberty.

5   He

17 *33* Teach me, O Lord,
 the way | of your statutes
 and I shall keep it | to the end.
  34 Give me understanding
   and I shall | keep your law;
   I shall keep it with | my whole heart.

18 *35* Lead me in the path
 of | your commandments,
 for therein is | my delight.
  36 Incline my heart | to your testimonies
   and not to | unjust gain.

19 *37* Turn away my eyes
 lest they | gaze on vanities;
 O give me life | in your ways.
  38 Confirm to your ser | vant your promise,
   which stands for | all who fear you.

20 *39* Turn away the reproach | which I dread,
 because your judge | ments are good.
  40 Behold, I long
   for | your commandments;
   in your righteousness | give me life.

6   Waw

21 *41* Let your faithful love
 come unto | me, O Lord,
 even your salvation,
 according | to your promise.
  42 Then shall I answer | those who taunt me,
   for my trust is | in your word.

22 *43* O take not the word of truth
 utterly out | of my mouth,
 for my hope is | in your judgements.
  44 So shall I always | keep your law;
   I shall keep it for e | ver and ever.

23 *45* I will | walk at liberty,
 because I study | your commandments.
  46 I will tell of your testimonies,
   even | before kings,
   and will not | be ashamed.

24 *47* My delight shall be
 in | your commandments,
 which I have | greatly loved.
  48 My hands will I lift up to your
   commandments, | which I love,
   and I will meditate | on your statutes.

Psalm 119 (continued)

Richard Lloyd

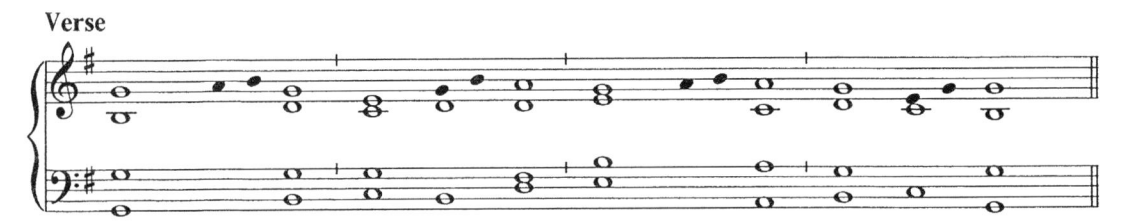

Response

cf. v. 35 Lead me, O Lord, in the path of your commandments.

Verse

K.D.

7 Zayin

25 ₄₉ Remember your word | to your servant,
   on which you have | built my hope.
   ₅₀ This is my comfort | in my trouble,
   that your promise | gives me life.

26 ₅₁ The proud have deri | ded me cruelly,
   but I have not turned aside | from your law.
   ₅₂ I have remembered your
   everlasting judge | ments, O Lord,
   and | have been comforted.

27 ₅₃ I am seized with indignation | at the wicked,
   for they have forsa | ken your law.
   ₅₄ Your statutes have | been like songs to me
   in the house | of my pilgrimage.

28 ₅₅ I have thought on your name
   in the | night, O Lord,
   and so have I | kept your law.
   ₅₆ These blessings | have been mine,
   for I have kept | your commandments.

8 Heth

29 ₅₇ You only are my por | tion, O Lord;
   I have promised to | keep your words.
   ₅₈ I entreat you with | all my heart,
   be merciful to me according | to your promise.

30 ₅₉ I have consi | dered my ways
   and turned my feet back | to your testimonies.
   ₆₀ I made haste and did | not delay
   to keep | your commandments.

31 ₆₁ Though the cords
   of the wic | ked entangle me,
   I do not for | get your law.
   ₆₂ At midnight I will
   rise to | give you thanks,
   because of your | righteous judgements.

32 ₆₃ I am a companion
   of all | those who fear you,
   those who keep | your commandments.
   ₆₄ The earth, O Lord,
   is full of your | faithful love;
   instruct me | in your statutes.

9 Teth

33 ₆₅ You have dealt
   graciously | with your servant,
   according to your | word, O Lord.
   ₆₆ O teach me true
   understand | ing and knowledge,
   for I have trusted
   in | your commandments.

34 ₆₇ Before I was afflicted I | went astray,
   but now I | keep your word.
   ₆₈ You are gracious | and do good;
   O Lord, teach | me your statutes.

35 ₆₉ The proud have
   smeared | me with lies,
   but I will keep your commandments
   with | my whole heart.
   ₇₀ Their heart has become | gross with fat,
   but my delight is | in your law.

36 *71* It is good for me that I have | been afflicted,
    that I may | learn your statutes.
  72 The law of your mouth is dear | er to me
    than a hoard of | gold and silver.

10 Yodh

37 *73* Your hands have made | me and fashioned me;
    give me understanding,
    that I may learn | your commandments.
  74 Those who fear you
    will be glad | when they see me,
    because I have hoped | in your word.

38 *75* I know, O Lord,
    that your judge | ments are right,
    and that in very faithfulness
    you caused me | to be troubled.
  76 Let your faithful love | be my comfort,
    according to your promise | to your servant.

39 *77* Let your tender mercies come to me,
    that | I may live,
    for your law is | my delight.
  78 Let the proud be put to shame,
    for they wrong | me with lies;
    but I will meditate on | your commandments.

40 *79* Let those who fear you | turn to me,
    even those who | know your testimonies.
  80 Let my heart be sound | in your statutes,
    that I may not be | put to shame.

11 Kaph

41 *81* My soul is pining for | your salvation;
    I have hoped | in your word.
  82 My eyes fail with watching | for your word,
    while I say, 'O when | will you comfort me?'

42 *83* I have become like a wineskin | in the smoke,
    yet I do not for | get your statutes.
  84 How many are the days | of your servant?
    When will you bring judgement
    on | those who persecute me?

43 *85* The proud | have dug pits for me
    in defiance | of your law.
  86 All your command | ments are true;
    help me, for they
    persecute | me with falsehood.

44 *87* They had almost made an
    end of | me on earth,
    but I have not forsaken
    | your commandments.
  88 Give me life according
    to your | loving-kindness;
    so shall I keep the testimonies | of your mouth.

12 Lamedh

45 *89* O Lord, your word is | everlasting;
    it ever stands firm | in the heavens.
  90 Your faithfulness also remains
    from one generation | to another;
    you have established the earth
    and | it abides.

46 *91* So also your judgements
    stand | firm this day,
    for all things | are your servants.
  92 If your law had not been | my delight,
    I should have perished | in my trouble.

47 *93* I will never forget | your commandments,
    for by them you have gi | ven me life.
  94 I am | yours, O save me!
    For I have sought | your commandments.

48 *95* The wicked have waited for me
    | to destroy me,
    but I will meditate | on your testimonies.
  96 I have seen an end of | all perfection,
    but your commandment | knows no bounds.

13 Mem

49 *97* Lord, how I | love your law!
    All the day long it | is my study.
  98 Your commandments have
    made me wiser | than my enemies,
    for they are | ever with me.

50 *99* I have more understanding
    than | all my teachers,
    for your testimonies are my | meditation.
  100 I am wiser | than the aged,
    because I keep | your commandments.

51 *101* I restrain my feet from every | evil way,
    that I may | keep your word.
  102 I have not turned aside
    | from your judgements,
    for you have | been my teacher.

52 *103* How sweet are your words | on my tongue!
    They are sweeter than honey | to my mouth.
  104 Through your commandments
    I get | understanding;
    therefore I hate all | lying ways.

Psalm 119 (continued)

Richard Lloyd

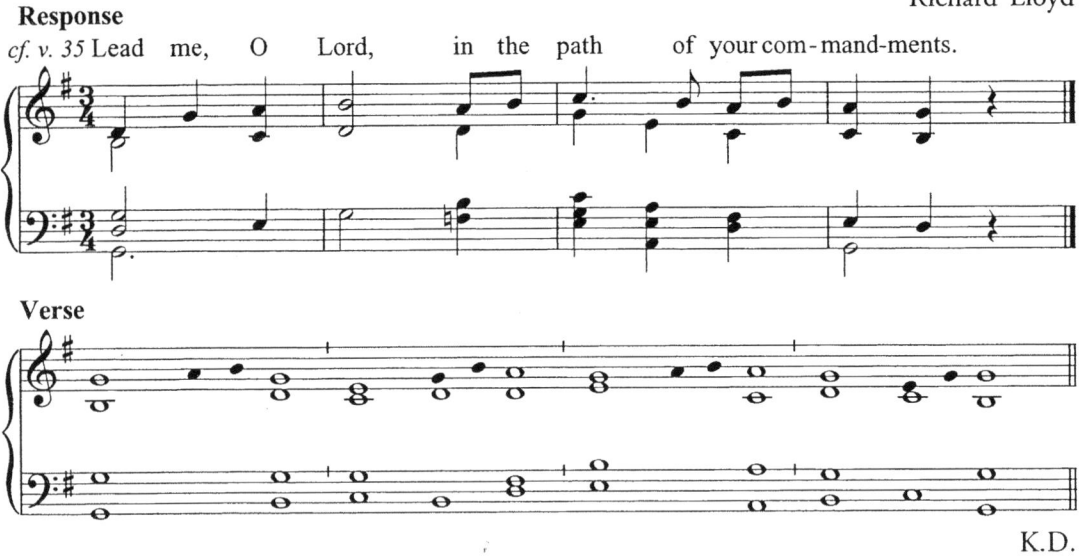

Response
cf. v. 35 Lead me, O Lord, in the path of your commandments.

Verse

K.D.

14 Nun

53 105 Your word is a lantern | to my feet
 and a light u | pon my path.
 106 I have sworn and | will fulfil it,
 to keep your | righteous judgements.

54 107 I am troubled | above measure;
 give me life, O Lord,
 according | to your word.
 108 Accept the freewill offering of my
 | mouth, O Lord,
 and teach | me your judgements.

55 109 My soul is ever | in my hand,
 yet I do not for | get your law.
 110 The wicked have | laid a snare for me,
 but I have not strayed from
 | your commandments.

56 111 Your testimonies have I
 claimed as my heri | tage for ever;
 for they are the very joy | of my heart.
 112 I have applied my heart
 to ful | fil your statutes:
 always, even | to the end.

15 Samekh

57 113 I hate those who are | double-minded,
 but your law | do I love.
 114 You are my hiding place | and my shield
 and my hope is | in your word.

58 115 Away from | me, you wicked!
 I will keep the commandments | of my God.
 116 Sustain me according
 to your promise, that | I may live,
 and let me not be disappointed | in my hope.

59 117 Hold me up and I | shall be saved,
 and my delight shall be
 ever | in your statutes.
 118 You set at nought those
 who depart | from your statutes,
 for their deceiving | is in vain.

60 119 You consider all the wic | ked as dross;
 therefore I | love your testimonies.
 120 My flesh trem | bles for fear of you
 and I am afraid | of your judgements.

16 Ayin

61 121 I have done what is | just and right;
 O give me not over to | my oppressors.
 122 Stand surety for your | servant's good;
 let not the | proud oppress me.

62 123 My eyes fail with watching
 for | your salvation
 and for your | righteous promise.
 124 O deal with your servant
 according to your | faithful love
 and teach | me your statutes.

63 *125* I am your servant;
O grant me | understanding,
that I may | know your testimonies.
126 It is time for you to | act, O Lord,
for they frus | trate your law.

64 *127* Therefore I love | your commandments
above gold, even | much fine gold.
128 Therefore I direct my steps
by | all your precepts,
and all false ways I utter | ly abhor.

17 Pe

65 *129* Your testimo | nies are wonderful;
therefore | my soul keeps them.
130 The opening of your | word gives light;
it gives understanding | to the simple.

66 *131* I open my mouth and draw | in my breath,
as I long for | your commandments.
132 Turn to me and be gra | cious to me,
as is your way with those
who | love your name.

67 *133* Order my steps | by your word,
and let no wickedness
have do | minion over me.
134 Redeem me from earth | ly oppressors
so that I may keep | your commandments.

68 *135* Show the light of your countenance
u | pon your servant
and teach | me your statutes.
136 My eyes run down with | streams of water,
because the wicked do not | keep your law.

18 Tsadhe

69 *137* Righteous are | you, O Lord,
and true | are your judgements.
138 You have ordered
your de | crees in righteousness
and | in great faithfulness.

70 *139* My indigna | tion destroys me,
because my adversaries for | get your word.
140 Your word has been tried | to the uttermost
and so your | servant loves it.

71 *141* I am small and of no | reputation,
yet do I not forget | your commandments.
142 Your righteousness
is an ever | lasting righteousness
and your law | is the truth.

72 *143* Trouble and heaviness
have taken | hold upon me,
yet my delight is in | your commandments.
144 The righteousness of
your testimonies is | everlasting;
O grant me understanding and | I shall live.

19 Qoph

73 *145* I call with | my whole heart;
answer me, O Lord,
that I may | keep your statutes.
146 To you I | call, O save me!
And I shall | keep your testimonies.

74 *147* Early in the morning I | cry to you,
for in your word | is my trust.
148 My eyes are open before | the night watches,
that I may meditate | on your word.

75 *149* Hear my voice, O Lord,
according to your | faithful love;
according to your judgement,
| give me life.
150 They draw near that in
| malice persecute me,
who are far | from your law.

76 *151* You, O Lord, are | near at hand,
and all your command | ments are true.
152 Long have I known | of your testimonies,
that you have founded | them for ever.

20 Resh

77 *153* O consider my affliction | and deliver me,
for I do not for | get your law.
154 Plead my cause | and redeem me;
according to your promise, | give me life.

78 *155* Salvation is far | from the wicked,
for they do not | seek your statutes.
156 Great is your compas | sion, O Lord;
give me life, according | to your judgements.

79 *157* Many there are that persecute | and oppress me,
yet do I not swerve | from your testimonies.
158 It grieves me when I | see the treacherous,
for they do not | keep your word.

80 *159* Consider, O Lord,
how I love | your commandments;
give me life according to your | loving-kindness.
160 The sum of your | word is truth,
and all your righteous judgements
endure for | evermore.

Psalm 119 (continued)

Richard Lloyd

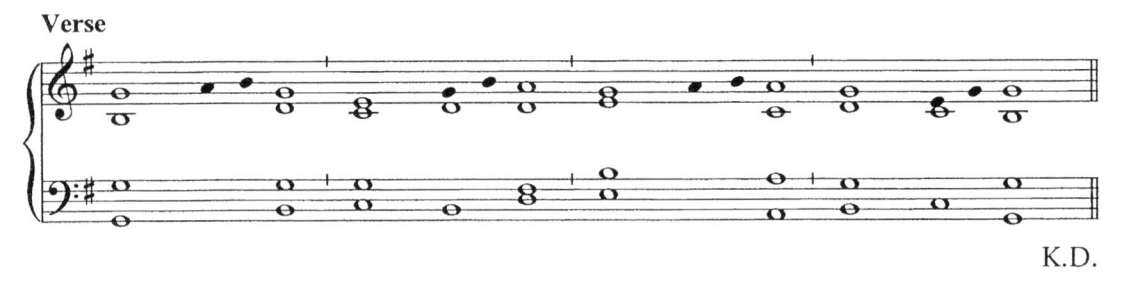

Response (cf. v. 35) Lead me, O Lord, in the path of your commandments.

Verse

K.D.

21 Shin

81 ¹⁶¹ Princes have persecuted
me with | out a cause,
but my heart stands in awe | of your word.
¹⁶² I am as glad | of your word
as one who | finds great spoils.

82 ¹⁶³ As for lies, I hate | and abhor them,
but your law | do I love.
¹⁶⁴ Seven times a day | do I praise you,
because of your | righteous judgements.

83 ¹⁶⁵ Great peace have they who | love your law;
nothing shall | make them stumble.
¹⁶⁶ Lord, I have looked for | your salvation
and I have fulfilled | your commandments.

84 ¹⁶⁷ My soul has | kept your testimonies
and greatly | have I loved them.
¹⁶⁸ I have kept your command
| ments and testimonies,
for all my ways | are before you.

22 Taw

85 ¹⁶⁹ Let my cry come before | you, O Lord;
give me understanding,
according | to your word.
¹⁷⁰ Let my supplication | come before you;
deliver me, according | to your promise.

86 ¹⁷¹ My lips shall pour | forth your praise,
when you have taught | me your statutes.
¹⁷² My tongue shall sing | of your word,
for all your command | ments are righteous.

87 ¹⁷³ Let your hand reach | out to help me,
for I have chosen | your commandments.
¹⁷⁴ I have longed for your salva | tion, O Lord,
and your law is | my delight.

88 ¹⁷⁵ Let my soul live and | it shall praise you,
and let your judgements | be my help.
¹⁷⁶ I have gone astray like a sheep | that is lost;
O seek your servant, for I do not
forget | your commandments.

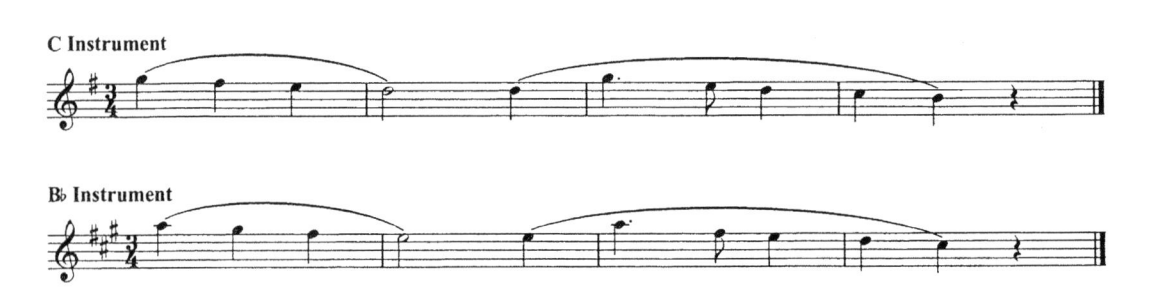

C Instrument

B♭ Instrument

Psalm 120

PRINCIPAL SERVICE   2ND SERVICE   3RD SERVICE
Proper 18 C
Proper 21 AB

Response   Geoff Nobes
cf. v. 1 In my trou-ble I called to the Lord.

Verse

T.B.

1 *1* When I was in trouble I called | to the Lord;
    I called to the Lord | and he answered me.
  2 Deliver me, O Lord, from | lying lips
    and from a de | ceitful tongue.

2 *3* What | shall be given to you?
    What more shall be done to you, de | ceitful tongue?
  4 The sharp arrows of a warrior,
    tempered in | burning coals!
  5 Woe is me, that I must lodge in Meshech
    and dwell among the | tents of Kedar.

3 *6* My soul has | dwelt too long
    with ene | mies of peace.
  7 I am for | making peace,
    but when I speak of it, they make rea | dy for war.

C Instrument

B♭ Instrument

Psalm 121

PRINCIPAL SERVICE
2 Lent A
Proper 24 C (related)

2ND SERVICE
Proper 18 C
Proper 21 B

3RD SERVICE

Andrew Moore

Response

v. 2 My help comes from the Lord, the mak-er of heav'n and earth.

Verse

T.B.

1. 1 I lift up my eyes | to the hills;
   from where is my | help to come?
   2 My help comes | from the Lord,
   the maker of hea | ven and earth.

2. 3 He will not suffer your | foot to stumble;
   he who watches over you | will not sleep.
   4 Behold, he who keeps watch | over Israel
   shall neither slum | ber nor sleep.

3. 5 The Lord himself | watches over you;
   the Lord is your shade | at your right hand,
   6 So that the sun shall not strike | you by day,
   neither the | moon by night.

4. 7 The Lord shall keep you | from all evil;
   it is he who shall | keep your soul.
   8 The Lord shall keep watch over your going out
   and your | coming in,
   from this time forth for | evermore.

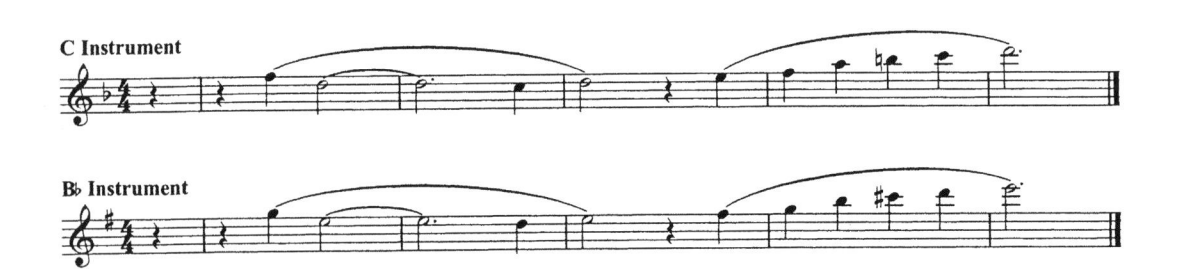

C Instrument

B♭ Instrument

Psalm 122

PRINCIPAL SERVICE
1 Advent A
Dedication ABC

2ND SERVICE
Presentation ABC

3RD SERVICE
Proper 18 C
Proper 21 B

Andrew Wright

Response

cf. v. 1   I was glad when they said, 'Let us go to the house of the Lord.'

Verse

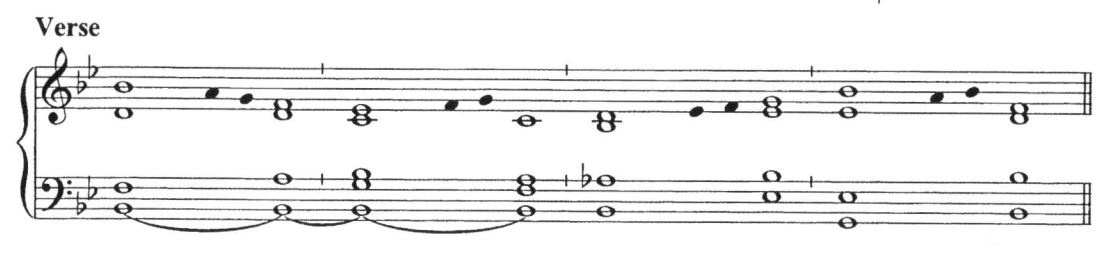

S.L.

1   *1* I was glad | when they said to me,
     'Let us go to the house | of the Lord.'
   2 And now our | feet are standing
     within your gates, | O Jerusalem;

2   *3* Jerusalem, built as a city
     that is at unity | in itself.
   4 Thither the tribes go up, the tribes | of the Lord,
     as is decreed for Israel,
     to give thanks to the name | of the Lord.
   5 For there are set the thrones of judgement,
     the thrones of the | house of David.

3   *6* O pray for the peace | of Jerusalem:
     'May they pros | per who love you.
   7 'Peace be with | in your walls
     and tranquillity with | in your palaces.'

4   *8* For my kindred and com | panions' sake,
     I will pray that | peace be with you.
   9 For the sake of the house of the | Lord our God,
     I will seek to | do you good.

C Instrument

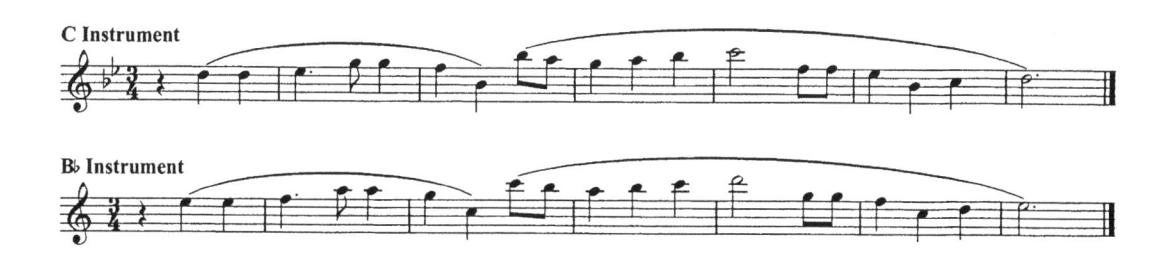

B♭ Instrument

Psalm 123

PRINCIPAL SERVICE
Proper 9 B (related)

2ND SERVICE
4 Advent C
Proper 21 A

3RD SERVICE
Proper 18 C
Proper 22 B

Keith Duke

Response

v. 4a Have mer-cy up-on us, O Lord, have mer - cy.

Verse

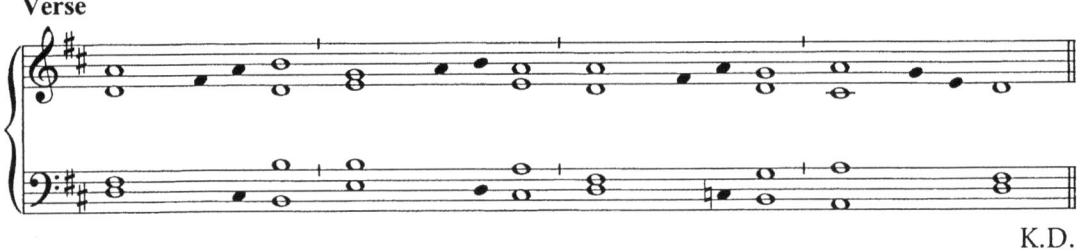

K.D.

1 *1* To you I lift up my eyes,
 to you that are enthroned | in the heavens.
 2 As the eyes of servants look to the hand | of their master,
 or the eyes of a maid to the hand | of her mistress,
 3 So our eyes wait upon the Lord our God,
 until he have mer | cy upon us.

2 *4* Have mercy upon us, O Lord, have mer | cy upon us,
 for we have had more than enough | of contempt.
 5 Our soul has had more than enough of the scorn | of the arrogant,
 and of the contempt | of the proud.

C Instrument

B♭ Instrument

Psalm 124

PRINCIPAL SERVICE
Proper 16 A
Proper 21 B

2ND SERVICE
Proper 19 C
Proper 21 A

3RD SERVICE
Proper 22 B

Colin Mawby

Response

cf. v. 7 Our help is in the name of the Lord, who made hea-ven and earth.

Verse

T.B.

1 ₁ If the Lord himself had not been on our side,
   now may Is | rael say;
 ₂ If the Lord had not been on our side,
   when enemies rose | up against us;
 ₃ Then would they have swallowed | us alive
   when their anger | burned against us;

2 ₄ Then would the waters have overwhelmed us
   and the torrent gone o | ver our soul;
   over our soul would have swept the | raging waters.
 ₅ But blessed | be the Lord
   who has not given us over to be a prey | for their teeth.

3 ₆ Our soul has escaped
   as a bird from the snare | of the fowler;
   the snare is broken and we | are delivered.
 ₇ Our help is in the name | of the Lord,
   who has made hea | ven and earth.

C Instrument

B♭ Instrument

Psalm 125

PRINCIPAL SERVICE
Proper 18 B

2ND SERVICE
Proper 19 C
Proper 22 B

3RD SERVICE
Proper 21 A

Andrew Wright

Response

cf. v. 1 Those who trust in the Lord are like Mount Zi - on that stands for e - ver.

Verse

* *Omit in verse 2*

K.D.

1 *1* Those who trust in the Lord are | like Mount Zion,
which cannot be moved, but stands | fast for ever.
2 As the hills stand about Jerusalem,
so the Lord stands round a | bout his people,
from this time forth for | evermore.

2 *3* The sceptre of wickedness shall | not hold sway
over the land allotted | to the righteous,
lest the righteous turn their | hands to evil.

3 *4* Do good, O Lord, to those | who are good,
and to those who are | true of heart.
5 Those who turn aside to crooked ways
the Lord shall take away with the | evildoers;
but let there be peace | upon Israel.

C Instrument

B♭ Instrument

Psalm 126

PRINCIPAL SERVICE
3 Advent B
5 Lent C
Proper 25 B (related)

2ND SERVICE
4 Advent A
6 Easter C
Proper 22 B

3RD SERVICE
Proper 19 C
Proper 21 A

Keith Duke

Response

cf. v. 4 The Lord has done great things for us and we rejoiced.

Verse

G.N.

1 *1* When the Lord restored the for | tunes of Zion,
   then were we like | those who dream.
  2 Then was our mouth | filled with laughter
   and our tongue with | songs of joy.

2 *3* Then said they among the nations,
   'The Lord has done great | things for them.'
  4 The Lord has indeed done great things for us,
   and therefore | we rejoiced.
  5 Restore again our for | tunes, O Lord,
   as the river beds | of the desert.

3 *6* Those who | sow in tears
   shall reap with | songs of joy.
  7 Those who go out weeping, bear | ing the seed,
   will come back with shouts of joy,
   bear | ing their sheaves with them.

C Instrument

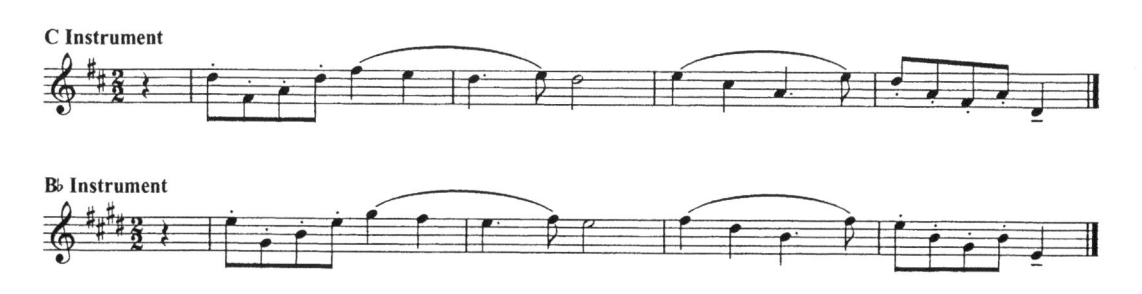

B♭ Instrument

Psalm 127

PRINCIPAL SERVICE
Mothering Sunday ABC (vs. 1-4)

2ND SERVICE
6 Easter C
Proper 23 B

3RD SERVICE
Proper 19 C
Proper 21 A

Andrew Moore

Response

v. 4 Child-ren are a he-ri-tage from the Lord.

Verse

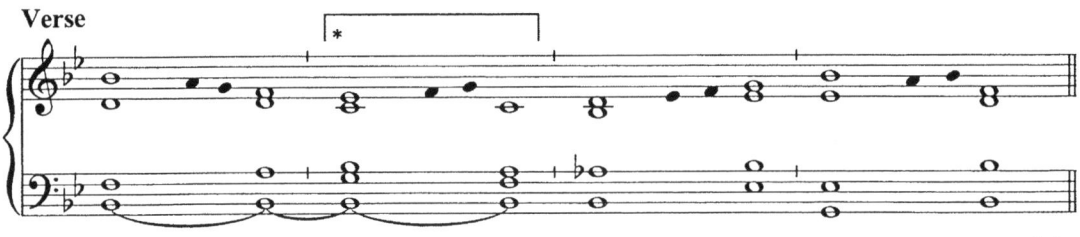

* Omit in verses 2 and 4

S.L.

1 *1* Unless the Lord | builds the house,
   those who build it la | bour in vain.
 2 Unless the Lord | keeps the city,
   the guard keeps | watch in vain.

2 *3* It is in vain that you hasten to | rise up early
   and go so late to rest, eating the | bread of toil,
   for he gives his be | loved sleep.

3 *4* Children are a heritage | from the Lord
   and the fruit of the womb | is his gift.
 5 Like arrows in the hand | of a warrior,
   so are the children | of one's youth.

4 *6* Happy are those who have their | quiver full of them:
   they shall not be | put to shame
   when they dispute with their enemies | in the gate.

C Instrument

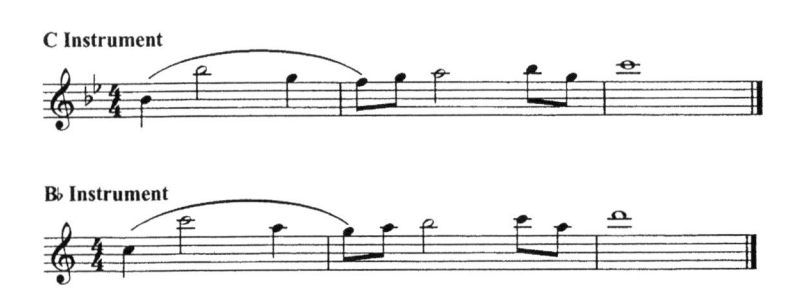

B♭ Instrument

Psalm 128

PRINCIPAL SERVICE
3 Epiphany B
Proper 12 A

2ND SERVICE
Proper 20 C
Proper 23 B

3RD SERVICE
Proper 22 A

Colin Mawby

Response

cf. v. 5 May the Lord bless you all the days of your life.

* F♮ last time only

Verse

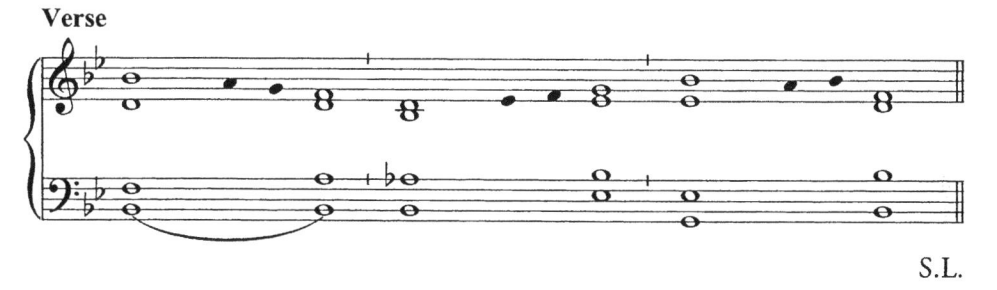

S.L.

1 *1* Blessed are all those who fear the Lord,
   and walk | in his ways.
  2 You shall eat the fruit of the toil | of your hands;
   it shall go well with you, and happy | shall you be.

2 *3* Your wife within your house
   shall be like a | fruitful vine;
   your children round your table,
   like fresh | olive branches.
  4 Thus shall the one be blest
   who | fears the Lord.

3 *5* The Lord from out of | Zion bless you,
   that you may see Jerusalem in prosperity
   all the days | of your life.
  6 May you see your children's children,
   and may there be peace | upon Israel.

C Instrument

B♭ Instrument

Psalm 129

PRINCIPAL SERVICE

2ND SERVICE
Proper 20 C

3RD SERVICE
Proper 22 A
Proper 23 B

Richard Lloyd

Response

v. 8a The blessing of the Lord be upon you.

Verse

C.M.

1 *1* 'Many a time have they fought against me from my youth,'
   may Isra | el now say;
   2 'Many a time have they fought against me | from my youth,
   but they have not pre | vailed against me.'

2 *3* The ploughers ploughed u | pon my back
   and made their | furrows long.
   4 But the righteous Lord
   has cut the cords of the wic | ked in pieces.

3 *5* Let them be put to shame and turned backwards,
   as many as are ene | mies of Zion.
   6 Let them be like grass upon the housetops,
   which withers before | it can grow,
   7 So that no reaper can fill his hand,
   nor a binder of | sheaves his bosom;

4 *8* And none who go | by may say,
   'The blessing of the Lord | be upon you.
   We bless you in the name | of the Lord.'

C Instrument

B♭ Instrument

Psalm 130

PRINCIPAL SERVICE
5 Lent A
Proper 5 B (related)
Proper 8 B
Proper 14 B

2ND SERVICE
Good Friday ABC

3RD SERVICE
Proper 20 C
Proper 23 B

Andrew Wright

Response

v. 1 Out of the depths have I cried to you, O Lord.

Verse

S.L.

1. *1* Out of the depths have I cried to | you, O Lord;
   Lord, | hear my voice;
   let your ears con | sider well
   the voice of my | supplication.

2. *2* If you, Lord, were to mark what is | done amiss,
   O Lord, | who could stand?
   3 But there is forgive | ness with you,
   so that you | shall be feared.

3. *4* I wait for the Lord; | my soul waits for him;
   in his word | is my hope.
   5 My soul waits for the Lord,
   more than the night watch | for the morning,
   more than the night watch | for the morning.

4. *6* O Israel, wait | for the Lord,
   for with the Lord | there is mercy;
   7 With him is plente | ous redemption
   and he shall redeem Israel from | all their sins.

C Instrument

B♭ Instrument

New Psalms for Common Worship

Psalm 131

PRINCIPAL SERVICE   **2ND SERVICE**   **3RD SERVICE**
                                  4 Advent BC   Proper 20 C

Response — Gerry Fitzpatrick

cf. v. 3a   I have stilled and quiet-ed my soul.

Verse

K.D.

1 *1* O Lord, my heart | is not proud;
      my eyes are not raised in | haughty looks.
   2 I do not occupy myself | with great matters,
      with things that | are too high for me.

2 *3* But I have quieted and stilled my soul,
      like a weaned child on its | mother's breast;
      so my soul is quiet | ed within me.
   4 O Israel, trust | in the Lord,
      from this time forth for | evermore.

C Instrument

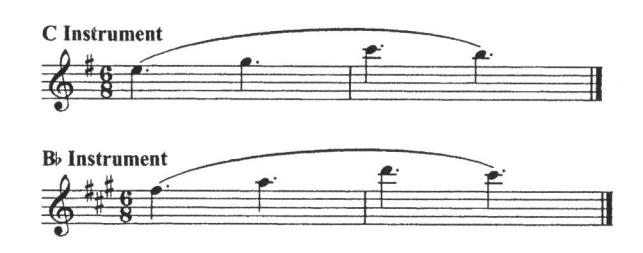

B♭ Instrument

Psalm 132

PRINCIPAL SERVICE

2ND SERVICE
1 Christmas ABC
Presentation ABC
Dedication ABC

3RD SERVICE
Epiphany ABC
Proper 21 C
2 before Advent C

Response
cf. vs. 14, 15

Colin Mawby

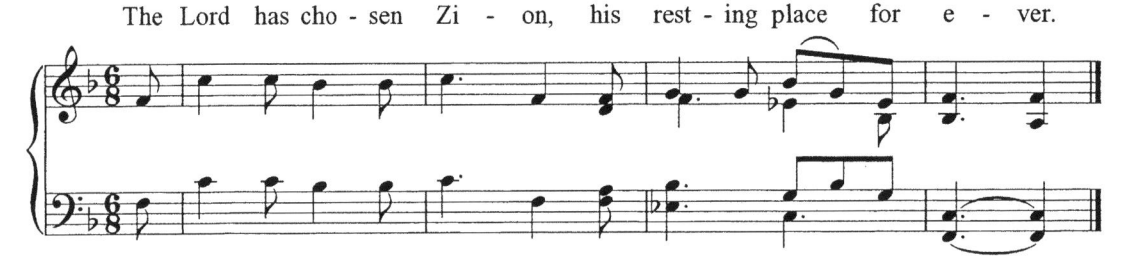

The Lord has cho-sen Zi - on, his rest-ing place for e - ver.

Verse

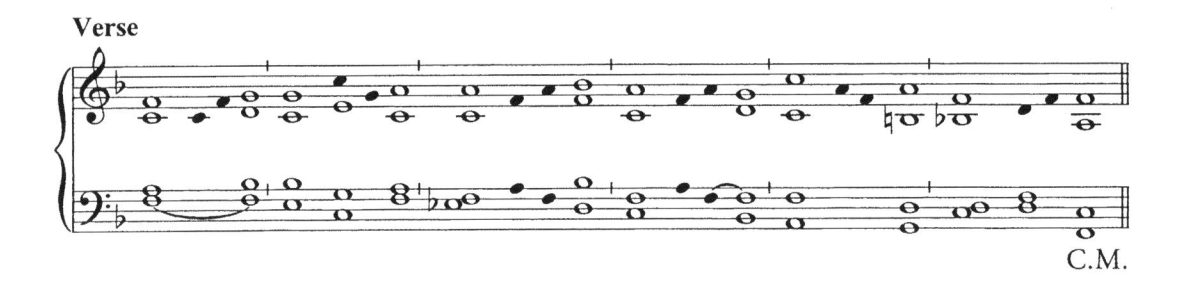

C.M.

1 *1* Lord, remember for David
　　all the hardships | he endured;
　2 How he swore an oath to the Lord
　　and vowed a vow to the Mighty | One of Jacob:
　3 'I will not come within the shelter of my house,
　　nor climb up in | to my bed;
　4 'I will not allow my eyes to sleep,
　　nor let my | eyelids slumber,
　5 'Until I find a place | for the Lord,
　　a dwelling for the Mighty | One of Jacob.'

2 *6* Now, we heard of the ark in Ephrathah
　　and found it in the | fields of Ja-ar.
　7 Let us enter his dwelling place
　　and fall low be | fore his footstool.
　8 Arise, O Lord, in | to your resting place,
　　you and the ark | of your strength.
　9 Let your priests be clothed with righteousness
　　and your faithful ones | sing with joy.
　10 For your servant David's sake,
　　turn not away the face of | your anointed.

3 *11* The Lord has sworn an | oath to David,
    a promise from which he | will not shrink:
 12 'Of the fruit | of your body
    shall I set u | pon your throne.
 13 'If your children keep my covenant and
    my testimonies that | I shall teach them,
    their children also shall
    sit upon your throne for | evermore.'

4 *14* For the Lord has chosen Zion | for himself;
    he has desired her for his | habitation:
 15 'This shall be my resting | place for ever;
    here will I dwell, for | I have longed for her.
 16 'I will abundantly bless | her provision;
    her poor will I satis | fy with bread.

5 *17* 'I will clothe her priests | with salvation,
    and her faithful ones shall re | joice and sing.
 18 'There will I make a horn to spring | up for David;
    I will keep a lantern burning for | my anointed.
 19 'As for his enemies, I will clothe | them with shame;
    but on him shall his | crown be bright.'

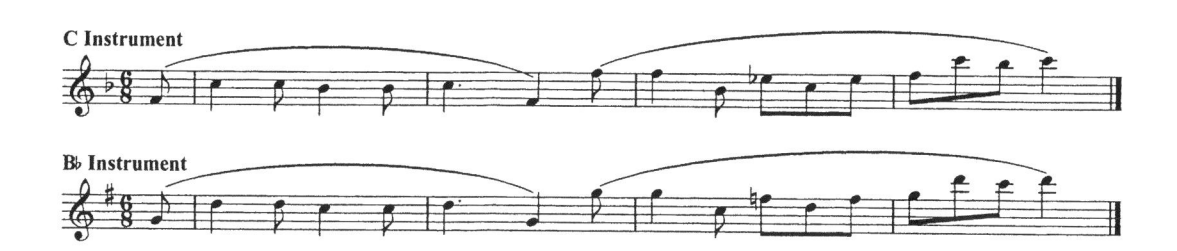

Psalm 133

PRINCIPAL SERVICE
2 Easter B
Proper 7 B
Proper 15 A

2ND SERVICE
Pentecost A

3RD SERVICE
Proper 24 B

John McCann

Response

cf. v. 5 The Lord's blessing is life for ever.

Verse

C.M.

1 1 Behold how good and plea | sant it is
to dwell toge | ther in unity.

2 2 It is like the precious oil u | pon the head,
running down u | pon the beard,

3 3 Even on | Aaron's beard,
running down upon the collar | of his clothing.

4 4 It is like the dew of Hermon
running down upon the | hills of Zion.
5 For there the Lord has promised his blessing:
even life for | evermore.

C Instrument

B♭ Instrument

Psalm 134

PRINCIPAL SERVICE

2ND SERVICE
Proper 21 C

3RD SERVICE
Proper 22 A
Proper 24 B

Alan Rees

Response
cf. v. 3 May the Lord bless you out of Zi-on.

Verse

A.M.

1 *1* Come, bless the Lord, all you servants | of the Lord,
you that by night stand in the house | of the Lord.

2 *2* Lift up your hands to | wards the sanctuary
and | bless the Lord.

3 *3* The Lord who made hea | ven and earth
give you blessing | out of Zion.

C Instrument

B♭ Instrument

Psalm 135

Verses 15-21 are omitted

PRINCIPAL SERVICE   2ND SERVICE   3RD SERVICE
                                    2 Christmas ABC
                                    2 Lent ABC
                                    Proper 21 C

Richard Lloyd

Response

cf. v. 3 Praise the Lord for he is good.

Verse

C.M.

1 *1* (Alleluia.)
   Praise the name of the Lord;
   give praise, you servants | of the Lord,
 2 You that stand in the house of the Lord,
   in the courts of the house | of our God.
 3 Praise the Lord, for the | Lord is good;
   make music to his name, for | it is lovely.
 4 For the Lord has chosen Jacob | for himself
   and Israel for his | own possession.

2 *5* For I know that the | Lord is great
   and that our Lord is a | bove all gods.
 6 The Lord does whatever he pleases
   in heaven | and on earth,
   in the seas and in | all the deeps.
 7 He brings up the clouds from the ends | of the earth;
   he makes lightning with the rain
   and brings the winds out | of his treasuries.

3 *8* He smote the firstborn of Egypt,
   the firstborn of | man and beast.
 9 He sent signs and wonders into your | midst, O Egypt,
   upon Pharaoh and | all his servants.
 10 He smote many nations
   and slew | mighty kings:
 11 Sihon, king of the Amorites,
   and Og, the | king of Bashan,
   and all the king | doms of Canaan.

4 *12* He gave their land | as a heritage,
   a heritage for Isra | el his people.
 13 Your name, O Lord, en | dures for ever
   and shall be remembered through all | generations.
 14 For the Lord will vindi | cate his people
   and have compassion | on his servants.

Psalm 136

This psalm is sung as a litany

PRINCIPAL SERVICE
2 before Lent A (vs. 1-9, 22-26)

2ND SERVICE
Proper 22 A (vs. 1-9)

3RD SERVICE
2 Easter C (vs. 1-16)
3 before Advent B

Also: Easter Vigil ABC (vs. 1-9, 23-26)

Keith Duke

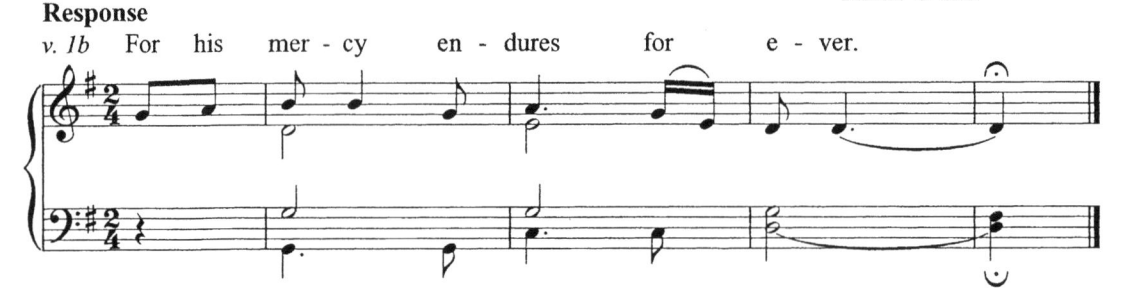

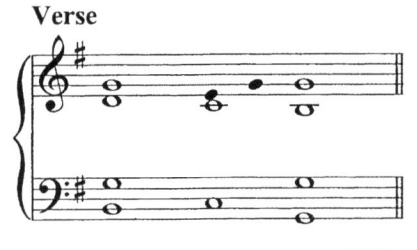

Response

v. 1b For his mercy endures for ever.

Verse

K.D.

1 Give thanks to the Lord, for | he is gracious,
   for his mercy endures for ever.
2 Give thanks to the | God of gods,
   for his mercy endures for ever.
3 Give thanks to the | Lord of lords,
   for his mercy endures for ever;
4 Who alone | does great wonders,
   for his mercy endures for ever;
5 Who by wisdom | made the heavens,
   for his mercy endures for ever;
6 Who laid out the earth u | pon the waters,
   for his mercy endures for ever;
7 Who made | the great lights,
   for his mercy endures for ever;
8 The sun to | rule the day,
   for his mercy endures for ever;
9 The moon and the stars to go | vern the night,
   for his mercy endures for ever;
10 Who smote the first | born of Egypt,
   for his mercy endures for ever;
11 And brought out Israel | from among them,
   for his mercy endures for ever;
12 With a mighty hand and | outstretched arm,
   for his mercy endures for ever;
13 Who divided the Red | Sea in two,
   for his mercy endures for ever;

14 And made Israel to pass | through the midst of it,
   for his mercy endures for ever;
15 But Pharaoh and his host he overthrew in | the Red Sea,
   for his mercy endures for ever;
16 Who led his people | through the wilderness,
   for his mercy endures for ever;
17 Who | smote great kings,
   for his mercy endures for ever;
18 And slew | mighty kings,
   for his mercy endures for ever;
19 Sihon, king | of the Amorites,
   for his mercy endures for ever;
20 And Og, the | king of Bashan,
   for his mercy endures for ever;
21 And gave away their land | for a heritage,
   for his mercy endures for ever;
22 A heritage for Isra | el his servant,
   for his mercy endures for ever;
23 Who remembered us when we | were in trouble,
   for his mercy endures for ever;
24 And delivered us | from our enemies,
   for his mercy endures for ever;
25 Who gives food | to all creatures,
   for his mercy endures for ever.
26 Give thanks to the | God of heaven,
   for his mercy endures for ever.

C Instrument

B♭ Instrument

Psalm 137

Verses 7-9 are omitted

PRINCIPAL SERVICE   2ND SERVICE   3RD SERVICE
Proper 22 C   Proper 24 B

Simon Lesley

Response

v. 4 How shall we sing the Lord's song in a strange land?

Verse

T.B.

1 *1* By the waters of Babylon we sat | down and wept,
    when we re | membered Zion.
 2 As for our lyres, we hung them up
    on the willows that grow | in that land.

2 *3* For there our captors asked | for a song,
    our tormentors | called for mirth:
    'Sing us one of the | songs of Zion.'

3 *4* How shall we sing the Lord's song
    in | a strange land?
 5 If I forget you, | O Jerusalem,
    let my right hand for | get its skill.

4 *6* Let my tongue cleave to the roof | of my mouth
    if I do | not remember you,
    if I set not Jerusalem above my | highest joy.

C Instrument

B♭ Instrument

Psalm 138

PRINCIPAL SERVICE
Proper 1 C
Proper 5 B
Proper 12 C (related)
Proper 16 A (related)

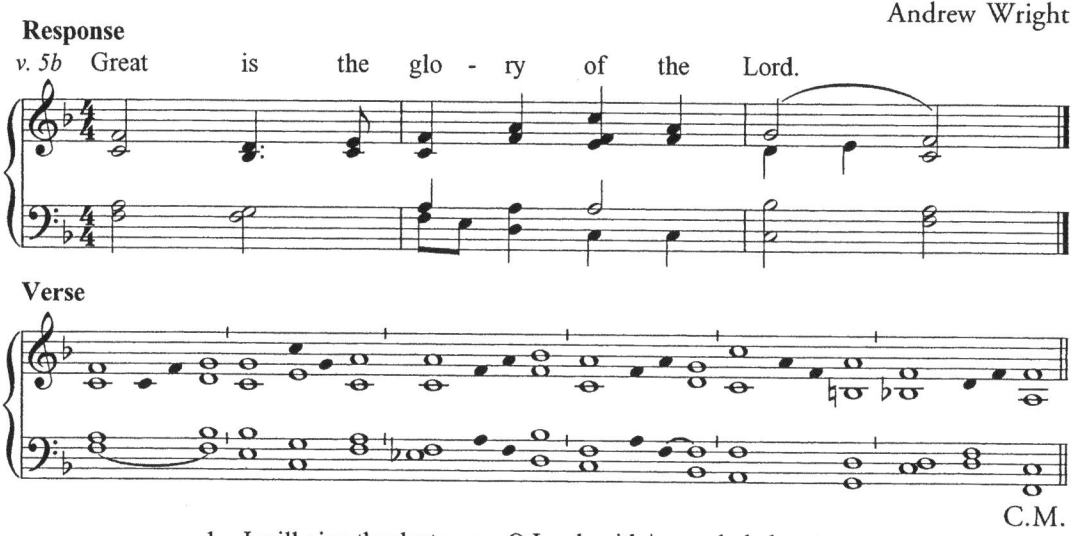

2ND SERVICE

3RD SERVICE
Proper 23 A

Andrew Wright

Response

v. 5b Great is the glo-ry of the Lord.

Verse

C.M.

1 *1* I will give thanks to you, O Lord, with | my whole heart;
   before the gods will | I sing praise to you.
  2 I will bow down towards your holy temple and praise your name,
   because of your | love and faithfulness;
   for you have glorified your name
   and your word a | bove all things.
  3 In the day that I called to | you, you answered me;
   you put new strength | in my soul.

2 *4* All the kings of the earth shall praise | you, O Lord,
   for they have heard the words | of your mouth.
  5 They shall sing of the ways | of the Lord,
   that great is the glory | of the Lord.
  6 Though the Lord be high, he watches o | ver the lowly;
   as for the proud, he regards them | from afar.

3 *7* Though I walk in the midst of trouble,
   you | will preserve me;
   you will stretch forth your hand against the fury | of my enemies;
   your right | hand will save me.
  8 The Lord shall make good his pur | pose for me;
   your loving-kindness, O Lord, en | dures for ever;
   forsake not the work | of your hands.

C Instrument

B♭ Instrument

Psalm 139

Verses 19-24 are omitted

PRINCIPAL SERVICE	2ND SERVICE	3RD SERVICE
2 Epiphany B (vs. 1-5, 12-18)	Pentecost B (vs. 1-11)	
Proper 4 B (vs. 1-5, 12-18)	Proper 23 A (vs. 1-11)	
Proper 11 A (vs. 1-11)		
Proper 18 C (vs. 1-7)		

Response — John McCann

cf. v. 13 How wonderful are your works, O Lord.

Verse

G.N.

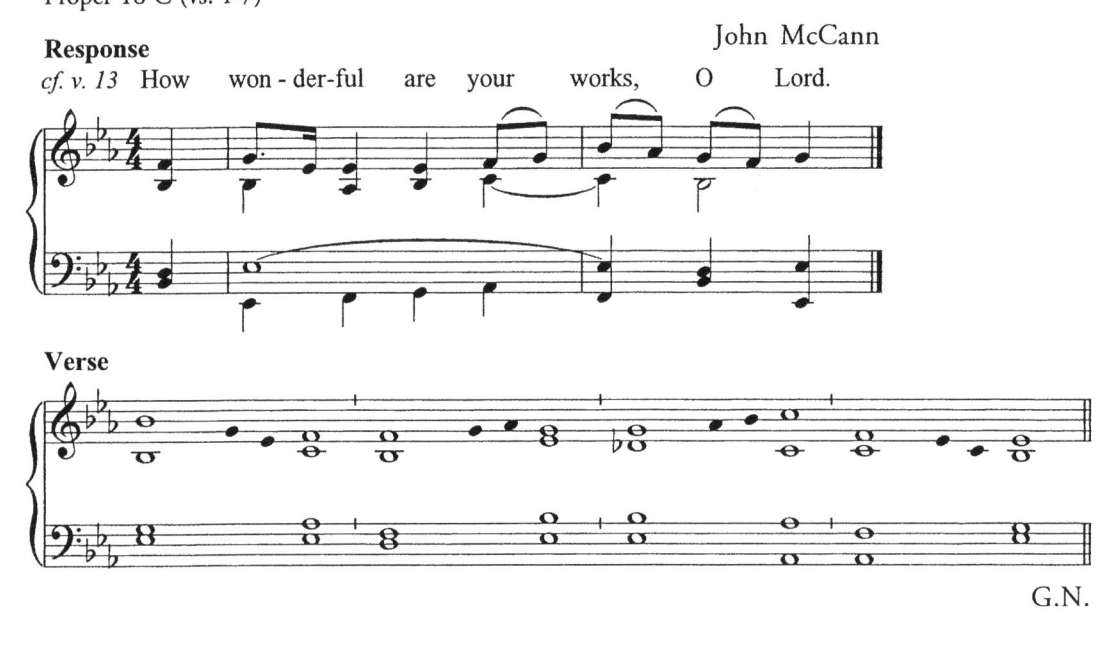

1 *1* O Lord, you have searched me out and known me;
  you know my sitting down and my | rising up;
  you discern my thoughts | from afar.
 2 You mark out my journeys | and my resting place
  and are acquainted with | all my ways.

2 *3* For there is not a word on my tongue,
  but you, O Lord, know it | altogether.
 4 You encompass me behind and before
  and lay your | hand upon me.
 5 Such knowledge | is too wonderful for me,
  so high that I can | not attain it.

3 *6* Where can I go then | from your spirit?
  Or where can I flee | from your presence?
 7 If I climb up to heaven, | you are there;
  if I make the grave my bed, you | are there also.

4 *8* If I take the wings | of the morning
  and dwell in the uttermost parts | of the sea,
 9 Even there your | hand shall lead me,
  your right hand | hold me fast.

5 *10* If I say, 'Surely the dark | ness will cover me
and the light around me | turn to night,'
  11 Even darkness is no darkness with you;
the night is as clear | as the day;
darkness and light to you are | both alike.

6 *12* For you yourself created my | inmost parts;
you knit me together in my | mother's womb.
  13 I thank you, for I am fearfully and wonder | fully made;
marvellous are your works, my | soul knows well.

7 *14* My frame was not hid | den from you,
when I was made in secret
and woven in the depths | of the earth.
  15 Your eyes beheld my form, as yet unfinished;
already in your book were all my | members written,
  16 As day by day they were fashioned
when as yet | there was none of them.

8 *17* How deep are your counsels to | me, O God!
How great is the | sum of them!
  18 If I count them, they are more in number | than the sand,
and at the end, I am still | in your presence.

Psalm 140 is omitted

Psalm 141

PRINCIPAL SERVICE   2ND SERVICE   3RD SERVICE
                                      Proper 24 B   Proper 22 C
                                                                   Proper 23 A

Geoff Nobes

Response
cf. v. 1b Hear my voice when I cry to you, O Lord.

Verse

S.L.

1 *1* O Lord, I call to you; come | to me quickly;
    hear my voice | when I cry to you.
  2 Let my prayer rise before | you as incense,
    the lifting up of my hands as the | evening sacrifice.

2 *3* Set a watch before my mouth, O Lord,
    and guard the door | of my lips;
  4 Let not my heart incline to | any evil thing;
    let me not be occupied in wicked | ness with evildoers,
    nor taste the pleasures | of their table.

3 *5* Let the | righteous smite me
    in friend | ly rebuke;
    but let not the oil of the unrighteous a | noint my head;
    for my prayer is continually against their | wicked deeds.

4 *6* Let their rulers be overthrown in | stony places;
    then they may know that my | words are sweet.
  7 As when a plough turns over the | earth in furrows,
    let their bones be scattered at the mouth | of the Pit.

5 *8* But my eyes are turned to | you, Lord God;
   in you I take refuge; do not leave | me defenceless.
  9 Protect me from the snare which they have laid for me
   and from the traps | of the evildoers.
  10 Let the wicked fall into their own nets,
   while I pass | by in safety.

New Psalms for Common Worship

Psalm 142

PRINCIPAL SERVICE   2ND SERVICE   3RD SERVICE
Easter Eve ABC
3 Easter B
Proper 22 C
Proper 24 A

Geoff Nobes

Response

cf. v. 5   I cry out to you, O Lord, 'You are my ref - uge.'

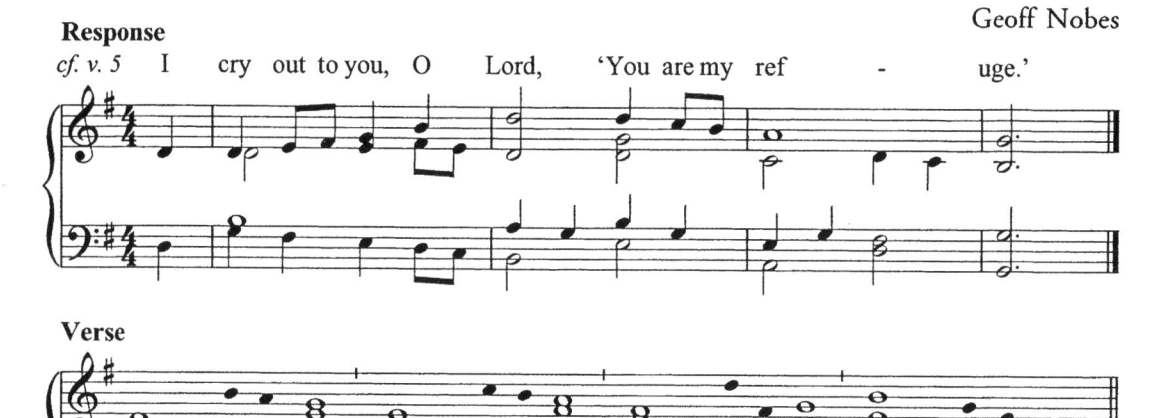

Verse

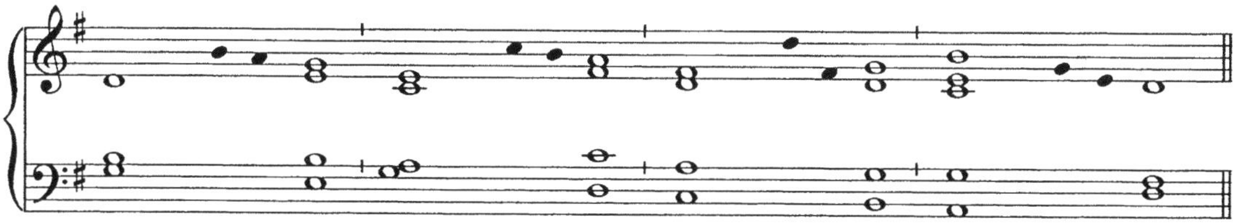

S.L.

1 *1* I cry aloud | to the Lord;
    to the Lord I make my | supplication.
  2 I pour out my com | plaint before him
    and tell him | of my trouble.

2 *3* When my spirit faints within me, you | know my path;
    in the way wherein I walk have they | laid a snare for me.
  4 I look to my right hand, and find no | one who knows me;
    I have no place to flee to, and no one cares | for my soul.

3 *5* I cry out to you, O | Lord, and say:
    'You are my refuge, my portion in the land | of the living.
  6 'Listen to my cry, for I am brought | very low;
    save me from my persecutors, for they | are too strong for me.

4 *7* 'Bring my soul | out of prison,
    that I may give thanks | to your name;
    when you have dealt bounti | fully with me,
    then shall the righteous ga | ther around me.'

C Instrument

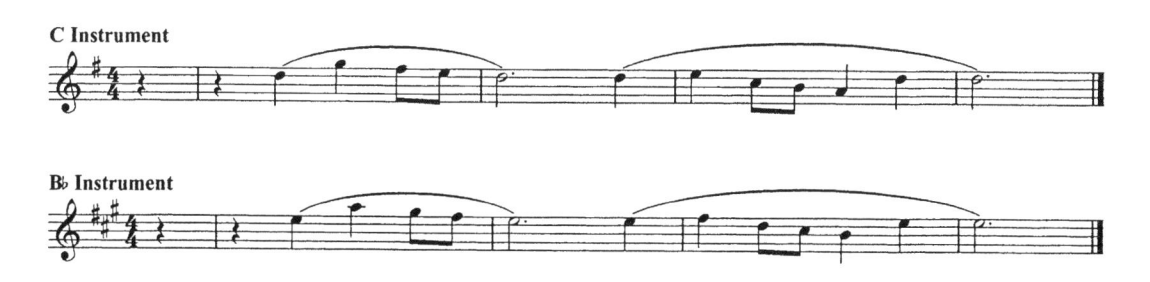

B♭ Instrument

Psalm 143

PRINCIPAL SERVICE

2ND SERVICE
Good Friday ABC
2 Easter B (vs. 1-11, 12b)
Proper 24 A (vs. 1-11, 12b)

3RD SERVICE
Proper 23 C

Also: Easter Vigil ABC

Andrew Moore

Response

v. 11 Re - vive me, O Lord, re - vive me, O Lord, for your name's sake.

Verse

*Omit in verse 6

K.D.

1 *1* Hear my prayer, O Lord,
 and in your faithfulness give ear to my | supplications;
 answer me | in your righteousness.
 2 Enter not into judgement | with your servant,
 for in your sight shall no one liv | ing be justified.

2 *3* For the enemy has pursued me,
 crushing my life | to the ground,
 making me sit in darkness like | those long dead.
 4 My spirit | faints within me;
 my heart within | me is desolate.

3 *5* I remember the time past;
 I muse upon | all your deeds;
 I consider the works | of your hands.
 6 I stretch out my | hands to you;
 my soul gasps for you like a | thirsty land.

4 *7* O Lord, make haste to answer me;
 my | spirit fails me;
 hide not your face from me
 lest I be like those who go down | to the Pit.
 8 Let me hear of your loving-kindness in the morning,
 for in you I | put my trust;
 show me the way I should walk in,
 for I lift up my | soul to you.

5 *9* Deliver me, O Lord, | from my enemies,
   for I flee to | you for refuge.
   10 Teach me to do what pleases you, for you | are my God;
   let your kindly spirit lead me on a | level path.

6 *11* Revive me, O Lord, | for your name's sake;
   for your righteousness' sake, bring me | out of trouble.
   [*12a* In your faithfulness, slay my enemies,
   and destroy all the adversaries | of my soul,]
   12b for truly I | am your servant.

Verse 12a may be omitted

Psalm 144

PRINCIPAL SERVICE   2ND SERVICE   3RD SERVICE
                           Proper 23 C   4 Advent ABC

Response — Geoff Nobes
v. 1 Bles-sed be the Lord, my rock.

Verse

G.N.

1 *1* Blessed be the | Lord my rock,
    who teaches my | hands for war
    and my fin | gers for battle;

2 *2* My steadfast help and my fortress,
    my stronghold and | my deliverer,
    my shield in | whom I trust,
    who subdues the | peoples under me.

3 *3* O Lord, what are mortals that you | should consider them;
    mere human beings, that you | should take thought for them?
  4 They are like a breath of wind;
    their days pass away | like a shadow.

4 *5* Bow your heavens, O Lord, | and come down;
    touch the mountains and | they shall smoke.
  6 Cast down your lightnings and scatter them;
    shoot out your arrows and let | thunder roar.

5 *7* Reach down your hand | from on high;
    deliver me and take me out of the great waters,
    from the hand of | foreign enemies,
  8 Whose mouth speaks wickedness
    and their right hand is the | hand of falsehood.

6 ⁹ O God, I will sing to | you a new song;
    I will play to you on a | ten-stringed harp,
  ¹⁰ You that give salvation to kings
    and have delivered Da | vid your servant.

7 ¹¹ Save me from the peril | of the sword
    and deliver me from the hand of | foreign enemies,
  ¹² Whose mouth speaks wickedness
    and whose right hand is the | hand of falsehood;

8 ¹³ So that our sons in their youth
    may be like well- | nurtured plants,
    and our daugh | ters like pillars
    carved for the corners | of the temple;

9 ¹⁴ Our barns be filled with all man | ner of store;
    our flocks bearing thousands,
    and ten thousands | in our fields;
  ¹⁵ Our cattle be hea | vy with young:

10 may there be no miscarriage or untimely birth,
    no cry of distress | in our streets.
  ¹⁶ Happy are the people whose bles | sing this is.
    Happy are the people who have the Lord | for their God.

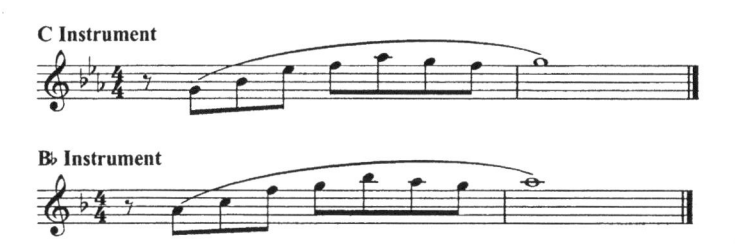

Psalm 145

PRINCIPAL SERVICE
Proper 9 A (related) (vs. 8-15)
Proper 12 B (related) (vs. 10-19)
Proper 13 A (related) (vs. 14-22)
Proper 20 A (related) (vs. 1-9)

2ND SERVICE
4 before Advent BC (vs. 1-9)

3RD SERVICE
2 Epiphany ABC (vs. 1-13)
Pentecost B
Proper 24 A
All Saints ABC

Gerry Fitzpatrick

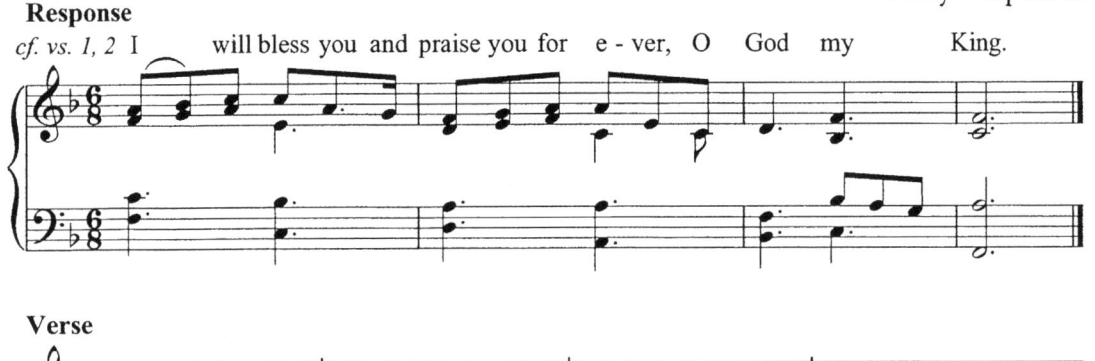

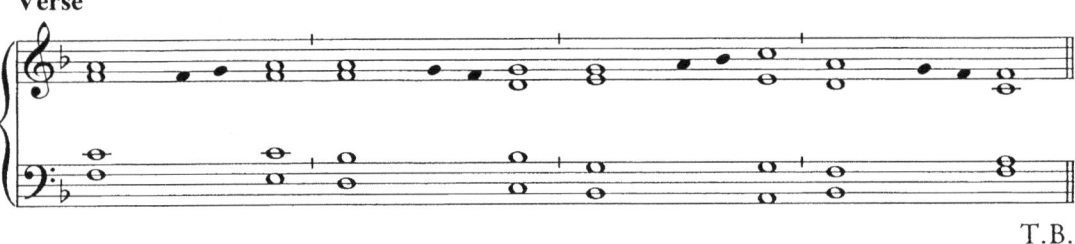

Response
cf. vs. 1, 2 I will bless you and praise you for e-ver, O God my King.

Verse

T.B.

1 *1* I will exalt you, O God my King,
    and bless your name for e | ver and ever.
 2 Every day will I bless you
    and praise your name for e | ver and ever.
 3 Great is the Lord and highly | to be praised;
    his greatness is beyond all | searching out.

2 *4* One generation shall praise your works | to another
    and declare your | mighty acts.
 5 They shall speak of the majesty | of your glory,
    and I will tell of all your won | derful deeds.

3 *6* They shall speak of the might of your mar | vellous acts,
    and I will also tell | of your greatness.
 7 They shall pour forth the story of your a | bundant kindness
    and joyfully sing | of your righteousness.

4 *8* The Lord is gra | cious and merciful,
    long-suffering and | of great goodness.
 9 The Lord is lov | ing to everyone
    and his mercy is over | all his creatures.

5 *10* All your works praise | you, O Lord,
    and your faithful | servants bless you.
 11 They tell of the glory | of your kingdom
    and speak of your | mighty power,

6 *12* To make known to all peoples your | mighty acts
    and the glorious splendour | of your kingdom.
  13 Your kingdom is an ever | lasting kingdom;
    your dominion endures through | out all ages.

7 *14* The Lord is sure in | all his words
    and faithful in | all his deeds.
  15 The Lord upholds all | those who fall
    and lifts up all those who | are bowed down.

8 *16* The eyes of all wait upon you, O Lord,
    and you give them their food | in due season.
  17 You open wide your hand
    and fill all things liv | ing with plenty.
  18 The Lord is righteous in | all his ways
    and loving in | all his works.

9 *19* The Lord is near to those who | call upon him,
    to all who call u | pon him faithfully.
  20 He fulfils the desire of | those who fear him;
    he hears their | cry and saves them.

10 *21* The Lord watches over | those who love him,
    but all the wicked shall | he destroy.
  22 My mouth shall speak the praise | of the Lord,
    and let all flesh bless his holy name for e | ver and ever.

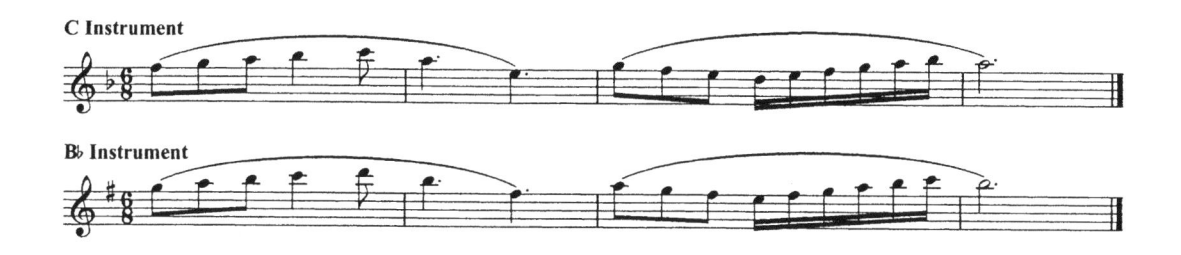

Psalm 146

PRINCIPAL SERVICE
3 Advent A (vs. 4-10)
Proper 5 C
Proper 18 B (related)
Proper 21 C (related)

2ND SERVICE
Proper 24 C

3RD SERVICE
4 Easter C

Simon Lesley

Response
cf. v. 1 I will praise the Lord as long as I live.

Verse

K.D.

1 *1* (Alleluia.)
   Praise the Lord, | O my soul:
   while I live will I | praise the Lord;
   as long as I have | any being,
   I will sing praises | to my God.

2 *2* Put not your trust in princes,
   nor in any | human power,
   for there | is no help in them.
   3 When their breath goes forth, they return | to the earth;
   on that day all | their thoughts perish.

3 *4* Happy are those who have the God of Jacob | for their help,
   whose hope is in the | Lord their God;
   5 Who made heaven and earth,
   the sea and all | that is in them;
   who keeps his pro | mise for ever;

4 *6* Who gives justice to those that | suffer wrong
   and bread to | those who hunger.
   7 The Lord looses those | that are bound;
   the Lord opens the eyes | of the blind;

5 *8* The Lord lifts up those who are bowed down;
    the Lord | loves the righteous;
  9 The Lord watches over the stranger in the land;
    he upholds the or | phan and widow;
    but the way of the wicked he turns | upside down.
  10 The Lord shall reign for ever,
    your God, O Zion, throughout all | generations.
    (Alleluia.)

C Instrument

B♭ Instrument

Psalm 147

PRINCIPAL SERVICE
2 Christmas ABC (vs. 13-21)
Proper 1 B (vs. 1-12)

2ND SERVICE
2 before Lent C (vs. 13-21)
5 Easter A (vs. 1-12)
7 Easter B (vs. 1-12)

3RD SERVICE
Proper 24 C

Also: Morning Prayer: Corpus Christi ABC

Keith Duke

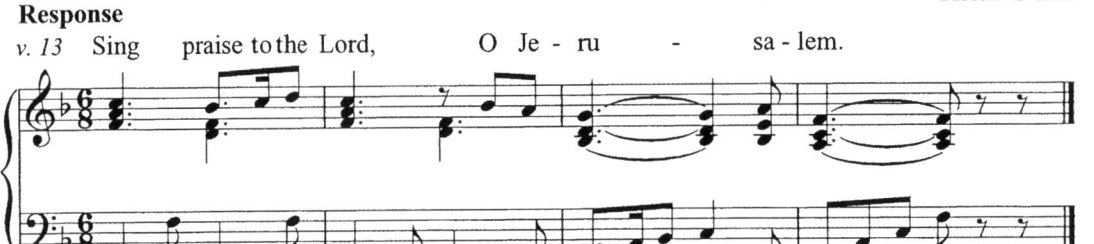

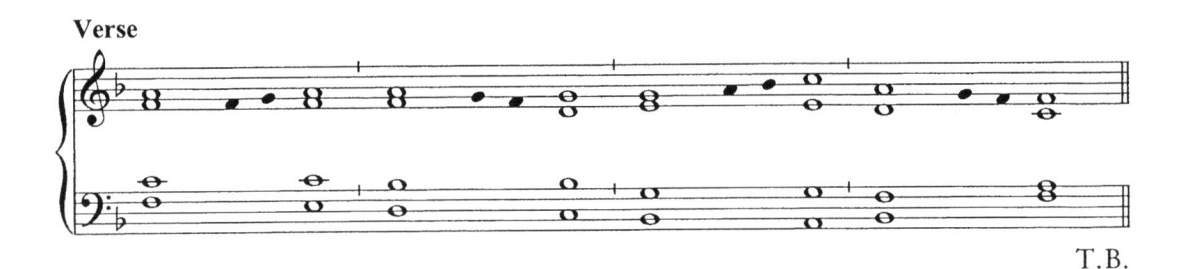

Response

v. 13 Sing praise to the Lord, O Jerusalem.

Verse

T.B.

1 *1* (Alleluia.)
   How good it is to make music | for our God,
   how joyful to honour | him with praise.
  2 The Lord builds up Jerusalem
   and gathers together the out | casts of Israel.
  3 He heals the brokenhearted
   and binds up | all their wounds.

2 *4* He counts the number | of the stars
   and calls them all | by their names.
  5 Great is our Lord and migh | ty in power;
   his wisdom is be | yond all telling.

3 *6* The Lord lifts | up the poor,
   but casts down the wicked | to the ground.
  7 Sing to the Lord | with thanksgiving;
   make music to our God u | pon the lyre;

4 *8* Who covers the heavens with clouds
   and prepares rain | for the earth;
  9 Who makes grass to grow upon the mountains
   and green plants to | serve our needs.
  10 He gives the | beasts their food
   and the young ravens | when they cry.

5 *11* He takes no pleasure in the power | of a horse,
   no delight in | human strength;
  12 But the Lord delights in | those who fear him,
   who put their trust in his | steadfast love.

6 *13* Sing praise to the Lord, | O Jerusalem;
 praise your | God, O Zion;
 14 For he has strengthened the bars | of your gates
  and has blest your chil | dren within you.

7 *15* He has established peace | in your borders
  and satisfies you with the | finest wheat.
 16 He sends forth his command | to the earth
  and his word runs | very swiftly.

8 *17* He gives snow like wool
  and scatters the hoar | frost like ashes.
 18 He casts down his hailstones like morsels of bread;
  who can en | dure his frost?
 19 He sends forth his | word and melts them;
  he blows with his wind and the | waters flow.

9 *20* He declares his | word to Jacob,
  his statutes and judge | ments to Israel.
 21 He has not dealt so with any | other nation;
  they do not | know his laws.
  (Alleluia.)

Psalm 148

PRINCIPAL SERVICE
1 Christmas ABC (vs. 7-14)
5 Easter C (vs. 1-6)

2ND SERVICE
2 before Lent A

3RD SERVICE
All Saints ABC

Colin Mawby

Response

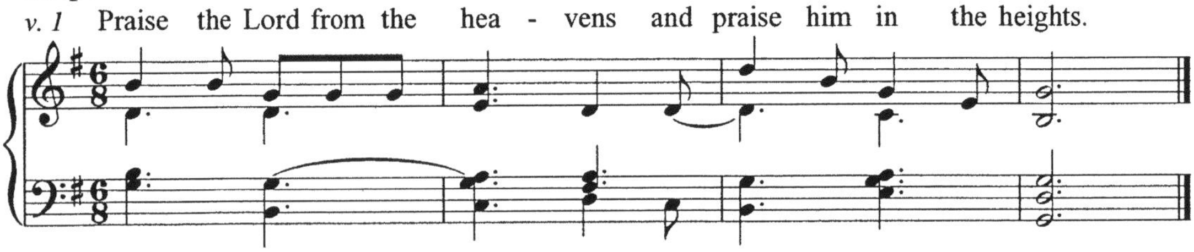

v. 1 Praise the Lord from the heavens and praise him in the heights.

Verse

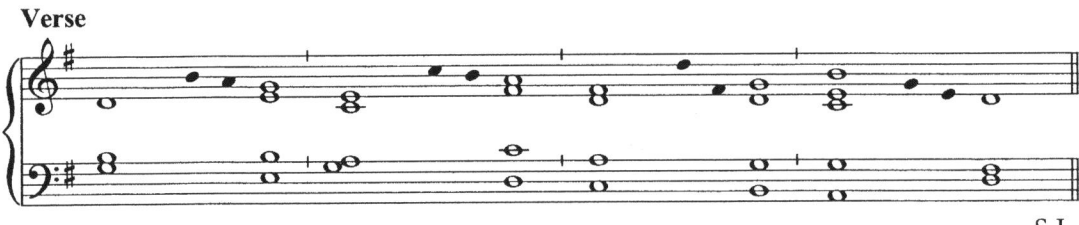

S.L.

1 *1* (Alleluia.)
   Praise the Lord | from the heavens;
   praise him | in the heights.
   2 Praise him, | all you his angels;
   praise him, | all his host.

2 *3* Praise him, | sun and moon;
   praise him, all you | stars of light.
   4 Praise him, hea | ven of heavens,
   and you waters a | bove the heavens.

3 *5* Let them praise the name | of the Lord,
   for he commanded and they | were created.
   6 He made them fast for e | ver and ever;
   he gave them a law which shall not | pass away.

4 *7* Praise the Lord | from the earth,
   you sea monsters | and all deeps;
   8 Fire and hail, | snow and mist,
   tempestuous wind, fulfil | ling his word;

5 *9* Mountains | and all hills,
   fruit trees | and all cedars;
   10 Wild beasts | and all cattle,
   creeping things and birds | on the wing;

6 *11* Kings of the earth | and all peoples,
   princes and all rulers | of the world;
   12 Young men and women,
   old and | young together;
   let them praise the name | of the Lord.

7 *13* For his name only | is exalted,
   his splendour above | earth and heaven.
   14 He has raised up the horn of his people
   and praise for all his | faithful servants,
   the children of Israel, a people | who are near him.
   (Alleluia.)

C Instrument

B♭ Instrument

Psalm 149

PRINCIPAL SERVICE
Proer 18 A
All Saints C

2ND SERVICE
Proper 24 C

3RD SERVICE
Proper 24 A
4 before Advent B

John McCann

Response

cf. v. 1 Sing, O sing to the Lord a new song: sing his praise.

Verse

K.D.

1 *1* (Alleluia.)
   O sing to the | Lord a new song;
   sing his praise in the congregation | of the faithful.
  2 Let Israel rejoice | in their maker;
   let the children of Zion be joyful | in their king.

2 *3* Let them praise his name | in the dance;
   let them sing praise to him with tim | brel and lyre.
  4 For the Lord has pleasure | in his people
   and adorns the poor | with salvation.

3 *5* Let the faithful be joy | ful in glory;
   let them rejoice | in their ranks,
  6 With the praises of God | in their mouths
   and a two-edged sword | in their hands;

4 *7* To execute vengeance on the nations
   and punishment | on the peoples;
  8 To bind their kings in chains
   and their nobles with fet | ters of iron;
  9 To execute on them the judge | ment decreed:
   such honour have all his | faithful servants.
   (Alleluia.)

C Instrument

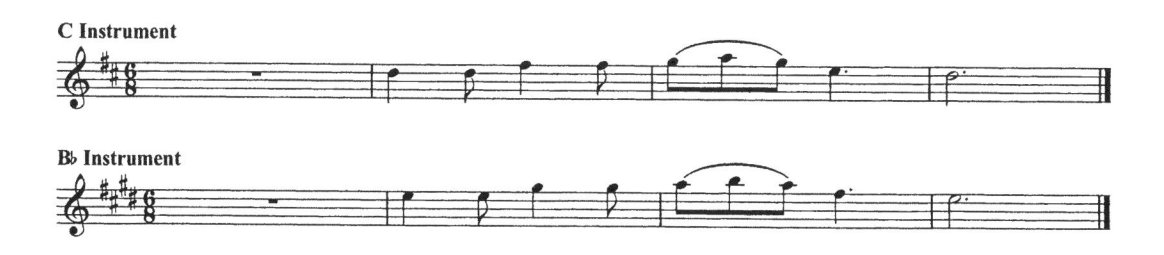

B♭ Instrument

Psalm 150

PRINCIPAL SERVICE
2 Easter C

2ND SERVICE
Pentecost C
Trinity A

3RD SERVICE
2 before Lent A
1 before Lent B
All Saints ABC

John McCann

Response

v. 6 Let ev-'ry-thing that has breath praise the Lord.

Verse

* *Omit in verse 3*

C.M.

1 *1* (Alleluia.)
   O praise God | in his holiness;
   praise him in the firmament | of his power.
  2 Praise him for his | mighty acts;
   praise him according to his ex | cellent greatness.

2 *3* Praise him with the blast | of the trumpet;
   praise him upon the | harp and lyre.
  4 Praise him with tim | brel and dances;
   praise him upon the | strings and pipe.

3 *5* Praise him with | ringing cymbals;
   praise him upon the | clashing cymbals.
  6 Let everything that has breath | praise the Lord.
   (Alleluia.)

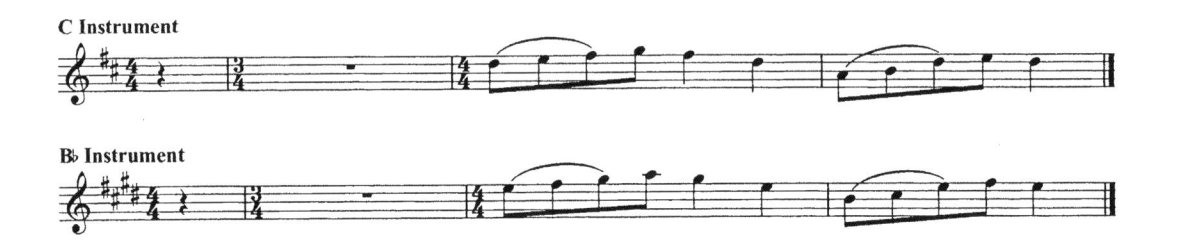

C Instrument

B♭ Instrument

Benedictus

Luke 1: 68-79
PRINCIPAL SERVICE
2 Advent C

John McCann

Response

v. 69 He has raised up for us a mighty Saviour.

Verse

G.N.

1 68 Blessed be the Lord the | God of Israel,
  who has come to his people
    and | set them free.
 69 He has raised up for us a | mighty Saviour,
  born of the house of his | servant David.

2 70 Through his holy prophets
    God pro | mised of old
 71 to save us from our enemies,
    from the hands of | all that hate us,
 72 to show mercy | to our ancestors,
    and to remember his | holy covenant.

3 73 This was the oath God swore
    to our | father Abraham:
 74 to set us free from the hands | of our enemies,
    free to worship him | without fear,
 75 holy and righteous in his sight
    all the days | of our life.

4 76 And you, child, shall be called
    the prophet of | the Most High,
  for you will go before the Lord
    to pre | pare his way,
 77 to give his people knowledge | of salvation
    by the forgiveness of | all their sins.

5 78 In the tender compassion | of our God
    the dawn from on high shall | break upon us,
 79 to shine on those who dwell
    in darkness and the sha | dow of death,
    and to guide our feet into the | way of peace.

Optional Gloria:
  Glory to the Father and | to the Son
  and to the | Holy Spirit;
  as it was in | the beginning
  is now and shall be for e | ver. Amen.

C Instrument

B♭ Instrument

Magnificat

Luke 1: 47-55
PRINCIPAL SERVICE
3 Advent AB
4 Advent BC

John McCann

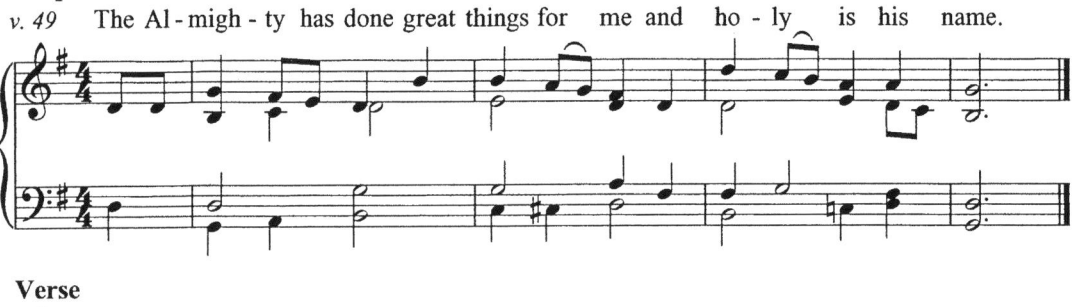

Response

v. 49 The Al-migh-ty has done great things for me and ho-ly is his name.

Verse

S.L.

1. ⁴⁷My soul proclaims the greatness | of the Lord,
   my spirit rejoices in | God my Saviour;
   ⁴⁸he has looked with favour on his | lowly servant.
   From this day all generations will | call me blessed;

2. ⁴⁹the Almighty has done great | things for me
   and holy | is his name.
   ⁵⁰He has mercy on | those who fear him,
   from generation to | generation.

3. ⁵¹He has shown strength | with his arm
   and has scattered the proud in | their conceit,
   ⁵²casting down the mighty | from their thrones
   and lifting | up the lowly.

4. ⁵³He has filled the hun | gry with good things
   and sent the rich | away empty.
   ⁵⁴He has come to the aid of his servant Israel,
   to remember his pro | mise of mercy.
   ⁵⁵The promise made to our ancestors,
   to Abraham and his child | ren for ever.

Optional Gloria:
Glory be to the Father, and | to the Son,
and to the | Holy Spirit;
as it was in the beginning
is now and shall be for e | ver. Amen.

Exodus

Exodus 15: 1b-21
PRINCIPAL SERVICE
Proper 19 A (vs. 1b-11, 20-21)
Also: Easter Vigil ABC (vs. 1b-13, 17-18)

Richard Lloyd

Response

v. 1b I will sing to the Lord for he has tri-umphed glo-rious-ly.

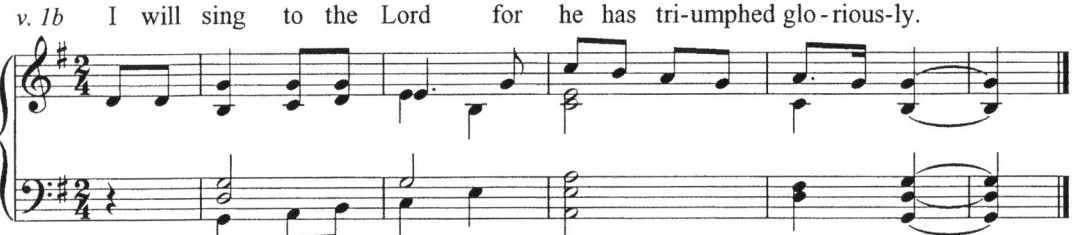

Verse

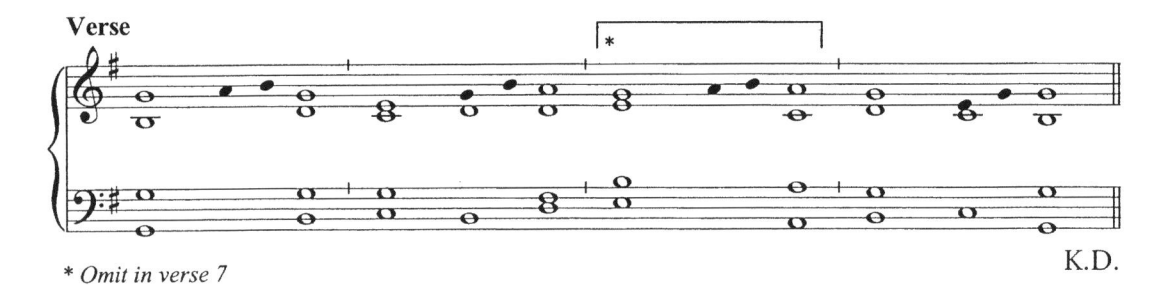

* Omit in verse 7

K.D.

1 *1b* I will sing to the Lord,
    for he has | triumphed gloriously;
    horse and rider he has thrown in | to the sea.
  2 The Lord is my strength | and my might,
    and he has become | my salvation;

2   this is my God, and | I will praise him,
    my father's God, and I | will exalt him.
  3 The Lord | is a warrior;
    the Lord | is his name.

3 *4* Pharaoh's chariots and his army he cast in | to the sea;
    his picked officers were sunk | in the Red Sea.
  5 The floods covered them;
    they went down into the depths | like a stone.
  6 Your right hand, O Lord, glorious in power —
    your right hand, O Lord, shat | tered the enemy.

4 *7* In the greatness of your majesty
    you over | threw your adversaries;
    you sent out your fury,
    it consumed | them like stubble.
  8 At the blast of your nostrils the wa | ters piled up,
    the floods stood up in a heap;
    the deeps congealed in the heart | of the sea.

5 *9* The enemy said, 'I will pursue,
I will | overtake,
I will divide the spoil,
my desire shall | have its fill of them.
I will | draw my sword,
my hand | shall destroy them.'

6 *10* You blew with your wind, the sea covered them;
they sank like lead in the | mighty waters.
  11 'Who is like you, O Lord, a | mong the gods?
Who is like you, majes | tic in holiness,
awesome in splendour, | doing wonders?

7 *12* You stretched out your right hand,
| the earth swallowed them.
  13 'In your steadfast love you led
the people whom | you redeemed;
you guided them by your strength
to your ho | ly abode.

8 *17* You brought them in and planted them
on the mountain of your | own possession,
the place, O Lord, that you made | your abode,
the sanctuary, O Lord,
that your hands | have established.
  18 The Lord will reign for e | ver and ever.'

9 *20* Then the prophet Miriam, Aaron's sister,
took a tambourine | in her hand;
and all the women went out after her
with tambourines | and with dancing.
  21 And Miriam sang to them: 'Sing to the Lord,
for he has | triumphed gloriously;
horse and rider he has thrown in | to the sea.'

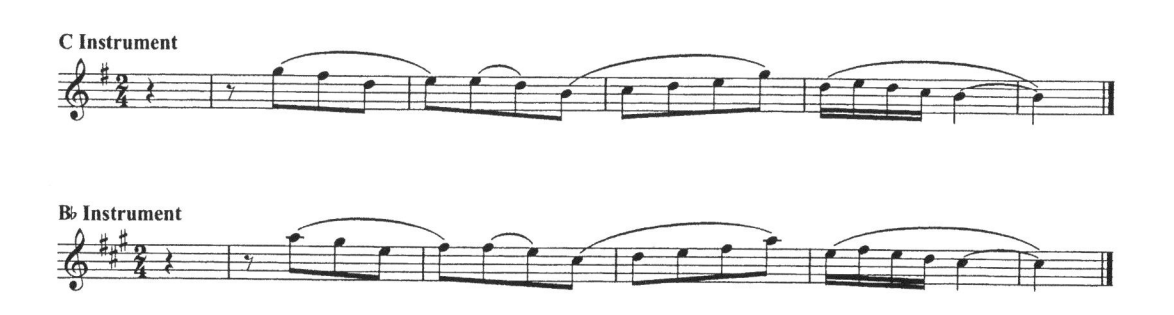

Isaiah

Isaiah 12: 2-6
PRINCIPAL SERVICE
3 Advent C
Also: Easter Vigil ABC

Alan Rees

Response

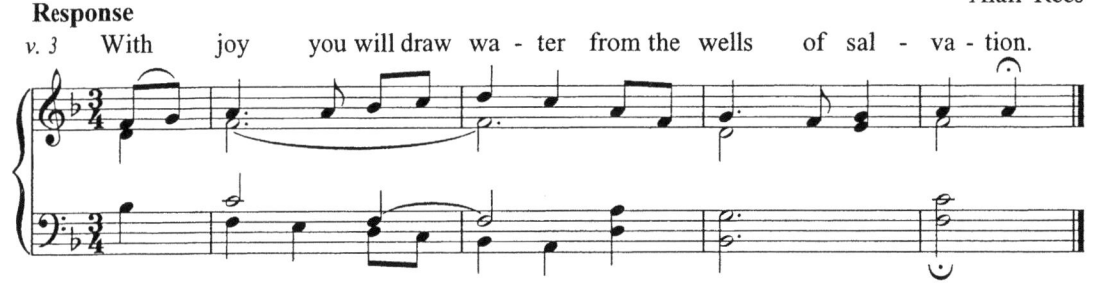

v. 3 With joy you will draw wa-ter from the wells of sal-va-tion.

Verse

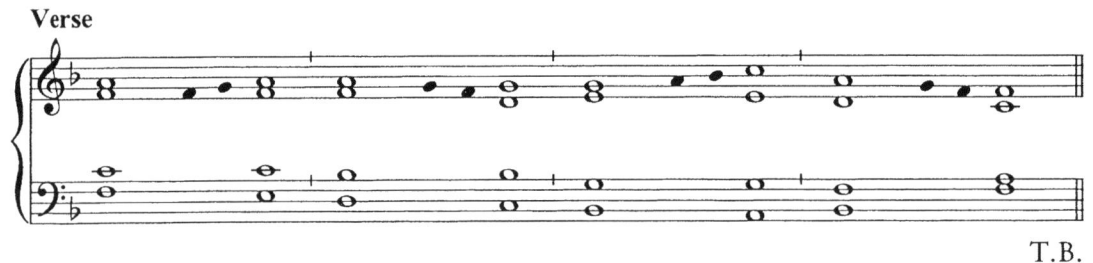

T.B.

1 ₂ Surely God is | my salvation;
 I will trust, and will not | be afraid,
 for the Lord God is my strength | and my might;
 he has become | my salvation.

2 ₃ With joy you will draw water
 from the wells | of salvation.
 ₄ And you will say | in that day:
 Give thanks to the Lord, call | on his name;
 make known his deeds among the nations;
 proclaim that his name | is exalted.

3 ₅ Sing praises to the Lord,
 for he | has done gloriously;
 let this be known in | all the earth.
 ₆ Shout aloud and sing for joy, O | royal Zion,
 for great in your midst is the Holy | One of Israel.

C Instrument

B♭ Instrument

Lamentations (A)

Lamentations 3: 19-26
PRINCIPAL SERVICE
Proper 22 C

Geoff Nobes

Response
cf. v. 22 The steadfast love of the Lord never comes to an end.

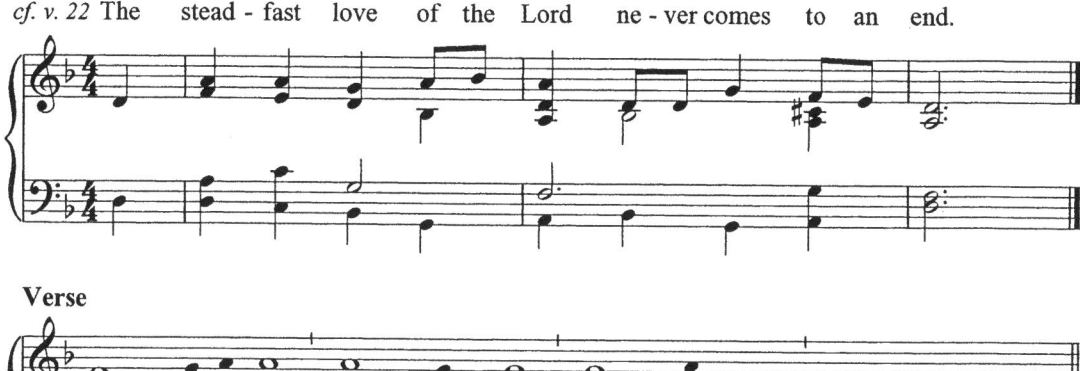

Verse

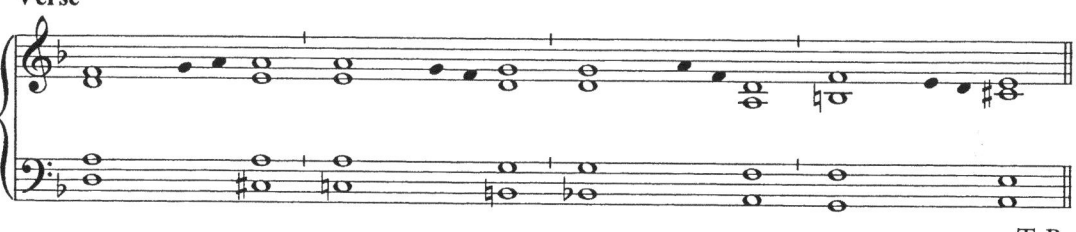

T.B.

1 19 The thought of my affliction | and my homelessness
　　 is worm | wood and gall!
　20 My soul continually thinks of it
　　 and is bowed | down within me.
　21 But this I call to mind,
　　 and therefore | I have hope:

2 22 The steadfast love of the Lord | never ceases,
　　 his mercies never come | to an end;
　23 they are new every morning;
　　 great | is your faithfulness.
　24 'The Lord is my portion,' says my soul,
　　 'therefore | I will hope in him.'

3 25 The Lord is good to | those who wait for him,
　　 to the | soul that seeks him.
　26 It is good that one | should wait quietly
　　 for the salvation | of the Lord.

C Instrument

B♭ Instrument

Lamentations (B)

Lamentations 3: 23-33
PRINCIPAL SERVICE
Proper 8 B (related)

Response Richard Lloyd

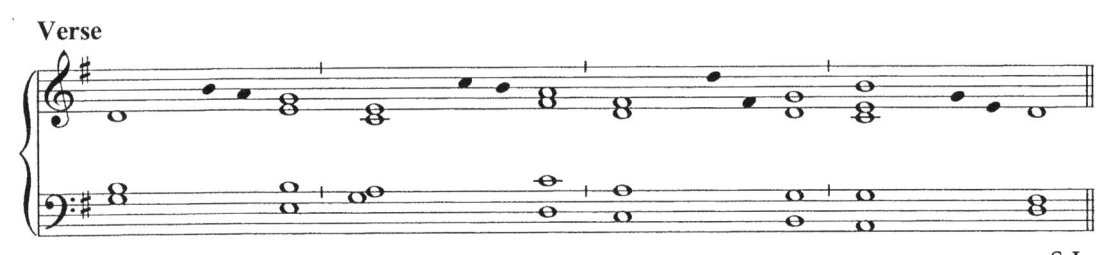

v. 25a The Lord is good to those who wait for him.

Verse

S.L.

1 ₂₃ They are new | ev'ry morning;
   great | is your faithfulness.
   ₂₄ 'The Lord is my portion,' | says my soul,
   'therefore | I will hope in him.'

2 ₂₅ The Lord is good to | those who wait for him,
   to the | soul that seeks him.
   ₂₆ It is good that one | should wait quietly
   for the salvation | of the Lord.

3 ₂₇ It is good for one to bear the | yoke in youth,
   ₂₈ to sit alone in silence when the Lord | has imposed it,
   ₂₉ to put one's mouth to the dust (there may | yet be hope),
   ₃₀ to give one's cheek to the smiter, and be | filled with insults.,

4 ₃₁ For the Lord will not re | ject for ever.
   ₃₂ Although he causes grief, he will | have compassion
   according to the abundance of his | steadfast love;
   ₃₃ for he does not willingly afflict | or grieve anyone.

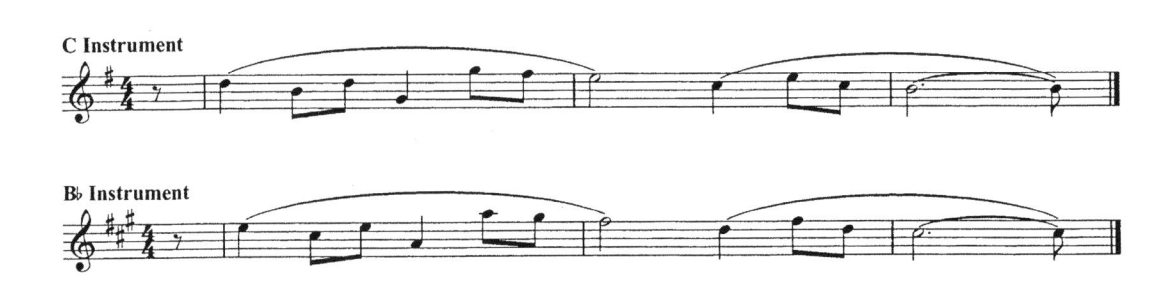

C Instrument

B♭ Instrument

Song of Solomon

Song of Solomon 2: 8-13
PRINCIPAL SERVICE
Proper 9 A

Geoff Nobes

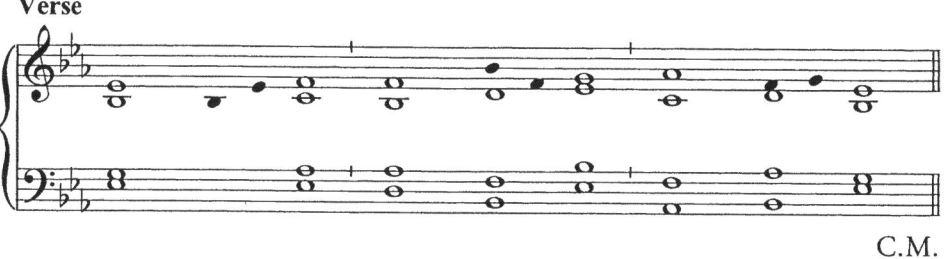

Response

v. 10b Arise, my love, my fair one, and come away.

Verse

C.M.

1 8 The voice of my beloved! | Look, he comes,
   leaping u | pon the mountains,
   bounding o | ver the hills.

2 9 My beloved is like a gazelle | or a young stag.
   Look, there he stands be | hind our wall,
   gazing in at the windows, looking | through the lattice.

3 10 My beloved | speaks and says to me:
   'Arise, my love, my fair one, and | come away;
   11 for now the winter is past, the rain is o | ver and gone.

4 12 The flowers appear | on the earth;
   the time of sing | ing has come,
   and the voice of the turtledove is heard | in our land.

5 13 The fig tree puts | forth its figs,
   and the vines | are in blossom;
   they give forth fragrance.
   Arise, my love, my fair one, and | come away.

C Instrument

B♭ Instrument

Wisdom (A)

Wisdom 6: 17-20
PRINCIPAL SERVICE
3 before Advent A

Response
cf. vs. 18, 19

Keith Duke

The love of wis-dom brings us near - er God.

Verse

C.M.

1 *17* The beginning of wisdom is
   the most sincere desire | for instruction,
   and concern for instruc | tion is love of her,

2 *18* and love of her is the keeping | of her laws,
   and giving heed to her laws is
   assurance of | immortality,

3 *19* and immortality brings one | near to God;
   20 so the desire for wisdom leads | to a kingdom.

C Instrument

B♭ Instrument

Wisdom (B)

Wisdom 7: 26-30; 8:1
PRINCIPAL SERVICE
19 Proper B

Andrew Wright

Response

cf. v. 28 God loves those who live with wis - dom.

Verse

* Omit in verse 3

T.B.

1 ²⁶ Wisdom is a reflection of e | ternal light,
    a spotless mirror of the working of God,
    and an image | of his goodness.
  ²⁷ Although she is but one, she | can do all things,
    and while remaining in herself, she re | news all things;

2 in every generation she passes into | holy souls
    and makes them friends of | God, and prophets;
  ²⁸ for God loves no | thing so much
    as the person who | lives with wisdom.

3 ²⁹ She is more beautiful | than the sun,
    and excels every constellation | of the stars.
    Compared with the light she is found to | be superior,

4 ³⁰ for it is succeeded | by the night,
    but against wisdom evil does | not prevail.
  ¹ She reaches mightily from one end of the earth | to the other,
    and she orders | all things well.

C Instrument

B♭ Instrument

New Psalms for Common Worship

Gospel Acclamations

Gospel Acclamations

Common Worship for the Celebration of Holy Communion introduces a Gospel Acclamation to be sung before the Gospel. Throughout the year, except from Ash Wednesday to Maundy Thursday, the form is as follows:

All	Alleluia
Cantor/Choir	sings a verse from scripture
All	Alleluia

From Ash Wednesday to Maundy Thursday the Alleluia is replaced by the response:
　　Praise to you, O Christ, King of eternal glory.

Below we give the texts for the Cantor/Choir verse; musical settings will be found on pages 290-295. Any setting may be chosen for any text.

Verses for Ordinary Time *(Turn to page 290 for musical settings)*

1
Speak, Lord, for your ser | vant is listening.
You have the words of e | ternal life.　　　　　　　　　　　　　　*1 Samuel 3:9; John 6:68*

2
I am the light of the world, | says the Lord.
Whoever follows me will never walk in darkness
　　but will have the | light of life.　　　　　　　　　　　　　　　　　*John 8:12*

3
My sheep hear my voice, | says the Lord.
I know them, and they | follow me.　　　　　　　　　　　　　　　　*John 10:27*

4
I am the way, the truth, and the life, | says the Lord.
No one comes to the Father ex | cept through me.　　　　　　　　　　*John 14:16*

5
We do not live by | bread alone,
but by every word that comes from the | mouth of God.　　　　　　　*Matthew 4:4*

6
Welcome with meekness the im | planted word
that has the power to | save your souls.　　　　　　　　　　　　　　　*James 1:21*

7
The word of the Lord en | dures for ever.
The word of the Lord is the good news an | nounced to you.　　　　　*cf. 1 Peter 1:25*

Verses for the seasons *(Turn to page 290 for musical settings)*

From the First Sunday of Advent until Christmas Eve
Prepare the way of the Lord, make | his paths straight,
and all flesh shall see the salva | tion of God. *cf. Isaiah 40:3-5*

From Christmas Day until the Eve of Epiphany
The Word became flesh and | dwelt among us,
and we have | seen his glory. *John 1:14*

From the Epiphany until the Eve of the Presentation
Christ was revealed in flesh, proclaimed a | mong the nations
and believed in through | out the world. *cf. 1 Timothy 3:16*

The Presentation of the Child in the Temple
This child is the light to enligh | ten the nations,
and the glory of your | people Israel. *cf. Luke 2:32*

From Ash Wednesday until the Saturday after the Fourth Sunday of Lent
The Lord is a great God, O that today you would listen | to his voice.
Harden | not your hearts. *cf. Psalm 95:3, 7-8*

The Annunciation of Our Lord
The Word has become flesh and | lived among us,
and we have | seen his glory. *John 1:14*

Note: if the Annunciation falls in Eastertide, use the text provided for Christmas.

From the Fifth Sunday of Lent until the Wednesday of Holy Week
Christ humbled himself and became obedient unto death,
  even death | on a cross.
Therefore God has highly exalted him
  and given him the name that is above | every name. *Philippians 2:8-9*

Maundy Thursday
I give you a new commandment, | says the Lord:
Love one another as I | have loved you. *cf. John 13:34*

From Easter Day until the Eve of the Ascension
I am the first and the last, says the Lord, and the | living one;
I was dead, and behold I am alive for | evermore. *cf. Revelation 1:17-18*

Ascension Day
Go and make disciples of all nations, | says the Lord.
Remember, I am with you always, to the end | of the age. *cf. Matthew 28:19-20*

From the day after Ascension Day until the Day of Pentecost
Come, Holy Spirit, fill the hearts of your | faithful people
and kindle in them the fire | of your love.

Trinity Sunday
Glory to the Father, and to the Son, and to the | Holy Spirit,
one God, who was, and who is, and who is to come, | the Almighty. *cf. Revelation 1:8*

All Saints' Day
You are a chosen race, a royal priesthood,
  a holy nation, | God's own people,
called out of darkness into his mar | vellous light. *1 Peter 2:9*

From the day after All Saints' Day until the day before the First Sunday of Advent
Blessed is the king who comes in the name | of the Lord.
Peace in heaven and glory in the | highest heaven. *Luke 19:38*

On Saints' Days
I have called you friends, | says the Lord,
for all that I have heard from my Father I have made | known to you. *cf. John 15:15*

See pages 288-290 for the proper texts Plainchant

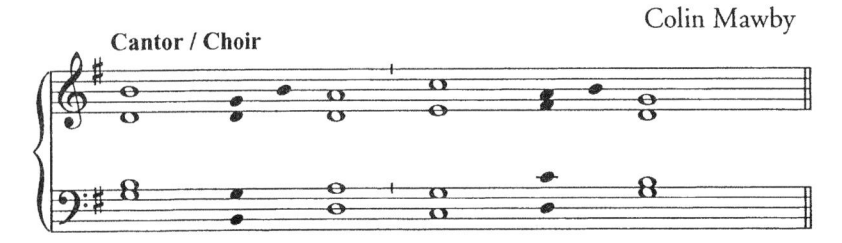

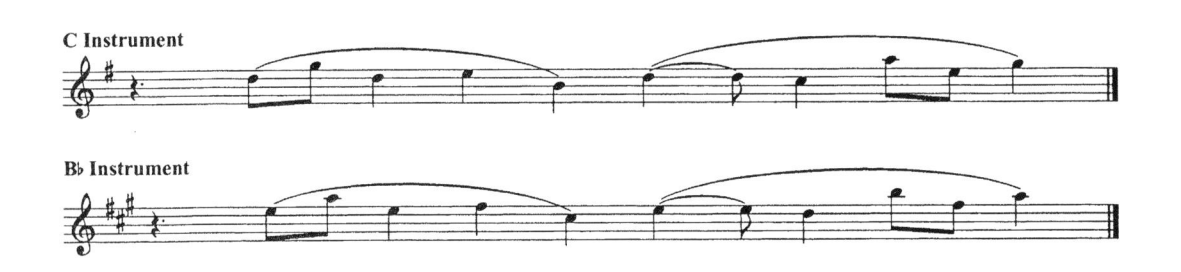

Colin Mawby

Unknown arr. John Ballantine

Keith Duke

Cantor / Choir

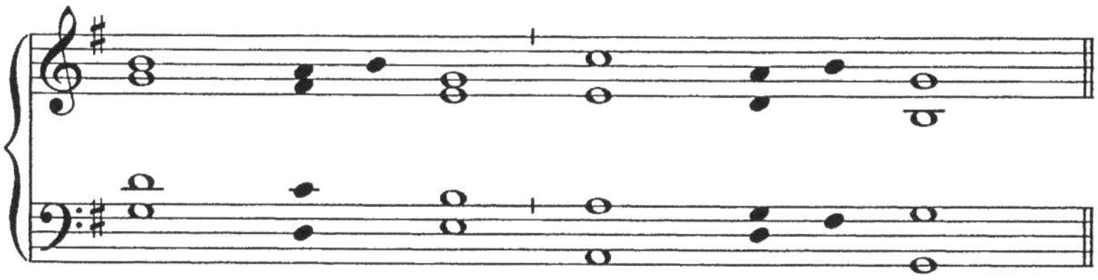

Colin Mawby

C Instrument

B♭ Instrument

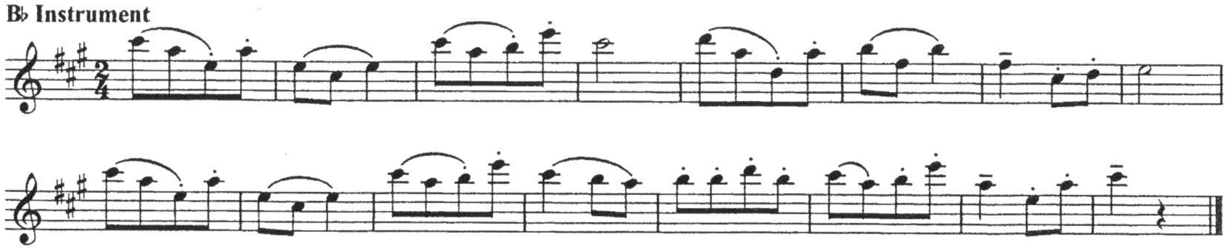

Colin Mawby

All Alleluia, alleluia, alleluia, alleluia.

Cantor / Choir Geoff Nobes

C Instrument

B♭ Instrument

Colin Mawby

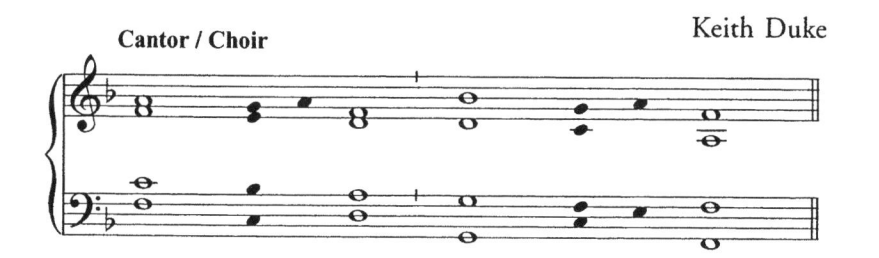

All Al-le-lu-ia, al-le-lu-ia, al-le-lu-ia, al-le-lu-ia.

Cantor / Choir

Keith Duke

C Instrument

B♭ Instrument

Fintan O'Carroll

All Al - le - lu - ia, al - le - lu - ia,

Al - le - lu - ia, al - le - lu - ia.

Simon Lesley

Cantor / Choir

Colin Mawby

C Instrument

B♭ Instrument

Easter Alleluia

Plainsong arr. Andrew Moore

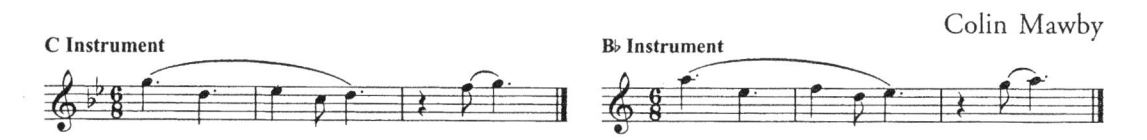

All Alleluia, alleluia, alleluia.

Cantor / Choir — Simon Lesley

C Instrument / *B♭ Instrument* — Colin Mawby

From Ash Wednesday to Maundy Thursday

Colin Mawby

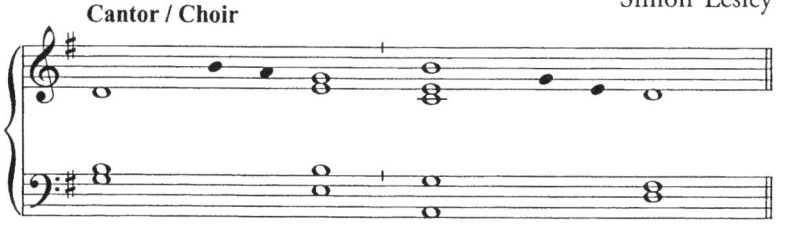

All Praise to you, O Christ, King of eternal glory.

Cantor / Choir — Simon Lesley

C Instrument

B♭ Instrument